SPORTS ALMANAC

COMPLETES SPORTS STATISTICS

1950—2000

ISBN: 978-1981435449

The rights of Replica Books, to be identified as the Creator of this Work have been asserted in accordance with the Copyrights, Designs & Patents Act 1988.
We gratefully acknowledge the following for the material and assistance they have provided: Universal Pictures, Amblin Entertainment.

CONTENTS

1950 .... Page 7

1951 .... Page 9

1952 .... Page 11

1953 .... Page 13

1954 .... Page 15

1955 .... Page 17

1956 .... Page 19

1957 .... Page 21

1958 .... Page 23

1959 .... Page 25

1960 .... Page 27

1961 .... Page 29

1962 .... Page 31

1963 .... Page 33

1964 .... Page 35

1965 .... Page 37

1966 .... Page 39

1967 .... Page 41

1968 .... Page 44

1969 .... Page 47

1970	Page 50
1971	Page 53
1972	Page 56
1973	Page 59
1974	Page 62
1975	Page 65
1976	Page 68
1977	Page 71
1978	Page 74
1979	Page 77
1980	Page 80
1981	Page 83
1982	Page 86
1983	Page 89
1984	Page 92
1985	Page 95
1986	Page 98
1987	Page 101
1988	Page 104
1989	Page 107
1990	Page 110

1991 .... **Page 114**

1992 .... **Page 118**

1993 .... **Page 122**

1994 .... **Page 126**

1995 .... **Page 130**

1996 .... **Page 134**

1997 .... **Page 138**

1998 .... **Page 142**

1999 .... **Page 146**

2000 .... **Page 150**

1950

1950 NATIONAL FOOTBALL LEAGUE SEASON
STANDINGS

AMERICAN	W	L	T	NATIONAL	W	L	T
Cleveland	10	2	0	Los Angeles	9	3	0
NY Giants	10	2	0	Chi. Bears	9	3	0
Philadelphia	6	6	0	NY Yanks	7	5	0
Pittsburgh	6	6	0	Detroit	6	6	0
Chi. Cardinals	5	7	0	Green Bay	3	9	0
Washington	3	9	0				

1950 U.S. NATIONAL BADMINTON CHAMPIONSHIPS
WINNERS

Year	Men's singles	Women's singles	Men's doubles	Women's doubles	Mixed doubles
1950	Marten Mendez	Ethel Marshall	Barney McCay Wynn Rogers	Thelma Scovil Janet Wright	Wynn Rogers Loma Moulton Smith

1950 NBA STANDINGS
DIVISION STANDINGS

Team	W	L	W/L%	GB	PS/G	PA/G	SRS
Central Division							
Minneapolis Lakers*	51	17	.750	—	84.1	75.7	8.25
Rochester Royals*	51	17	.750	—	82.4	74.6	7.72
Fort Wayne Pistons*	40	28	.588	11.0	79.3	77.9	1.84
Chicago Stags*	40	28	.588	11.0	78.7	77.1	2.06
St. Louis Bombers	26	42	.382	25.0	73.7	76.5	-2.01
Eastern Division							
Syracuse Nationals*	51	13	.797	—	84.8	76.7	6.48
New York Knicks*	40	28	.588	13.0	80.7	78.6	2.53
Washington Capitols*	32	36	.471	21.0	76.5	77.4	-0.28
Philadelphia Warriors*	26	42	.382	27.0	73.3	76.4	-2.27
Baltimore Bullets	25	43	.368	28.0	73.1	78.7	-4.55
Boston Celtics	22	46	.324	31.0	79.7	82.2	-1.73
Western Division							
Indianapolis Olympians*	39	25	.609	—	85.8	82.1	2.59
Anderson Packers*	37	27	.578	2.0	87.3	83.5	2.42
Tri-Cities Blackhawks*	29	35	.453	10.0	83.0	83.6	-1.43
Sheboygan Red Skins*	22	40	.355	16.0	82.4	87.8	-5.85
Waterloo Hawks	19	43	.306	19.0	79.4	84.9	-5.96
Denver Nuggets	11	51	.177	27.0	77.7	89.2	-11.31

AMERICAN HORSE OF THE YEAR
1950 ECLIPSE AWARD

Year	Horse	Trainer	Owner	Age	Gender
1950	Hill Prince	Casey Hayes	Christopher Chenery	3	C

1950- NHL SEASON
FINAL STANDINGS

National Hockey League	GP	W	L	T	Pts	GF	GA	PIM
Detroit Red Wings	70	44	13	13	101	236	139	566
Toronto Maple Leafs	70	41	16	13	95	212	138	823
Montreal Canadiens	70	25	30	15	65	173	184	835
Boston Bruins	70	22	30	18	62	178	197	656
New York Rangers	70	20	29	21	61	169	201	774
Chicago Black Hawks	70	13	47	10	36	171	280	615

1950 MAJOR LEAGUE BASEBALL SEASON HISTORY

1950 American League Standings									
TEAM	W	L	PCT	GB	HOME	ROAD	RS	RA	DIFF
*-New York	98	56	.632	--	--	--	914	691	+223
Detroit	95	59	.605	3	--	--	837	713	+124
Boston	94	60	.610	4	--	--	1027	804	+223
Cleveland	92	62	.594	6	--	--	806	654	+152
Washington	67	87	.432	31	--	--	690	813	-123
Chicago	60	94	.385	38	--	--	625	749	-124
St. Louis	58	96	.377	40	--	--	684	916	-232
Philadelphia	52	102	.338	46	--	--	670	913	-243
1950 National League Standings									
TEAM	W	L	PCT	GB	HOME	ROAD	RS	RA	DIFF
*-Philadelphia	91	63	.580	--	--	--	722	624	+98
Brooklyn	89	65	.574	2	--	--	847	724	+123
New York	86	68	.558	5	--	--	735	643	+92
Boston	83	71	.532	8	--	--	785	736	+49
St. Louis	78	75	.510	12.5	--	--	693	670	+23
Cincinnati	66	87	.431	24.5	--	--	654	734	-80
Chicago	64	89	.416	26.5	--	--	643	772	-129
Pittsburgh	57	96	.370	33.5	--	--	681	857	-176

1950 U.S. NATIONAL TENNIS CHAMPIONSHIPS

Men's Singles
Art Larsen defeated Herb Flam 6–3, 4–6, 5–7, 6–4, 6–3
Women's Singles
Margaret Osborne duPont defeated Doris Hart 6–3, 6–3
Men's doubles
John Bromwich / Frank Sedgman defeated Bill Talbert / Gardnar Mulloy 7–5, 8–6, 3–6, 6–1
Women's doubles
Louise Brough / Margaret Osborne defeated Shirley Fry / Doris Hart 6–2, 6–3
Mixed doubles
Margaret Osborne duPont / Ken McGregor defeated Doris Hart / Frank Sedgman 6–4, 3–6, 6–3

1951

1951 NATIONAL FOOTBALL LEAGUE SEASON
STANDINGS

AMERICAN	W	L	T	NATIONAL	W	L	T
Cleveland	11	1	0	Los Angeles	8	4	0
NY Giants	9	2	1	Detroit	7	4	1
Washington	5	7	0	San Francisco	7	4	1
Pittsburgh	4	7	1	Chi. Bears	7	5	0
Philadelphia	4	8	0	Green Bay	3	9	0
Chi. Cardinals	3	9	0	NY Yanks	1	9	2

1951 U.S. NATIONAL BADMINTON CHAMPIONSHIPS
WINNERS

Year	Men's singles	Women's singles	Men's doubles	Women's doubles	Mixed doubles
1951	Joseph Cameron Alston	Ethel Marshall	Joe Alston Wynn Rogers	Dorothy Hann Loma Moulton Smith	Wynn Rogers Loma Moulton Smith

1951 NBA STANDINGS
DIVISION STANDINGS

Team	W	L	W/L%	GB	PS/G	PA/G	SRS
Eastern Division							
Philadelphia Warriors*	40	26	.606	—	85.4	81.6	3.40
Boston Celtics*	39	30	.565	2.5	85.2	85.5	-0.41
New York Knicks*	36	30	.545	4.0	85.8	85.4	0.49
Syracuse Nationals*	32	34	.485	8.0	86.1	85.5	0.62
Baltimore Bullets	24	42	.364	16.0	82.0	84.3	-1.94
Washington Capitols	10	25	.286	14.5	81.3	86.0	-4.63
Western Division							
Minneapolis Lakers*	44	24	.647	—	82.8	77.4	4.79
Rochester Royals*	41	27	.603	3.0	84.6	81.7	2.54
Fort Wayne Pistons*	32	36	.471	12.0	84.1	86.0	-1.81
Indianapolis Olympians*	31	37	.456	13.0	81.7	84.1	-2.00
Tri-Cities Blackhawks	25	43	.368	19.0	84.3	88.1	-3.22

AMERICAN HORSE OF THE YEAR
1951 ECLIPSE AWARD

Year	Horse	Trainer	Owner	Age	Gender
1951	Counterpoint	Sylvester Veitch	C. V. Whitney	3	C

1951- NHL SEASON
FINAL STANDINGS

National Hockey League	GP	W	L	T	Pts	GF	GA	PIM
Detroit Red Wings	70	44	14	12	100	215	133	694
Montreal Canadiens	70	34	26	10	78	195	164	661
Toronto Maple Leafs	70	29	25	16	74	168	157	841
Boston Bruins	70	25	29	16	66	162	176	601
New York Rangers	70	23	34	13	59	192	219	532
Chicago Black Hawks	70	17	44	9	43	158	241	627

1951 MAJOR LEAGUE BASEBALL SEASON HISTORY

1951 American League Standings									
TEAM	W	L	PCT	GB	HOME	ROAD	RS	RA	DIFF
*-New York	98	56	.636	--	--	--	798	621	+177
Cleveland	93	61	.600	5	--	--	696	594	+102
Boston	87	67	.565	11	--	--	804	725	+79
Chicago	81	73	.523	17	--	--	714	644	+70
Detroit	73	81	.474	25	--	--	685	741	-56
Philadelphia	70	84	.455	28	--	--	736	745	-9
Washington	62	92	.403	36	--	--	672	764	-92
St. Louis	52	102	.338	46	--	--	611	882	-271

1951 National League Standings									
TEAM	W	L	PCT	GB	HOME	ROAD	RS	RA	DIFF
*-New York	98	59	.624	--	--	--	781	641	+140
Brooklyn	97	60	.614	1	--	--	855	672	+183
St. Louis	81	73	.523	15.5	--	--	683	671	+12
Boston	76	78	.490	20.5	--	--	723	662	+61
Philadelphia	73	81	.474	23.5	--	--	648	644	+4
Cincinnati	68	86	.439	28.5	--	--	559	667	-108
Pittsburgh	64	90	.413	32.5	--	--	689	845	-156
Chicago	62	92	.400	34.5	--	--	614	750	-136

1951 U.S. NATIONAL TENNIS CHAMPIONSHIPS

Men's Singles
Frank Sedgman defeated Vic Seixas 6–4, 6–1, 6–1
Women's Singles
Maureen Connolly defeated Shirley Fry 6–3, 1–6, 6–4
Men's doubles
Ken McGregor / Frank Sedgman defeated Don Candy / Mervyn Rose 10–8, 6–4, 4–6, 7–5
Women's doubles
Shirley Fry / Doris Hart defeated Nancy Chaffee / Patricia Todd 6–4, 6–2
Mixed doubles
Doris Hart / Frank Sedgman defeated Shirley Fry / Mervyn Rose 6–3, 6–2

1952

1952 NATIONAL FOOTBALL LEAGUE SEASON
STANDINGS

EAST	W	L	T	WEST	W	L	T
Cleveland	11	1	0	Detroit	10	2	0
Philadelphia	7	4	1	San Francisco	9	3	0
Washington	6	5	1	Los Angeles	8	3	1
Pittsburgh	6	6	0	Chi. Bears	3	8	1
NY Giants	3	9	0	Baltimore	3	9	0
Chi. Cardinals	1	10	1	Green Bay	2	9	1

1952 U.S. NATIONAL BADMINTON CHAMPIONSHIPS
WINNERS

Year	Men's singles	Women's singles	Men's doubles	Women's doubles	Mixed doubles
1952	Marten Mendez	Ethel Marshall	Joe Alston Wynn Rogers	Ethel Marshall Beatrice Massman	Wynn Rogers Helen Tibbetts

1952 NBA STANDINGS
DIVISION STANDINGS

Team	W	L	W/L%	GB	PS/G	PA/G	SRS
Eastern Division							
Syracuse Nationals*	40	26	.606	—	86.7	82.2	3.94
Boston Celtics*	39	27	.591	1.0	91.3	87.2	3.60
New York Knicks*	37	29	.561	3.0	85.0	84.2	0.67
Philadelphia Warriors*	33	33	.500	7.0	86.5	87.8	-1.08
Baltimore Bullets	20	46	.303	20.0	81.5	89.0	-6.60
Western Division							
Rochester Royals*	41	25	.621	—	86.2	82.8	2.92
Minneapolis Lakers*	40	26	.606	1.0	85.6	79.5	5.28
Indianapolis Olympians*	34	32	.515	7.0	82.9	82.8	0.08
Fort Wayne Pistons*	29	37	.439	12.0	78.0	80.1	-1.83
Milwaukee Hawks	17	49	.258	24.0	73.2	81.2	-7.04

AMERICAN HORSE OF THE YEAR
1952 ECLIPSE AWARD

Year	Horse	Trainer	Owner	Age	Gender
1952	Native Dancer	William C. Winfrey	Alfred G. Vanderbilt II	2	C

1952- NHL SEASON
FINAL STANDINGS

National Hockey League	GP	W	L	T	Pts	GF	GA	PIM
Detroit Red Wings	70	36	16	18	90	222	133	645
Montreal Canadiens	70	28	23	19	75	155	148	777
Boston Bruins	70	28	29	13	69	152	172	528
Chicago Black Hawks	70	27	28	15	69	169	175	736
Toronto Maple Leafs	70	27	30	13	67	156	167	812
New York Rangers	70	17	37	16	50	152	211	548

1952 MAJOR LEAGUE BASEBALL SEASON HISTORY

1952 American League Standings									
TEAM	W	L	PCT	GB	HOME	ROAD	RS	RA	DIFF
*-New York	95	59	.617	--	--	--	727	557	+170
Cleveland	93	61	.600	2	--	--	763	606	+157
Chicago	81	73	.519	14	--	--	610	568	+42
Philadelphia	79	75	.510	16	--	--	664	723	-59
Washington	78	76	.497	17	--	--	598	608	-10
Boston	76	78	.494	19	--	--	668	658	+10
St. Louis	64	90	.413	31	--	--	604	733	-129
Detroit	50	104	.321	45	--	--	557	738	-181
1952 National League Standings									
TEAM	W	L	PCT	GB	HOME	ROAD	RS	RA	DIFF
*-Brooklyn	96	57	.619	--	--	--	775	603	+172
New York	92	62	.597	4.5	--	--	722	639	+83
St. Louis	88	66	.571	8.5	--	--	677	630	+47
Philadelphia	87	67	.565	9.5	--	--	657	552	+105
Chicago	77	77	.497	19.5	--	--	628	631	-3
Cincinnati	69	85	.448	27.5	--	--	615	659	-44
Boston	64	89	.413	32	--	--	569	651	-82
Pittsburgh	42	112	.271	54.5	--	--	515	793	-278

1952 U.S. NATIONAL TENNIS CHAMPIONSHIPS

Men's Singles
Frank Sedgman defeated Gardnar Mulloy 6–1, 6–2, 6–3
Women's Singles
Maureen Connolly defeated Doris Hart 6–3, 7–5
Men's doubles
Mervyn Rose / Vic Seixas defeated Ken McGregor / Frank Sedgman 3–6, 10–8, 10–8, 6–8, 8–6
Women's doubles
Shirley Fry / Doris Hart defeated Louise Brough / Maureen Connolly 10–8, 6–4
Mixed doubles
Doris Hart / Frank Sedgman defeated Thelma Coyne Long / Lew Hoad 6–3, 7–5

1953

1953 NATIONAL FOOTBALL LEAGUE SEASON
STANDINGS

EAST	W	L	T	WEST	W	L	T
Cleveland	11	1	0	Detroit	10	2	0
Philadelphia	7	4	1	San Francisco	9	3	0
Washington	6	5	1	Los Angeles	8	3	1
Pittsburgh	6	6	0	Chi. Bears	3	8	1
NY Giants	3	9	0	Baltimore	3	9	0
Chi. Cardinals	1	10	1	Green Bay	2	9	1

1953 U.S. NATIONAL BADMINTON CHAMPIONSHIPS
WINNERS

Year	Men's singles	Women's singles	Men's doubles	Women's doubles	Mixed doubles
1953	David G. Freeman	Ethel Marshall	Joe Alston Wynn Rogers	Judy Devlin Sue Devlin	Joe Alston Lois Alston

1953 NBA STANDINGS
DIVISION STANDINGS

Team	W	L	W/L%	GB	PS/G	PA/G	SRS
Eastern Division							
New York Knicks*	47	23	.671	—	85.5	80.3	4.39
Syracuse Nationals*	47	24	.662	0.5	85.6	81.3	3.62
Boston Celtics*	46	25	.648	1.5	88.1	85.8	1.94
Baltimore Bullets*	16	54	.229	31.0	84.4	90.9	-5.80
Philadelphia Warriors	12	57	.174	34.5	80.2	87.4	-7.75
Western Division							
Minneapolis Lakers*	48	22	.686	—	85.3	79.2	5.54
Rochester Royals*	44	26	.629	4.0	86.3	83.5	2.62
Fort Wayne Pistons*	36	33	.522	11.5	81.0	81.1	0.17
Indianapolis Olympians*	28	43	.394	20.5	74.6	77.4	-2.30
Milwaukee Hawks	27	44	.380	21.5	75.9	77.4	-2.49

AMERICAN HORSE OF THE YEAR
1953 ECLIPSE AWARD

Year	Horse	Trainer	Owner	Age	Gender
1953	Tom Fool	John M. Gaver, Sr.	Greentree Stable	4	C

1953- NHL SEASON
FINAL STANDINGS

National Hockey League	GP	W	L	T	Pts	GF	GA	PIM
Detroit Red Wings	70	37	19	14	88	191	132	814
Montreal Canadiens	70	35	24	11	81	195	141	1064
Toronto Maple Leafs	70	32	24	14	78	152	131	1022
Boston Bruins	70	32	28	10	74	177	181	685
New York Rangers	70	29	31	10	68	161	182	717
Chicago Black Hawks	70	12	51	7	31	133	242	797

1953 MAJOR LEAGUE BASEBALL SEASON HISTORY

1953 American League Standings									
TEAM	W	L	PCT	GB	HOME	ROAD	RS	RA	DIFF
*-New York	99	52	.656	--	--	--	801	547	+254
Cleveland	92	62	.594	8.5	--	--	770	627	+143
Chicago	89	65	.571	11.5	--	--	716	592	+124
Boston	84	69	.549	16	--	--	656	632	+24
Washington	76	76	.500	23.5	--	--	687	614	+73
Detroit	60	94	.380	40.5	--	--	695	923	-228
Philadelphia	59	95	.376	41.5	--	--	632	799	-167
St. Louis	54	100	.351	46.5	--	--	555	778	-223
1953 National League Standings									
TEAM	W	L	PCT	GB	HOME	ROAD	RS	RA	DIFF
*-Brooklyn	105	49	.677	--	--	--	955	689	+266
Milwaukee	92	62	.586	13	--	--	738	589	+149
St. Louis	83	71	.529	22	--	--	768	713	+55
Philadelphia	83	71	.532	22	--	--	716	666	+50
New York	70	84	.452	35	--	--	768	747	+21
Cincinnati	68	86	.439	37	--	--	714	788	-74
Chicago	65	89	.419	40	--	--	633	835	-202
Pittsburgh	50	104	.325	55	--	--	622	887	-265

1953 U.S. NATIONAL TENNIS CHAMPIONSHIPS

Men's Singles
Tony Trabert defeated Vic Seixas 6–3, 6–2, 6–3
Women's Singles
Maureen Connolly defeated Doris Hart 6–2, 6–4
Men's doubles
Rex Hartwig / Mervyn Rose defeated Bill Talbert / Gardnar Mulloy 6–4, 4–6, 6–2, 6–4
Women's doubles
Shirley Fry / Doris Hart defeated Louise Brough / Margaret Osborne duPont 6–2, 7–9, 9–7
Mixed doubles
Doris Hart / Vic Seixas defeated Julia Sampson / Rex Hartwig 6–2, 4–6, 6–4

1954

1954 NATIONAL FOOTBALL LEAGUE SEASON
STANDINGS

EAST	W	L	T	WEST	W	L	T
Cleveland	9	3	0	Detroit	9	2	1
Philadelphia	7	4	1	Chi. Bears	8	4	0
NY Giants	7	5	0	San Francisco	7	4	1
Pittsburgh	5	7	0	Los Angeles	6	5	1
Washington	3	9	0	Green Bay	4	8	0
Chi. Cardinals	2	10	0	Baltimore	3	9	0

1954 U.S. OPEN BADMINTON CHAMPIONSHIPS
WINNERS

Year	Men's singles	Women's singles	Men's doubles	Women's doubles	Mixed doubles
1954	Eddy B. Choong	Judy Devlin	Ooi Teik Hock Ong Poh Lim	Judy Devlin Susan Devlin	Joseph Cameron Alston Lois Alston

1954 NBA STANDINGS
DIVISION STANDINGS

Team	W	L	W/L%	GB	PS/G	PA/G	SRS
Eastern Division							
New York Knicks*	44	28	.611	—	79.0	79.1	-0.16
Syracuse Nationals*	42	30	.583	2.0	83.5	78.6	4.27
Boston Celtics*	42	30	.583	2.0	87.7	85.4	1.97
Philadelphia Warriors	29	43	.403	15.0	78.2	80.4	-1.89
Baltimore Bullets	16	56	.222	28.0	78.3	85.1	-5.98
Western Division							
Minneapolis Lakers*	46	26	.639	—	81.7	78.6	2.71
Rochester Royals*	44	28	.611	2.0	79.8	77.3	2.24
Fort Wayne Pistons*	40	32	.556	6.0	77.7	76.1	1.45
Milwaukee Hawks	21	51	.292	25.0	70.0	75.3	-4.55

AMERICAN HORSE OF THE YEAR
1954 ECLIPSE AWARD

Year	Horse	Trainer	Owner	Age	Gender
1954	Native Dancer	William C. Winfrey	Alfred G. Vanderbilt II	4	C

1954- NHL SEASON
FINAL STANDINGS

National Hockey League	GP	W	L	T	Pts	GF	GA	PIM
Detroit Red Wings	70	42	17	11	95	204	134	827
Montreal Canadiens	70	41	18	11	93	228	157	890
Toronto Maple Leafs	70	24	24	22	70	147	135	990
Boston Bruins	70	23	26	21	67	169	188	863
New York Rangers	70	17	35	18	52	150	210	690
Chicago Black Hawks	70	13	40	17	43	161	235	733

1954 MAJOR LEAGUE BASEBALL SEASON HISTORY

1954 American League Standings									
TEAM	W	L	PCT	GB	HOME	ROAD	RS	RA	DIFF
*-Cleveland	111	43	.712	--	--	--	746	504	+242
New York	103	51	.665	8	--	--	805	563	+242
Chicago	94	60	.606	17	--	--	711	521	+190
Boston	69	85	.442	42	--	--	700	728	-28
Detroit	68	86	.439	43	--	--	584	664	-80
Washington	66	88	.426	45	--	--	632	680	-48
Baltimore	54	100	.351	57	--	--	483	668	-185
Philadelphia	51	103	.327	60	--	--	542	875	-333
1954 National League Standings									
TEAM	W	L	PCT	GB	HOME	ROAD	RS	RA	DIFF
*-New York	97	57	.630	--	--	--	732	550	+182
Brooklyn	92	62	.597	5	--	--	778	740	+38
Milwaukee	89	65	.578	8	--	--	670	556	+114
Philadelphia	75	79	.487	22	--	--	659	614	+45
Cincinnati	74	80	.481	23	--	--	729	763	-34
St. Louis	72	82	.468	25	--	--	799	790	+9
Chicago	64	90	.416	33	--	--	700	766	-66
Pittsburgh	53	101	.344	44	--	--	557	845	-288

1954 U.S. NATIONAL TENNIS CHAMPIONSHIPS

Men's Singles
Vic Seixas defeated Rex Hartwig 3–6, 6–2, 6–4, 6–4
Women's Singles
Doris Hart defeated Louise Brough 6–8, 6–1, 8–6
Men's doubles
Vic Seixas / Tony Trabert defeated Lew Hoad / Ken Rosewall 3–6, 6–4, 8–6, 6–3
Women's doubles
Shirley Fry / Doris Hart defeated Louise Brough / Margaret Osborne duPont 6–4, 6–4
Mixed doubles
Doris Hart / Vic Seixas defeated Margaret Osborne duPont / Ken Rosewall 4–6, 6–1, 6–1

1955

1955 NATIONAL FOOTBALL LEAGUE SEASON
STANDINGS

EAST	W	L	T	WEST	W	L	T
Cleveland	9	2	1	Los Angeles	8	3	1
Washington	8	4	0	Chi. Bears	8	4	0
NY Giants	6	5	1	Green Bay	6	6	0
Chi. Cardinals	4	7	1	Baltimore	5	6	1
Philadelphia	4	7	1	San Francisco	4	8	0
Pittsburgh	4	8	0	Detroit	3	9	0

1955 U.S. OPEN BADMINTON CHAMPIONSHIPS
WINNERS

Year	Men's singles	Women's singles	Men's doubles	Women's doubles	Mixed doubles
1955	Joseph C. Alston	Margaret Varner	Joe Alston T. Wynn Rogers	Judy Devlin Susan Devlin	Wynn Rogers Dorothy Hann

1955 NBA STANDINGS
DIVISION STANDINGS

Team	W	L	W/L%	GB	PS/G	PA/G	SRS
Eastern Division							
Syracuse Nationals*	43	29	.597	—	91.1	89.7	1.23
New York Knicks*	38	34	.528	5.0	92.7	92.6	0.11
Boston Celtics*	36	36	.500	7.0	101.5	101.5	-0.03
Philadelphia Warriors	33	39	.458	10.0	93.2	93.5	-0.19
Baltimore Bullets							
Western Division							
Fort Wayne Pistons*	43	29	.597	—	92.4	90.0	2.01
Minneapolis Lakers*	40	32	.556	3.0	95.6	94.5	0.96
Rochester Royals*	29	43	.403	14.0	90.8	92.4	-1.43
Milwaukee Hawks	26	46	.361	17.0	87.4	90.4	-2.66

AMERICAN HORSE OF THE YEAR
1955 ECLIPSE AWARD

Year	Horse	Trainer	Owner	Age	Gender
1955	Nashua	Jim Fitzsimmons	Belair Stud	3	C

1955- NHL SEASON
FINAL STANDINGS

National Hockey League	GP	W	L	T	Pts	GF	GA	PIM
Montreal Canadiens	70	45	15	10	100	222	131	977
Detroit Red Wings	70	30	24	16	76	183	148	794
New York Rangers	70	32	28	10	74	204	203	911
Toronto Maple Leafs	70	24	33	13	61	153	181	1051
Boston Bruins	70	23	34	13	59	147	185	929
Chicago Black Hawks	70	19	39	12	50	155	216	826

1955 MAJOR LEAGUE BASEBALL SEASON HISTORY

1955 American League Standings									
TEAM	W	L	PCT	GB	HOME	ROAD	RS	RA	DIFF
*-New York	96	58	.623	--	--	--	762	569	+193
Cleveland	93	61	.604	3	--	--	698	601	+97
Chicago	91	63	.587	5	--	--	725	557	+168
Boston	84	70	.545	12	--	--	755	652	+103
Detroit	79	75	.513	17	--	--	775	658	+117
Kansas City	63	91	.406	33	--	--	638	911	-273
Baltimore	57	97	.365	39	--	--	540	754	-214
Washington	53	101	.344	43	--	--	598	789	-191
1955 National League Standings									
TEAM	W	L	PCT	GB	HOME	ROAD	RS	RA	DIFF
*-Brooklyn	98	55	.636	--	--	--	857	650	+207
Milwaukee	85	69	.552	13.5	--	--	743	668	+75
New York	80	74	.519	18.5	--	--	702	673	+29
Philadelphia	77	77	.500	21.5	--	--	675	666	+9
Cincinnati	75	79	.487	23.5	--	--	761	684	+77
Chicago	72	81	.468	26	--	--	626	713	-87
St. Louis	68	86	.442	30.5	--	--	654	757	-103
Pittsburgh	60	94	.390	38.5	--	--	560	767	-207

1955 U.S. NATIONAL TENNIS CHAMPIONSHIPS

Men's Singles
Tony Trabert (USA) defeated Ken Rosewall (AUS) 9–7, 6–3, 6–3
Women's Singles
Doris Hart (USA) defeated Patricia Ward Hales (GBR) 6–4, 6–2
Men's doubles
Kosei Kamo (JPN) / Atsushi Miyagi (JPN) defeated Gerald Moss (USA) / Bill Quillian (USA) 6–3, 6–3, 3–6, 1–6, 6–4
Women's doubles
Louise Brough (USA) / Margaret Osborne (USA) defeated Shirley Fry (USA) / Doris Hart (USA) 6–3, 1–6, 6–3
Mixed doubles
Doris Hart (USA) / Vic Seixas (USA) defeated Shirley Fry (USA) / Gardnar Mulloy (USA) 7–5, 5–7, 6–2

1956

1956 NATIONAL FOOTBALL LEAGUE SEASON
STANDINGS

EAST	W	L	T	WEST	W	L	T
NY Giants	8	3	1	Chi. Bears	9	2	1
Chi. Cardinals	7	5	0	Detroit	9	3	0
Washington	6	6	0	San Francisco	5	6	1
Cleveland	5	7	0	Baltimore	5	7	0
Pittsburgh	5	7	0	Green Bay	4	8	0
Philadelphia	3	8	1	Los Angeles	4	8	0

1956 U.S. OPEN BADMINTON CHAMPIONSHIPS
WINNERS

Year	Men's singles	Women's singles	Men's doubles	Women's doubles	Mixed doubles
1956	Finn Kobberø	Judy Devlin	Finn Kobberø Jørgen Hammergaard Hansen	Ethel Marshall Beatrice Massman	Finn Kobberø Judy Devlin

1956 NBA STANDINGS
DIVISION STANDINGS

Team	W	L	W/L%	GB	PS/G	PA/G	SRS
Eastern Division							
Philadelphia Warriors*	45	27	.625	—	103.1	98.8	3.82
Boston Celtics*	39	33	.542	6.0	106.0	105.3	0.72
Syracuse Nationals*	35	37	.486	10.0	96.9	96.9	0.17
New York Knicks*	35	37	.486	10.0	100.2	100.6	-0.20
Western Division							
Fort Wayne Pistons*	37	35	.514	—	94.4	93.7	0.45
Minneapolis Lakers*	33	39	.458	4.0	99.3	100.2	-0.92
St. Louis Hawks*	33	39	.458	4.0	96.6	98.0	-1.42
Rochester Royals	31	41	.431	6.0	95.8	98.7	-2.61

AMERICAN HORSE OF THE YEAR
1956 ECLIPSE AWARD

Year	Horse	Trainer	Owner	Age	Gender
1956	Swaps	Mesh Tenney	Rex C. Ellsworth	4	C

1956- NHL SEASON
FINAL STANDINGS

National Hockey League	GP	W	L	T	Pts	GF	GA	PIM
Detroit Red Wings	70	38	20	12	88	198	157	656
Montreal Canadiens	70	35	23	12	82	210	155	870
Boston Bruins	70	34	24	12	80	195	174	978
New York Rangers	70	26	30	14	66	184	227	870
Toronto Maple Leafs	70	21	34	15	57	174	192	829
Chicago Black Hawks	70	16	39	15	47	169	225	809

1956 MAJOR LEAGUE BASEBALL SEASON HISTORY

1956 American League Standings									
TEAM	W	L	PCT	GB	HOME	ROAD	RS	RA	DIFF
*-New York	97	57	.630	--	--	--	857	631	+226
Cleveland	88	66	.568	9	--	--	712	581	+131
Chicago	85	69	.552	12	--	--	776	634	+142
Boston	84	70	.542	13	--	--	780	751	+29
Detroit	82	72	.529	15	--	--	789	699	+90
Baltimore	69	85	.448	28	--	--	571	705	-134
Washington	59	95	.381	38	--	--	652	924	-272
Kansas City	52	102	.338	45	--	--	619	831	-212

1956 National League Standings									
TEAM	W	L	PCT	GB	HOME	ROAD	RS	RA	DIFF
*-Brooklyn	93	61	.604	--	--	--	720	601	+119
Milwaukee	92	62	.594	1	--	--	709	569	+140
Cincinnati	91	63	.587	2	--	--	775	658	+117
St. Louis	76	78	.487	17	--	--	678	698	-20
Philadelphia	71	83	.461	22	--	--	668	738	-70
New York	67	87	.435	26	--	--	540	650	-110
Pittsburgh	66	88	.420	27	--	--	588	653	-65
Chicago	60	94	.382	33	--	--	597	708	-111

1956 U.S. NATIONAL TENNIS CHAMPIONSHIPS

Men's Singles
Ken Rosewall (AUS) defeated Lew Hoad (AUS) 4–6, 6–2, 6–3, 6–3
Women's Singles
Shirley Fry (USA) defeated Althea Gibson (USA) 6–3, 6–4
Men's doubles
Lew Hoad (AUS) / Ken Rosewall (AUS) defeated Ham Richardson (USA) / Vic Seixas (USA) 6–2, 6–2, 3–6, 6–4
Women's doubles
Louise Brough (USA) / Margaret Osborne (USA) defeated Shirley Fry (USA) / Betty Pratt (USA) 6–3, 6–0
Mixed doubles
Margaret Osborne (USA) / Ken Rosewall (AUS) defeated Darlene Hard (USA) / Lew Hoad (AUS) 9–7, 6–1

1957

1957 NATIONAL FOOTBALL LEAGUE SEASON
STANDINGS

EAST	W	L	T	WEST	W	L	T
Cleveland	9	2	1	Detroit	8	4	0
NY Giants	7	5	0	San Francisco	8	4	0
Pittsburgh	6	6	0	Baltimore	7	5	0
Washington	5	6	1	Los Angeles	6	6	0
Philadelphia	4	8	0	Chi. Bears	5	7	0
Chi. Cardinals	3	9	0	Green Bay	3	9	0

1957 U.S. OPEN BADMINTON CHAMPIONSHIPS
WINNERS

Year	Men's singles	Women's singles	Men's doubles	Women's doubles	Mixed doubles
1957	Finn Kobberø	Judy Devlin	Finn Kobberø Jørgen Hammergaard Hansen	Judy Devlin Susan Devlin	Finn Kobberø Judy Devlin

1957 NBA STANDINGS
DIVISION STANDINGS

Team	W	L	W/L%	GB	PS/G	PA/G	SRS
Eastern Division							
Boston Celtics*	44	28	.611	—	105.5	100.2	4.78
Syracuse Nationals*	38	34	.528	6.0	99.7	101.1	-1.03
Philadelphia Warriors*	37	35	.514	7.0	100.4	98.8	1.54
New York Knicks	36	36	.500	8.0	100.8	100.9	0.07
Western Division							
St. Louis Hawks*	34	38	.472	—	98.5	98.6	-0.27
Minneapolis Lakers*	34	38	.472	—	102.3	103.1	-0.89
Fort Wayne Pistons*	34	38	.472	—	96.4	98.7	-2.18
Rochester Royals	31	41	.431	3.0	93.4	95.6	-2.08

AMERICAN HORSE OF THE YEAR
1957 ECLIPSE AWARD

Year	Horse	Trainer	Owner	Age	Gender
1957	Bold Ruler (DRF) (TSD)	Jim Fitzsimmons	Wheatley Stable	3	C

1957- NHL SEASON
FINAL STANDINGS

National Hockey League	GP	W	L	T	Pts	GF	GA	PIM
Montreal Canadiens	70	43	17	10	96	250	158	945
New York Rangers	70	32	25	13	77	195	188	781
Detroit Red Wings	70	29	29	12	70	176	207	758
Boston Bruins	70	27	28	15	69	199	194	849
Chicago Black Hawks	70	24	39	7	55	163	202	906
Toronto Maple Leafs	70	21	38	11	53	192	226	861

1957 MAJOR LEAGUE BASEBALL SEASON HISTORY

1957 American League Standings									
TEAM	W	L	PCT	GB	HOME	ROAD	RS	RA	DIFF
*-New York	98	56	.636	--	--	--	723	534	+189
Chicago	90	64	.581	8	--	--	707	566	+141
Boston	82	72	.532	16	--	--	721	668	+53
Detroit	78	76	.506	20	--	--	614	614	0
Baltimore	76	76	.494	21	--	--	597	588	+9
Cleveland	76	77	.497	21.5	--	--	682	722	-40
Kansas City	59	94	.383	38.5	--	--	563	710	-147
Washington	55	99	.357	43	--	--	603	808	-205
1957 National League Standings									
TEAM	W	L	PCT	GB	HOME	ROAD	RS	RA	DIFF
*-Milwaukee	95	59	.613	--	--	--	772	613	+159
St. Louis	87	67	.565	8	--	--	737	666	+71
Brooklyn	84	70	.545	11	--	--	690	591	+99
Cincinnati	80	74	.519	15	--	--	747	781	-34
Philadelphia	77	77	.494	18	--	--	623	656	-33
New York	69	85	.448	26	--	--	643	701	-58
Pittsburgh	62	92	.400	33	--	--	586	696	-110
Chicago	62	92	.397	33	--	--	628	722	-94

1957 U.S. NATIONAL TENNIS CHAMPIONSHIPS

Men's Singles
Malcolm Anderson (AUS) defeated Ashley Cooper (AUS) 10–8, 7–5, 6–4
Women's Singles
Althea Gibson (USA) defeated Louise Brough (USA) 6–3, 6–2
Men's doubles
Ashley Cooper (AUS) / Neale Fraser (AUS) defeated Gardnar Mulloy (USA) / Budge Patty (USA) 4–6, 6–3, 9–7, 6–3
Women's doubles
Louise Brough (USA) / Margaret Osborne (USA) defeated Althea Gibson (USA) / Darlene Hard (USA) 6–2, 7–5
Mixed doubles
Althea Gibson (USA) / Kurt Nielsen (DEN) defeated Darlene Hard (USA) / Bob Howe (AUS) 6–3, 9–7

1958

1958 NATIONAL FOOTBALL LEAGUE SEASON
STANDINGS

EAST	W	L	T	WEST	W	L	T
NY Giants	9	3	0	Baltimore	9	3	0
Cleveland	9	3	0	Chi. Bears	8	4	0
Pittsburgh	7	4	1	Los Angeles	8	4	0
Washington	4	7	1	San Francisco	6	6	0
Chi. Cardinals	2	9	1	Detroit	4	7	1
Philadelphia	2	9	1	Green Bay	1	10	1

1958 U.S. OPEN BADMINTON CHAMPIONSHIPS
WINNERS

Year	Men's singles	Women's singles	Men's doubles	Women's doubles	Mixed doubles
1958	Jim Poole	Judy Devlin	Finn Kobberø Jørgen Hammergaard Hansen	Judy Devlin Susan Devlin	Finn Kobberø Judy Devlin

1958 NBA STANDINGS
DIVISION STANDINGS

Team	W	L	W/L%	GB	PS/G	PA/G	SRS
Eastern Division							
Boston Celtics*	49	23	.681	—	109.9	104.4	5.02
Syracuse Nationals*	41	31	.569	8.0	107.2	105.1	2.18
Philadelphia Warriors*	37	35	.514	12.0	104.3	104.4	0.21
New York Knicks	35	37	.486	14.0	112.1	110.8	1.35
Western Division							
St. Louis Hawks*	41	31	.569	—	107.5	106.2	0.82
Detroit Pistons*	33	39	.458	8.0	105.3	107.7	-2.32
Cincinnati Royals*	33	39	.458	8.0	101.7	103.1	-1.47
Minneapolis Lakers	19	53	.264	22.0	105.1	111.5	-5.78

AMERICAN HORSE OF THE YEAR
1958 ECLIPSE AWARD

Year	Horse	Trainer	Owner	Age	Gender
1958	Round Table	William Molter	Kerr Stable	4	C

1958- NHL SEASON
FINAL STANDINGS

National Hockey League	GP	W	L	T	Pts	GF	GA	PIM
Montreal Canadiens	70	39	18	13	91	258	158	760
Boston Bruins	70	32	29	9	73	205	215	838
Chicago Black Hawks	70	28	29	13	69	197	208	921
Toronto Maple Leafs	70	27	32	11	65	189	201	846
New York Rangers	70	26	32	12	64	201	217	860
Detroit Red Wings	70	25	37	8	58	167	218	613

1958 MAJOR LEAGUE BASEBALL SEASON HISTORY

1958 American League Standings									
TEAM	W	L	PCT	GB	HOME	ROAD	RS	RA	DIFF
*-New York	92	62	.594	--	--	--	759	577	+182
Chicago	82	72	.529	10	--	--	634	615	+19
Boston	79	75	.510	13	--	--	697	691	+6
Cleveland	77	76	.503	14.5	--	--	694	635	+59
Detroit	77	77	.500	15	--	--	659	606	+53
Baltimore	74	79	.481	17.5	--	--	521	575	-54
Kansas City	73	81	.468	19	--	--	642	713	-71
Washington	61	93	.391	31	--	--	553	747	-194
1958 National League Standings									
TEAM	W	L	PCT	GB	HOME	ROAD	RS	RA	DIFF
*-Milwaukee	92	62	.597	--	--	--	675	541	+134
Pittsburgh	84	70	.545	8	--	--	662	607	+55
San Francisco	80	74	.519	12	--	--	727	698	+29
Cincinnati	76	78	.494	16	--	--	695	621	+74
St. Louis	72	82	.468	20	--	--	619	704	-85
Chicago	72	82	.468	20	--	--	709	725	-16
Los Angeles	71	83	.461	21	--	--	668	761	-93
Philadelphia	69	85	.448	23	--	--	664	762	-98

1958 U.S. NATIONAL TENNIS CHAMPIONSHIPS

Men's Singles
Ashley Cooper defeated Malcolm Anderson 6–2, 3–6, 4–6, 10–8, 8–6

Women's Singles
Althea Gibson defeated Darlene Hard 3–6, 6–1, 6–2

Men's doubles
Alex Olmedo (USA) / Ham Richardson (USA) defeated Sam Giammalva (USA) / Barry MacKay (USA) 3–6, 6–3, 6–4, 6–4

Women's doubles
Jeanne Arth (USA) / Darlene Hard (USA) defeated Althea Gibson (USA) / Maria Bueno (BRA) 2–6, 6–3, 6–4

Mixed doubles
Margaret Osborne (USA) / Neale Fraser (AUS) defeated Maria Bueno (BRA) / Alex Olmedo (USA) 6–3, 3–6, 9–7

1959

1959 NATIONAL FOOTBALL LEAGUE SEASON
STANDINGS

EAST	W	L	T	WEST	W	L	T
NY Giants	10	2	0	Baltimore	9	3	0
Cleveland	7	5	0	Chi. Bears	8	4	0
Philadelphia	7	5	0	Green Bay	7	5	0
Pittsburgh	6	5	1	San Francisco	7	5	0
Washington	3	9	0	Detroit	3	8	1
Chi. Cardinals	2	10	0	Los Angeles	2	10	0

1959 U.S. OPEN BADMINTON CHAMPIONSHIPS
WINNERS

Year	Men's singles	Women's singles	Men's doubles	Women's doubles	Mixed doubles
1959	Tan Joe Hok	Judy Devlin	Teh Kew San / Lim Say Hup	Judy Devlin / Susan Devlin	Michael Roche / Judy Devlin

1959 NBA STANDINGS
DIVISION STANDINGS

Team	W	L	W/L%	GB	PS/G	PA/G	SRS
Eastern Division							
Boston Celtics*	52	20	.722	—	116.4	109.9	5.84
New York Knicks*	40	32	.556	12.0	110.3	110.1	0.49
Syracuse Nationals*	35	37	.486	17.0	113.1	109.1	3.74
Philadelphia Warriors	32	40	.444	20.0	103.3	106.3	-2.29
Western Division							
St. Louis Hawks*	49	23	.681	—	108.8	105.1	2.89
Minneapolis Lakers*	33	39	.458	16.0	106.0	107.3	-1.42
Detroit Pistons*	28	44	.389	21.0	105.1	106.3	-1.36
Cincinnati Royals	19	53	.264	30.0	103.1	111.9	-7.89

AMERICAN HORSE OF THE YEAR
1959 ECLIPSE AWARD

Year	Horse	Trainer	Owner	Age	Gender
1959	Sword Dancer	J. Elliott Burch	Brookmeade Stable	3	C

1959- NHL SEASON
FINAL STANDINGS

National Hockey League	GP	W	L	T	Pts	GF	GA	PIM
Montreal Canadiens	70	40	18	12	92	255	178	756
Toronto Maple Leafs	70	35	26	9	79	199	195	859
Chicago Black Hawks	70	28	29	13	69	191	180	970
Detroit Red Wings	70	26	29	15	67	186	197	538
Boston Bruins	70	28	34	8	64	220	241	932
New York Rangers	70	17	38	15	49	187	247	850

1959 MAJOR LEAGUE BASEBALL SEASON HISTORY

1959 American League Standings									
TEAM	W	L	PCT	GB	HOME	ROAD	RS	RA	DIFF
*-Chicago	94	60	.603	--	--	--	669	588	+81
Cleveland	89	65	.578	5	--	--	745	646	+99
New York	79	75	.510	15	--	--	687	647	+40
Detroit	76	78	.494	18	--	--	713	732	-19
Boston	75	79	.487	19	--	--	726	696	+30
Baltimore	74	80	.477	20	--	--	551	621	-70
Kansas City	66	88	.429	28	--	--	681	760	-79
Washington	63	91	.409	31	--	--	619	701	-82
1959 National League Standings									
TEAM	W	L	PCT	GB	HOME	ROAD	RS	RA	DIFF
*-Los Angeles	88	68	.564	--	--	--	705	670	+35
Milwaukee	86	70	.548	2	--	--	724	623	+101
San Francisco	83	71	.539	4	--	--	705	613	+92
Pittsburgh	78	76	.503	9	--	--	651	680	-29
Cincinnati	74	80	.481	13	--	--	764	738	+26
Chicago	74	80	.477	13	--	--	673	688	-15
St. Louis	71	83	.461	16	--	--	641	725	-84
Philadelphia	64	90	.413	23	--	--	599	725	-126

1959 U.S. NATIONAL TENNIS CHAMPIONSHIPS

Men's Singles
Neale Fraser (AUS) defeated Alex Olmedo (USA) 6–3, 5–7, 6–2, 6–4
Women's Singles
Maria Bueno (BRA) defeated Christine Truman (UK) 6–1, 6–4
Men's doubles
Neale Fraser (AUS) / Roy Emerson (AUS) defeated Alex Olmedo (USA) / Earl Buchholz (USA) 3–6, 6–3, 5–7, 6–4, 7–5
Women's doubles
Jeanne Arth (USA) / Darlene Hard (USA) defeated Althea Gibson (USA) / Sally Moore (USA) 6–2, 6–3
Mixed doubles
Margaret Osborne (USA) / Neale Fraser (AUS) defeated Janet Hopps (USA) / Bob Mark (AUS) 7–5, 13–15, 6–2

1960

1960 NATIONAL FOOTBALL LEAGUE SEASON
STANDINGS

EAST	W	L	WEST	W	L	T
Philadelphia	10	2	Green Bay	8	4	0
Cleveland	8	3	Detroit	7	5	0
NY Giants	6	4	San Francisco	7	5	0
St. Louis	6	5	Baltimore	6	6	0
Pittsburgh	5	6	Chicago	5	6	1
Washington	1	9	Los Angeles	4	7	1
			Dallas	0	11	1

1960 U.S. OPEN BADMINTON CHAMPIONSHIPS
WINNERS

Year	Men's singles	Women's singles	Men's doubles	Women's doubles	Mixed doubles
1960	Tan Joe Hok	Judy Devlin	Finn Kobberø Charoen Wattanasin	Judy Devlin Susan Devlin	Finn Kobberø Margaret Varner

1960 NBA STANDINGS
DIVISION STANDINGS

Team	W	L	W/L%	GB	PS/G	PA/G	SRS
Eastern Division							
Boston Celtics*	59	16	.787	—	124.5	116.2	7.62
Philadelphia Warriors*	49	26	.653	10.0	118.6	116.0	2.77
Syracuse Nationals*	45	30	.600	14.0	118.9	116.3	2.77
New York Knicks	27	48	.360	32.0	117.3	119.6	-1.43
Western Division							
St. Louis Hawks*	46	29	.613	—	113.4	110.7	1.77
Detroit Pistons*	30	45	.400	16.0	111.6	115.0	-3.45
Minneapolis Lakers*	25	50	.333	21.0	107.3	111.5	-4.14
Cincinnati Royals	19	56	.253	27.0	111.1	117.4	-5.92

AMERICAN HORSE OF THE YEAR
1960 ECLIPSE AWARD

Year	Horse	Trainer	Owner	Age	Gender
1960	Kelso	Carl Hanford	Bohemia Stable	3	G

1960- NHL SEASON
FINAL STANDINGS

National Hockey League	GP	W	L	T	Pts	GF	GA	PIM
Montreal Canadiens	70	41	19	10	92	254	188	811
Toronto Maple Leafs	70	39	19	12	90	234	176	844
Chicago Black Hawks	70	29	24	17	75	198	180	1072
Detroit Red Wings	70	25	29	16	66	195	215	655
New York Rangers	70	22	38	10	54	204	248	591
Boston Bruins	70	15	42	13	43	176	254	810

1960 MAJOR LEAGUE BASEBALL SEASON HISTORY

1960 American League Standings									
TEAM	W	L	PCT	GB	HOME	ROAD	RS	RA	DIFF
*-New York	97	57	.626	--	--	--	746	627	+119
Baltimore	89	65	.578	8	--	--	682	606	+76
Chicago	87	67	.565	10	--	--	741	617	+124
Cleveland	76	78	.494	21	--	--	667	693	-26
Washington	73	81	.474	24	--	--	672	696	-24
Detroit	71	83	.461	26	--	--	633	644	-11
Boston	65	89	.422	32	--	--	658	775	-117
Kansas City	58	96	.374	39	--	--	615	756	-141
1960 National League Standings									
TEAM	W	L	PCT	GB	HOME	ROAD	RS	RA	DIFF
*-Pittsburgh	95	59	.613	--	--	--	734	593	+141
Milwaukee	88	66	.571	7	--	--	724	658	+66
St. Louis	86	68	.555	9	--	--	639	616	+23
Los Angeles	82	72	.532	13	--	--	662	593	+69
San Francisco	79	75	.506	16	--	--	671	631	+40
Cincinnati	67	87	.435	28	--	--	640	692	-52
Chicago	60	94	.385	35	--	--	634	776	-142
Philadelphia	59	95	.383	36	--	--	546	691	-145

1960 U.S. NATIONAL TENNIS CHAMPIONSHIPS

Men's Singles
Neale Fraser defeated Rod Laver 6–4, 6–4, 9–7
Women's Singles
Darlene Hard defeated Maria Bueno 6–4, 10–12, 6–4
Men's doubles
Neale Fraser / Roy Emerson defeated Rod Laver / Bob Mark 9–7, 6–, 6–4, 13–11
Women's doubles
Maria Bueno / Darlene Hard defeated Ann Haydon Jones / Deidre Catt 6–1, 6–1
Mixed doubles
Margaret Osborne / Neale Fraser defeated Maria Bueno / Antonio Palafox 6–3, 6–2

1961

1961 NATIONAL FOOTBALL LEAGUE SEASON
STANDINGS

EAST	W	L	T	WEST	W	L	T
NY Giants	10	3	1	Green Bay	11	3	0
Philadelphia	10	4	0	Detroit	8	5	1
Cleveland	8	5	1	Baltimore	8	6	0
St. Louis	7	7	0	Chicago	8	6	0
Pittsburgh	6	8	0	San Francisco	7	6	1
Dallas	4	9	1	Los Angeles	4	10	0
Washington	1	12	1	Minnesota	3	11	0

1961 U.S. OPEN BADMINTON CHAMPIONSHIPS
WINNERS

Year	Men's singles	Women's singles	Men's doubles	Women's doubles	Mixed doubles
1961	Jim Poole	Judy Devlin	Joe Alston Wynn Rogers	Judy Devlin Hashman Susan Devlin Peard	Wynn Rogers Judy Devlin Hashman

1961 NBA STANDINGS
DIVISION STANDINGS

Team	W	L	W/L%	GB	PS/G	PA/G	SRS
Eastern Division							
Boston Celtics*	57	22	.722	—	119.7	114.1	4.94
Philadelphia Warriors*	46	33	.582	11.0	121.0	120.1	0.89
Syracuse Nationals*	38	41	.481	19.0	121.3	119.2	1.93
New York Knicks	21	58	.266	36.0	113.7	120.1	-5.43
Western Division							
St. Louis Hawks*	51	28	.646	—	118.8	115.2	2.99
Los Angeles Lakers*	36	43	.456	15.0	114.0	114.1	-0.11
Detroit Pistons*	34	45	.430	17.0	118.6	121.0	-2.11
Cincinnati Royals	33	46	.418	18.0	117.9	121.3	-3.04

AMERICAN HORSE OF THE YEAR
1961 ECLIPSE AWARD

Year	Horse	Trainer	Owner	Age	Gender
1961	Kelso	Carl Hanford	Bohemia Stable	4	G

1961- NHL SEASON
FINAL STANDINGS

National Hockey League	GP	W	L	T	Pts	GF	GA	PIM
Montreal Canadiens	70	42	14	14	98	259	166	818
Toronto Maple Leafs	70	37	22	11	85	232	180	762
Chicago Black Hawks	70	31	26	13	75	217	186	894
New York Rangers	70	26	32	12	64	195	207	668
Detroit Red Wings	70	23	33	14	60	184	219	684
Boston Bruins	70	15	47	8	38	177	306	712

1961 MAJOR LEAGUE BASEBALL SEASON HISTORY

1961 American League Standings									
TEAM	W	L	PCT	GB	HOME	ROAD	RS	RA	DIFF
*-New York	109	53	.669	--	--	--	827	612	+215
Detroit	101	61	.620	8	--	--	841	671	+170
Baltimore	95	67	.583	14	--	--	691	588	+103
Chicago	86	76	.528	23	--	--	765	726	+39
Cleveland	78	83	.484	30.5	--	--	737	752	-15
Boston	76	86	.466	33	--	--	729	792	-63
Minnesota	70	90	.435	38	--	--	707	778	-71
Los Angeles	70	91	.432	38.5	--	--	744	784	-40
Washington	61	100	.379	47.5	--	--	618	776	-158
Kansas City	61	100	.377	47.5	--	--	683	863	-180
1961 National League Standings									
TEAM	W	L	PCT	GB	HOME	ROAD	RS	RA	DIFF
*-Cincinnati	93	61	.604	--	--	--	710	653	+57
Los Angeles	89	65	.578	4	--	--	735	697	+38
San Francisco	85	69	.548	8	--	--	773	655	+118
Milwaukee	83	71	.535	10	--	--	712	656	+56
St. Louis	80	74	.516	13	--	--	703	668	+35
Pittsburgh	75	79	.487	18	--	--	694	675	+19
Chicago	64	90	.410	29	--	--	689	800	-111
Philadelphia	47	107	.303	46	--	--	584	796	-212

1961 U.S. NATIONAL TENNIS CHAMPIONSHIPS

Men's Singles
Roy Emerson defeated Rod Laver 7–5, 6–3, 6–2
Women's Singles
Darlene Hard defeated Ann Haydon Jones 6–3, 6–4
Men's doubles
Chuck McKinley / Dennis Ralston defeated Rafael Osuna / Antonio Palafox 6–3, 6–4, 2–6, 13–11
Women's doubles
Darlene Hard / Lesley Turner defeated Edda Buding / Yola Ramírez 6–4, 5–7, 6–0
Mixed doubles
Margaret Smith / Bob Mark defeated Darlene Hard / Dennis Ralston default

1962

1962 NATIONAL FOOTBALL LEAGUE SEASON
STANDINGS

EAST	W	L	T	WEST	W	L	T
NY Giants	12	2	0	Green Bay	13	1	0
Pittsburgh	9	5	0	Detroit	11	3	0
Cleveland	7	6	1	Chicago	9	5	0
Washington	5	7	2	Baltimore	7	7	0
Dallas	5	8	1	San Francisco	6	8	0
St. Louis	4	9	1	Minnesota	2	11	1
Philadelphia	3	10	1	Los Angeles	1	12	1

1962 U.S. OPEN BADMINTON CHAMPIONSHIPS
WINNERS

Year	Men's singles	Women's singles	Men's doubles	Women's doubles	Mixed doubles
1962	Ferry Sonneville	Judy Devlin	Joe Alston Wynn Rogers	Judy Hashman Patsy Stephens	Wynn Rogers Judy Hashman

1962 NBA STANDINGS
DIVISION STANDINGS

Team	W	L	W/L%	GB	PS/G	PA/G	SRS
Eastern Division							
Boston Celtics*	60	20	.750	—	121.1	111.9	8.25
Philadelphia Warriors*	49	31	.613	11.0	125.4	122.7	2.63
Syracuse Nationals*	41	39	.513	19.0	120.7	118.4	2.24
New York Knicks	29	51	.363	31.0	114.8	119.7	-3.98
Western Division							
Los Angeles Lakers*	54	26	.675	—	118.5	116.3	1.80
Cincinnati Royals*	43	37	.538	11.0	123.1	121.3	1.28
Detroit Pistons*	37	43	.463	17.0	115.4	117.1	-1.72
St. Louis Hawks	29	51	.363	25.0	118.9	122.1	-2.96
Chicago Packers	18	62	.225	36.0	110.9	119.4	-7.54

AMERICAN HORSE OF THE YEAR
1962 ECLIPSE AWARD

Year	Horse	Trainer	Owner	Age	Gender
1962	Kelso	Carl Hanford	Bohemia Stable	5	G

1962- NHL SEASON
FINAL STANDINGS

National Hockey League	GP	W	L	T	Pts	GF	GA	PIM
Toronto Maple Leafs	70	35	23	12	82	221	180	816
Chicago Black Hawks	70	32	21	17	81	194	178	906
Montreal Canadiens	70	28	19	23	79	225	183	751
Detroit Red Wings	70	32	25	13	77	200	194	964
New York Rangers	70	22	36	12	56	211	233	657
Boston Bruins	70	14	39	17	45	198	281	636

1962 MAJOR LEAGUE BASEBALL SEASON HISTORY

1962 American League Standings									
TEAM	W	L	PCT	GB	HOME	ROAD	RS	RA	DIFF
*-New York	96	66	.593	--	--	--	817	680	+137
Minnesota	91	71	.558	5	--	--	798	713	+85
Los Angeles	86	76	.531	10	--	--	718	706	+12
Detroit	85	76	.528	10.5	--	--	758	692	+66
Chicago	85	77	.525	11	--	--	707	658	+49
Cleveland	80	82	.494	16	--	--	682	745	-63
Baltimore	77	85	.475	19	--	--	652	680	-28
Boston	76	84	.475	19	--	--	707	756	-49
Kansas City	72	90	.444	24	--	--	745	837	-92
Washington	60	101	.370	35.5	--	--	599	716	-117
1962 National League Standings									
TEAM	W	L	PCT	GB	HOME	ROAD	RS	RA	DIFF
*-San Francisco	103	62	.624	--	--	--	878	690	+188
Los Angeles	102	63	.618	1	--	--	842	697	+145
Cincinnati	98	64	.605	3.5	--	--	802	685	+117
Pittsburgh	93	68	.578	8	--	--	706	626	+80
Milwaukee	86	76	.531	15.5	--	--	730	665	+65
St. Louis	84	78	.515	17.5	--	--	774	664	+110
Philadelphia	81	80	.503	20	--	--	705	759	-54
Houston	64	96	.395	36.5	--	--	592	717	-125
Chicago	59	103	.364	42.5	--	--	632	827	-195
New York	40	120	.248	60.5	--	--	617	948	-331

1962 U.S. NATIONAL TENNIS CHAMPIONSHIPS

Men's Singles
Rod Laver defeated Roy Emerson 6–2, 6–4, 5–7, 6–4
Women's Singles
Margaret Smith defeated Darlene Hard 9–7, 6–4
Men's doubles
Rafael Osuna / Antonio Palafox defeated Chuck McKinley / Dennis Ralston 6–4, 10–12, 1–6, 9–7, 6–3
Women's doubles
Darlene Hard / Maria Bueno defeated Karen Hantze Susman / Billie Jean Moffitt, 4–6, 6–3, 6–2
Mixed doubles
Margaret Smith / Fred Stolle defeated Lesley Turner / Frank Froehling 7–5, 6–2

1963

1963 NATIONAL FOOTBALL LEAGUE SEASON
STANDINGS

EAST	W	L	T	WEST	W	L	T
NY Giants	11	3	0	Chicago	11	1	2
Cleveland	10	4	0	Green Bay	11	2	1
St. Louis	9	5	0	Baltimore	8	6	0
Pittsburgh	7	4	3	Detroit	5	8	1
Dallas	4	10	0	Minnesota	5	8	1
Washington	3	11	0	Los Angeles	5	9	0
Philadelphia	2	10	2	San Francisco	2	12	0

1963 U.S. OPEN BADMINTON CHAMPIONSHIPS
WINNERS

Year	Men's singles	Women's singles	Men's doubles	Women's doubles	Mixed doubles
1963	Erland Kops	Judy Devlin	Erland Kops Bob McCoig	Judy Hashman Susan Peard	Sangob Rattanusorn Margaret Barrand

1963 NBA STANDINGS
DIVISION STANDINGS

Team	W	L	W/L%	GB	PS/G	PA/G	SRS
Eastern Division							
Boston Celtics*	58	22	.725	—	118.8	111.6	6.38
Syracuse Nationals*	48	32	.600	10.0	121.6	117.8	3.40
Cincinnati Royals*	42	38	.525	16.0	119.1	117.8	1.24
New York Knicks	21	59	.263	37.0	110.5	117.7	-6.20
Western Division							
Los Angeles Lakers*	53	27	.663	—	115.5	112.4	2.67
St. Louis Hawks*	48	32	.600	5.0	109.6	107.8	1.38
Detroit Pistons*	34	46	.425	19.0	113.9	117.6	-3.38
San Francisco Warriors	31	49	.388	22.0	118.5	120.6	-1.86
Chicago Zephyrs	25	55	.313	28.0	109.9	114.0	-3.63

AMERICAN HORSE OF THE YEAR
1963 ECLIPSE AWARD

Year	Horse	Trainer	Owner	Age	Gender
1963	Kelso	Carl Hanford	Bohemia Stable	6	G

1963- NHL SEASON
FINAL STANDINGS

National Hockey League	GP	W	L	T	Pts	GF	GA	PIM
Montreal Canadiens	70	36	21	13	85	209	167	982
Chicago Black Hawks	70	36	22	12	84	218	169	1116
Toronto Maple Leafs	70	33	25	12	78	192	172	928
Detroit Red Wings	70	30	29	11	71	191	204	771
New York Rangers	70	22	38	10	54	186	242	715
Boston Bruins	70	18	40	12	48	170	212	858

1963 MAJOR LEAGUE BASEBALL SEASON HISTORY

1963 American League Standings									
TEAM	W	L	PCT	GB	HOME	ROAD	RS	RA	DIFF
*-New York	104	57	.646	--	--	--	714	547	+167
Chicago	94	68	.580	10.5	--	--	683	544	+139
Minnesota	91	70	.565	13	--	--	767	602	+165
Baltimore	86	76	.531	18.5	--	--	644	621	+23
Detroit	79	83	.488	25.5	--	--	700	703	-3
Cleveland	79	83	.488	25.5	--	--	635	702	-67
Boston	76	85	.472	28	--	--	666	704	-38
Kansas City	73	89	.451	31.5	--	--	615	704	-89
Los Angeles	70	91	.435	34	--	--	597	660	-63
Washington	56	106	.346	48.5	--	--	578	812	-234

1963 National League Standings									
TEAM	W	L	PCT	GB	HOME	ROAD	RS	RA	DIFF
*-Los Angeles	99	63	.607	--	--	--	640	550	+90
St. Louis	93	69	.574	6	--	--	747	628	+119
San Francisco	88	74	.543	11	--	--	725	641	+84
Philadelphia	87	75	.537	12	--	--	642	578	+64
Cincinnati	86	76	.531	13	--	--	648	594	+54
Milwaukee	84	78	.515	15	--	--	677	603	+74
Chicago	82	80	.506	17	--	--	570	578	-8
Pittsburgh	74	88	.457	25	--	--	567	595	-28
Houston	66	96	.407	33	--	--	464	640	-176
New York	51	111	.315	48	--	--	501	774	-273

1963 U.S. NATIONAL TENNIS CHAMPIONSHIPS

Men's Singles
Rafael Osuna defeated Frank Froehling 7–5, 6–4, 6–2
Women's Singles
Maria Bueno defeated Margaret Smith 7–5, 6–4
Men's doubles
Chuck McKinley / Dennis Ralston defeated Rafael Osuna / Antonio Palafox 9–7, 4–6, 5–7, 6–3, 11–9
Women's doubles
Robyn Ebbern / Margaret Smith defeated Darlene Hard / Maria Bueno, 4–6, 10–8, 6–3
Mixed doubles
Margaret Smith / Ken Fletcher defeated Judy Tegart / Ed Rubinoff 3–6, 8–6, 6–2

1964

1964 NATIONAL FOOTBALL LEAGUE SEASON
STANDINGS

EAST	W	L	T	WEST	W	L	T
Cleveland	10	3	1	Baltimore	12	2	0
St. Louis	9	3	2	Green Bay	8	5	1
Philadelphia	6	8	0	Minnesota	8	5	1
Washington	6	8	0	Detroit	7	5	2
Dallas	5	8	1	Los Angeles	5	7	2
Pittsburgh	5	9	0	Chicago	5	9	0
NY Giants	2	10	2	San Francisco	4	10	0

1964 U.S. OPEN BADMINTON CHAMPIONSHIPS
WINNERS

Year	Men's singles	Women's singles	Men's doubles	Women's doubles	Mixed doubles
1964	Channarong Ratanaseangsuang	Dorothy O'Neil	Joe Alston Wynn Rogers	Tyna Barinaga Caroline Jensen	Channarong Ratanaseangsuang Margaret Barrand

1960 NBA STANDINGS
DIVISION STANDINGS

Team	W	L	W/L%	GB	PS/G	PA/G	SRS
Eastern Division							
Boston Celtics*	59	21	.738	—	113.0	105.1	6.93
Cincinnati Royals*	55	25	.688	4.0	114.7	109.7	4.43
Philadelphia 76ers*	34	46	.425	25.0	112.2	116.5	-3.75
New York Knicks	22	58	.275	37.0	112.2	119.0	-5.91
Western Division							
San Francisco Warriors*	48	32	.600	—	107.7	102.6	4.41
St. Louis Hawks*	46	34	.575	2.0	110.0	108.4	1.39
Los Angeles Lakers*	42	38	.525	6.0	109.7	108.7	0.87
Baltimore Bullets	31	49	.388	17.0	111.9	113.6	-1.59
Detroit Pistons	23	57	.288	25.0	107.8	115.5	-6.77

AMERICAN HORSE OF THE YEAR
1964 ECLIPSE AWARD

Year	Horse	Trainer	Owner	Age	Gender
1964	Kelso	Carl Hanford	Bohemia Stable	7	G

1964- NHL SEASON
FINAL STANDINGS

National Hockey League	GP	W	L	T	Pts	GF	GA	PIM
Detroit Red Wings	70	40	23	7	87	224	175	1121
Montreal Canadiens	70	36	23	11	83	211	185	1033
Chicago Black Hawks	70	34	28	8	76	224	176	1051
Toronto Maple Leafs	70	30	26	14	74	204	173	1068
New York Rangers	70	20	38	12	52	179	246	760
Boston Bruins	70	21	43	6	48	166	253	946

1964 MAJOR LEAGUE BASEBALL SEASON HISTORY

1964 American League Standings									
TEAM	W	L	PCT	GB	HOME	ROAD	RS	RA	DIFF
*-New York	99	63	.604	--	--	--	730	577	+153
Chicago	98	64	.605	1	--	--	642	501	+141
Baltimore	97	65	.595	2	--	--	679	567	+112
Detroit	85	77	.521	14	--	--	699	678	+21
Los Angeles	82	80	.506	17	--	--	544	551	-7
Minnesota	79	83	.485	20	--	--	737	678	+59
Cleveland	79	83	.482	20	--	--	689	693	-4
Boston	72	90	.444	27	--	--	688	793	-105
Washington	62	100	.383	37	--	--	578	733	-155
Kansas City	57	105	.350	42	--	--	621	836	-215
1964 National League Standings									
TEAM	W	L	PCT	GB	HOME	ROAD	RS	RA	DIFF
*-St. Louis	93	69	.574	--	--	--	715	652	+63
Philadelphia	92	70	.568	1	--	--	693	632	+61
Cincinnati	92	70	.564	1	--	--	660	566	+94
San Francisco	90	72	.556	3	--	--	656	587	+69
Milwaukee	88	74	.543	5	--	--	803	744	+59
Pittsburgh	80	82	.494	13	--	--	663	636	+27
Los Angeles	80	82	.488	13	--	--	614	572	+42
Chicago	76	86	.469	17	--	--	649	724	-75
Houston	66	96	.407	27	--	--	495	628	-133
New York	53	109	.325	40	--	--	569	776	-207

1964 U.S. NATIONAL TENNIS CHAMPIONSHIPS

Men's Singles
Roy Emerson defeated Fred Stolle 6–4, 6–2, 6–4
Women's Singles
Maria Bueno defeated Carole Caldwell Graebner 6–1, 6–0
Men's doubles
Chuck McKinley / Dennis Ralston defeated Graham Stilwell / Mike Sangster 6–3, 6–2, 6–4
Women's doubles
Billie Jean Moffitt / Karen Susman defeated Margaret Smith / Lesley Turner 3–6, 6–2, 6–4
Mixed doubles
Margaret Smith / John Newcombe defeated Judy Tegart / Ed Rubinoff 10–6, 4–6, 6–3

1965

1965 NATIONAL FOOTBALL LEAGUE SEASON
STANDINGS

EAST	W	L	T	WEST	W	L	T
Cleveland	11	3	0	Green Bay	10	3	1
Dallas	7	7	0	Baltimore	10	3	1
NY Giants	7	7	0	Chicago	9	5	0
Washington	6	8	0	San Francisco	7	6	1
Philadelphia	5	9	0	Minnesota	7	7	0
St. Louis	5	9	0	Detroit	6	7	1
Pittsburgh	2	12	0	Los Angeles	4	10	0

1965 U.S. OPEN BADMINTON CHAMPIONSHIPS
WINNERS

Year	Men's singles	Women's singles	Men's doubles	Women's doubles	Mixed doubles
1965	Erland Kops	Judy Devlin	Bob McCoig Tony Jordan	Margaret Barrand Jennifer Pritchard	Bob McCoig Margaret Barrand

1965 NBA STANDINGS
DIVISION STANDINGS

Team	W	L	W/L%	GB	PS/G	PA/G	SRS
Eastern Division							
Boston Celtics*	62	18	.775	—	112.8	104.4	7.46
Cincinnati Royals*	48	32	.600	14.0	114.2	111.9	2.04
Philadelphia 76ers*	40	40	.500	22.0	112.5	112.7	-0.13
New York Knicks	31	49	.388	31.0	107.4	111.1	-3.26
Western Division							
Los Angeles Lakers*	49	31	.613	—	111.9	109.9	1.70
St. Louis Hawks*	45	35	.563	4.0	108.8	105.8	2.68
Baltimore Bullets*	37	43	.463	12.0	113.6	115.8	-1.97
Detroit Pistons	31	49	.388	18.0	108.5	111.9	-3.03
San Francisco Warriors	17	63	.213	32.0	105.8	112.0	-5.49

AMERICAN HORSE OF THE YEAR
1965 ECLIPSE AWARD

Year	Horse	Trainer	Owner	Age	Gender
1965	Moccasin	Harry Trotsek	Claiborne Farm	2	F
1965	Roman Brother	Burley Parke	Harbor View Farm	4	G

1965- NHL SEASON
FINAL STANDINGS

National Hockey League	GP	W	L	T	Pts	GF	GA	PIM
Montreal Canadiens	70	41	21	8	90	239	173	884
Chicago Black Hawks	70	37	25	8	82	240	187	815
Toronto Maple Leafs	70	34	25	11	79	208	187	811
Detroit Red Wings	70	31	27	12	74	221	194	804
Boston Bruins	70	21	43	6	48	174	275	787
New York Rangers	70	18	41	11	47	195	261	894

1965 MAJOR LEAGUE BASEBALL SEASON HISTORY

1965 American League Standings

TEAM	W	L	PCT	GB	HOME	ROAD	RS	RA	DIFF
*-Minnesota	102	60	.630	--	--	--	774	600	+174
Chicago	95	67	.586	7	--	--	647	555	+92
Baltimore	94	68	.580	8	--	--	641	578	+63
Detroit	89	73	.549	13	--	--	680	602	+78
Cleveland	87	75	.537	15	--	--	663	613	+50
New York	77	85	.475	25	--	--	611	604	+7
California	75	87	.463	27	--	--	527	569	-42
Washington	70	92	.432	32	--	--	591	721	-130
Boston	62	100	.383	40	--	--	669	791	-122
Kansas City	59	103	.364	43	--	--	585	755	-170

1965 National League Standings

TEAM	W	L	PCT	GB	HOME	ROAD	RS	RA	DIFF
*-Los Angeles	97	65	.599	--	--	--	608	521	+87
San Francisco	95	67	.583	2	--	--	682	593	+89
Pittsburgh	90	72	.552	7	--	--	675	580	+95
Cincinnati	89	73	.549	8	--	--	825	704	+121
Milwaukee	86	76	.531	11	--	--	708	633	+75
Philadelphia	85	76	.525	11.5	--	--	654	667	-13
St. Louis	80	81	.494	16.5	--	--	707	674	+33
Chicago	72	90	.439	25	--	--	635	723	-88
Houston	65	97	.401	32	--	--	569	711	-142
New York	50	112	.305	47	--	--	495	752	-257

1965 U.S. NATIONAL TENNIS CHAMPIONSHIPS

Men's Singles
Manuel Santana defeated Cliff Drysdale 6–2, 7–9, 7–5, 6–1
Women's Singles
Margaret Smith defeated Billie Jean Moffitt 8–6, 7–5
Men's doubles
Roy Emerson / Fred Stolle defeated Frank Froehling / Charles Pasarell 6–4, 10–12, 7–5, 6–3
Women's doubles
Carole Graebner / Nancy Richey defeated Billie Jean Moffitt / Karen Susman 6–4, 6–4
Mixed doubles
Margaret Smith / Fred Stolle defeated Judy Tegart / Frank Froehling 6–2, 6–2

1966

1966 NATIONAL FOOTBALL LEAGUE SEASON
STANDINGS

EAST	W	L	T	WEST	W	L	T
Dallas	10	3	1	Green Bay	12	2	0
Cleveland	9	5	0	Baltimore	9	5	0
Philadelphia	9	5	0	Los Angeles	8	6	0
St. Louis	8	5	1	San Francisco	6	6	2
Washington	7	7	0	Chicago	5	7	2
Pittsburgh	5	8	1	Detroit	4	9	1
Atlanta	3	11	0	Minnesota	4	9	1
NY Giants	1	12	1				

1966 U.S. OPEN BADMINTON CHAMPIONSHIPS
WINNERS

Year	Men's singles	Women's singles	Men's doubles	Women's doubles	Mixed doubles
1966	Tan Aik Huang	Judy Devlin	Ng Boon Bee Tan Yee Khan	Judy Hashman Susan Peard	Wayne MacDonnell Tyna Barinaga

1966 NBA STANDINGS
DIVISION STANDINGS

Team	W	L	W/L%	GB	PS/G	PA/G	SRS
Eastern Division							
Philadelphia 76ers*	55	25	.688	—	117.3	112.7	4.16
Boston Celtics*	54	26	.675	1.0	112.7	107.8	4.34
Cincinnati Royals*	45	35	.563	10.0	117.8	116.6	1.03
New York Knicks	30	50	.375	25.0	116.7	119.3	-2.31
Western Division							
Los Angeles Lakers*	45	35	.563	—	119.5	116.4	2.76
Baltimore Bullets*	38	42	.475	7.0	118.3	119.5	-1.06
St. Louis Hawks*	36	44	.450	9.0	111.4	112.0	-0.50
San Francisco Warriors	35	45	.438	10.0	115.5	118.2	-2.36
Detroit Pistons	22	58	.275	23.0	110.3	117.2	-6.07

AMERICAN HORSE OF THE YEAR
1966 ECLIPSE AWARD

Year	Horse	Trainer	Owner	Age	Gender
1966	Buckpasser	Edward A. Neloy	Ogden Phipps	3	C

1966- NHL SEASON
FINAL STANDINGS

National Hockey League	GP	W	L	T	Pts	GF	GA	PIM
Chicago Black Hawks	70	41	17	12	94	264	170	757
Montreal Canadiens	70	32	25	13	77	202	188	879
Toronto Maple Leafs	70	32	27	11	75	204	211	736
New York Rangers	70	30	28	12	72	188	189	664
Detroit Red Wings	70	27	39	4	58	212	241	719
Boston Bruins	70	17	43	10	44	182	253	764

1966 MAJOR LEAGUE BASEBALL SEASON HISTORY

1966 American League Standings

TEAM	W	L	PCT	GB	HOME	ROAD	RS	RA	DIFF
*-Baltimore	97	63	.606	--	--	--	755	601	+154
Minnesota	89	73	.549	9	--	--	663	581	+82
Detroit	88	74	.543	10	--	--	719	698	+21
Chicago	83	79	.509	15	--	--	574	517	+57
Cleveland	81	81	.500	17	--	--	574	586	-12
California	80	82	.494	18	--	--	604	643	-39
Kansas City	74	86	.463	23	--	--	564	648	-84
Washington	71	88	.447	25.5	--	--	557	659	-102
Boston	72	90	.444	26	--	--	655	731	-76
New York	70	89	.438	26.5	--	--	611	612	-1

1966 National League Standings

TEAM	W	L	PCT	GB	HOME	ROAD	RS	RA	DIFF
*-Los Angeles	95	67	.586	--	--	--	606	490	+116
San Francisco	93	68	.578	1.5	--	--	675	626	+49
Pittsburgh	92	70	.568	3	--	--	759	641	+118
Philadelphia	87	75	.537	8	--	--	696	640	+56
Atlanta	85	77	.521	10	--	--	782	683	+99
St. Louis	83	79	.512	12	--	--	571	577	-6
Cincinnati	76	84	.475	18	--	--	692	702	-10
Houston	72	90	.442	23	--	--	612	695	-83
New York	66	95	.410	28.5	--	--	587	761	-174
Chicago	59	103	.364	36	--	--	644	809	-165

1966 U.S. NATIONAL TENNIS CHAMPIONSHIPS

Men's Singles
Fred Stolle defeated John Newcombe 4–6, 12–10, 6–3, 6–4
Women's Singles
Maria Bueno defeated Nancy Richey 6–3, 6–1
Men's doubles
Roy Emerson / Fred Stolle defeated Clark Graebner / Dennis Ralston 6–4, 6–4, 6–4
Women's doubles
Maria Bueno / Nancy Richey defeated Billie Jean King / Rosie Casals 6–3, 6–4
Mixed doubles
Donna Floyd / Owen Davidson defeated Carol Hanks / Ed Rubinoff 6–1, 6–3

1967

1967 NATIONAL FOOTBALL LEAGUE SEASON
STANDINGS

EAST CAPITOL	W	L	T	WEST COASTAL	W	L	T
Dallas	9	5	0	Los Angeles	11	1	2
Philadelphia	6	7	1	Baltimore	11	1	2
Washington	5	6	3	San Francisco	7	7	0
New Orleans	3	11	0	Atlanta	1	12	1
EAST CENTURY	W	L	T	WEST CENT	W	L	T
Cleveland	9	5	0	Green Bay	9	4	1
NY Giants	7	7	0	Chicago	7	6	1
St. Louis	6	7	1	Detroit	5	7	2
Pittsburgh	4	9	1	Minnesota	3	8	3

1967 U.S. OPEN BADMINTON CHAMPIONSHIPS
WINNERS

Year	Men's singles	Women's singles	Men's doubles	Women's doubles	Mixed doubles
1967	Erland Kops	Judy Devlin	Erland Kops Joe Alston	Judy Hashman Rosine Jones Lemon	Jim Sydie Judy Hashman

1967 NBA STANDINGS
DIVISION STANDINGS

Team	W	L	W/L%	GB	PS/G	PA/G	SRS
Eastern Division							
Philadelphia 76ers*	68	13	.840	—	125.2	115.8	8.50
Boston Celtics*	60	21	.741	8.0	119.3	111.3	7.24
Cincinnati Royals*	39	42	.481	29.0	117.1	117.4	-0.23
New York Knicks*	36	45	.444	32.0	116.4	119.4	-2.74
Baltimore Bullets	20	61	.247	48.0	115.5	122.0	-5.87
Western Division							
San Francisco Warriors*	44	37	.543	—	122.4	119.5	2.58
St. Louis Hawks*	39	42	.481	5.0	113.6	115.2	-1.44
Los Angeles Lakers*	36	45	.444	8.0	120.5	120.2	0.31
Chicago Bulls*	33	48	.407	11.0	113.2	116.9	-3.37
Detroit Pistons	30	51	.370	14.0	111.3	116.8	-4.98

AMERICAN HORSE OF THE YEAR
1967 ECLIPSE AWARD

Year	Horse	Trainer	Owner	Age	Gender
1967	Damascus	Frank Y. Whiteley, Jr.	Edith W. Bancroft	3	C

1967- NHL SEASON
FINAL STANDINGS

East Division	GP	W	L	T	Pts	GF	GA	PIM
Montreal Canadiens	74	42	22	10	94	236	167	700
New York Rangers	74	39	23	12	90	226	183	673
Boston Bruins	74	37	27	10	84	259	216	1043
Chicago Black Hawks	74	32	26	16	80	212	222	606
Toronto Maple Leafs	74	33	31	10	76	209	176	634
Detroit Red Wings	74	27	35	12	66	245	257	759
West Division	GP	W	L	T	Pts	GF	GA	PIM
Philadelphia Flyers	74	31	32	11	73	173	179	987
Los Angeles Kings	74	31	33	10	72	200	224	810
St. Louis Blues	74	27	31	16	70	177	191	792
Minnesota North Stars	74	27	32	15	69	191	226	738
Pittsburgh Penguins	74	27	34	13	67	195	216	554
Oakland Seals [3]	74	15	42	17	47	153	219	787

1967 MAJOR LEAGUE BASEBALL SEASON HISTORY

1967 American League Standings

TEAM	W	L	PCT	GB	HOME	ROAD	RS	RA	DIFF
*-Boston	92	70	.568	--	--	--	722	614	+108
Minnesota	91	71	.562	1	--	--	671	590	+81
Detroit	91	71	.562	1	--	--	683	587	+96
Chicago	89	73	.549	3	--	--	531	491	+40
California	84	77	.522	7.5	--	--	567	587	-20
Washington	76	85	.472	15.5	--	--	550	637	-87
Baltimore	76	85	.472	15.5	--	--	654	592	+62
Cleveland	75	87	.463	17	--	--	559	613	-54
New York	72	90	.444	20	--	--	522	621	-99
Kansas City	62	99	.385	29.5	--	--	533	660	-127

1967 National League Standings

TEAM	W	L	PCT	GB	HOME	ROAD	RS	RA	DIFF
*-St. Louis	101	60	.627	--	--	--	695	557	+138
San Francisco	91	71	.562	10.5	--	--	652	551	+101
Chicago	87	74	.540	14	--	--	702	624	+78
Cincinnati	87	75	.537	14.5	--	--	604	563	+41
Philadelphia	82	80	.506	19.5	--	--	612	581	+31
Pittsburgh	81	81	.500	20.5	--	--	679	693	-14
Atlanta	77	85	.475	24.5	--	--	631	640	-9
Los Angeles	73	89	.451	28.5	--	--	519	595	-76
Houston	69	93	.426	32.5	--	--	626	742	-116
New York	61	101	.377	40.5	--	--	498	672	-174

1967 U.S. NATIONAL TENNIS CHAMPIONSHIPS

Men's Singles
John Newcombe defeated Clark Graebner 6–4, 6–4, 8–6
Women's Singles
Billie Jean King defeated Ann Haydon Jones 11–9, 6–4
Men's doubles
John Newcombe / Tony Roche defeated William Bowrey / Owen Davidson 6–8, 9–7, 6–3, 6–3
Women's doubles
Rosie Casals / Billie Jean King defeated Mary-Ann Eisel / Donna Floyd, 4–6, 6–3, 6–4
Mixed doubles
Billie Jean King / Owen Davidson defeated Rosie Casals / Stan Smith 6–3, 6–2

1968

1968 NATIONAL FOOTBALL LEAGUE SEASON
STANDINGS

EAST CAPITOL	W	L	T	WEST COASTAL	W	L	T
Dallas	12	2	0	Baltimore	13	1	0
NY Giants	7	7	0	Los Angeles	10	3	1
Washington	5	9	0	San Francisco	7	6	1
Philadelphia	2	12	0	Atlanta	2	12	0
EAST CENTURY	W	L	T	WEST CENT	W	L	T
Cleveland	10	4	0	Minnesota	8	6	0
St. Louis	9	4	1	Chicago	7	7	0
New Orleans	4	9	1	Green Bay	6	7	1
Pittsburgh	2	11	1	Detroit	4	8	2

1968 U.S. OPEN BADMINTON CHAMPIONSHIPS
WINNERS

Year	Men's singles	Women's singles	Men's doubles	Women's doubles	Mixed doubles
1968	Channarong Ratanaseangsuang	Tyna Barinaga	Jim Poole Don Paup	Tyna Barinaga Helen Tibbetts	Larry Saben Carlene Starkey

1968 NBA STANDINGS
DIVISION STANDINGS

Team	W	L	W/L%	GB	PS/G	PA/G	SRS
Eastern Division							
Philadelphia 76ers*	62	20	.756	—	122.6	114.0	7.96
Boston Celtics*	54	28	.659	8.0	116.1	112.0	3.87
New York Knicks*	43	39	.524	19.0	116.1	114.3	1.78
Detroit Pistons*	40	42	.488	22.0	118.6	120.6	-1.70
Cincinnati Royals	39	43	.476	23.0	116.6	117.5	-0.64
Baltimore Bullets	36	46	.439	26.0	117.4	117.8	-0.23
Western Division							
St. Louis Hawks*	56	26	.683	—	113.0	110.3	2.37
Los Angeles Lakers*	52	30	.634	4.0	121.2	115.6	4.99
San Francisco Warriors*	43	39	.524	13.0	117.0	117.6	-0.66
Chicago Bulls*	29	53	.354	27.0	109.5	113.5	-3.76
Seattle SuperSonics	23	59	.280	33.0	118.7	125.1	-6.00
San Diego Rockets	15	67	.183	41.0	112.4	121.0	-7.94

AMERICAN HORSE OF THE YEAR
1968 ECLIPSE AWARD

Year	Horse	Trainer	Owner	Age	Gender
1968	Dr. Fager	John A. Nerud	Tartan Stable	4	C

AMERICAN HORSE OF THE YEAR
1968 ECLIPSE AWARD

East Division	GP	W	L	T	Pts	GF	GA	PIM
Montreal Canadiens	76	46	19	11	103	271	202	780
Boston Bruins	76	42	18	16	100	303	221	1297
New York Rangers	76	41	26	9	91	231	196	806
Toronto Maple Leafs	76	35	26	15	85	234	217	961
Detroit Red Wings	76	33	31	12	78	239	221	885
Chicago Black Hawks	76	34	33	9	77	280	246	842
West Division	**GP**	**W**	**L**	**T**	**Pts**	**GF**	**GA**	**PIM**
St. Louis Blues	76	37	25	14	88	204	157	838
Oakland Seals	76	29	36	11	69	219	251	811
Philadelphia Flyers	76	20	35	21	61	174	225	964
Los Angeles Kings	76	24	42	10	58	185	260	698
Pittsburgh Penguins	76	20	45	11	51	189	252	677
Minnesota North Stars	76	18	43	15	51	189	270	862

1968 MAJOR LEAGUE BASEBALL SEASON HISTORY

1968 American League Standings

TEAM	W	L	PCT	GB	HOME	ROAD	RS	RA	DIFF
*-Detroit	103	59	.628	--	--	--	671	492	+179
Baltimore	91	71	.562	12	--	--	579	497	+82
Cleveland	86	75	.531	16.5	--	--	516	504	+12
Boston	86	76	.531	17	--	--	614	611	+3
New York	83	79	.506	20	--	--	536	531	+5
Oakland	82	80	.503	21	--	--	569	544	+25
Minnesota	79	83	.488	24	--	--	562	546	+16
California	67	95	.414	36	--	--	498	615	-117
Chicago	67	95	.414	36	--	--	463	527	-64
Washington	65	96	.404	37.5	--	--	524	665	-141

1968 National League Standings

TEAM	W	L	PCT	GB	HOME	ROAD	RS	RA	DIFF
*-St. Louis	97	65	.599	--	--	--	583	472	+111
San Francisco	88	74	.540	9	--	--	599	529	+70
Chicago	84	78	.515	13	--	--	612	611	+1
Cincinnati	83	79	.509	14	--	--	690	673	+17
Atlanta	81	81	.497	16	--	--	514	549	-35
Pittsburgh	80	82	.491	17	--	--	583	532	+51
Philadelphia	76	86	.469	21	--	--	543	615	-72
Los Angeles	76	86	.469	21	--	--	470	509	-39
New York	73	89	.448	24	--	--	473	499	-26
Houston	72	90	.444	25	--	--	510	588	-78

1968 U.S. NATIONAL TENNIS CHAMPIONSHIPS

Men's singles
Arthur Ashe defeated Tom Okker, 14–12, 5–7, 6–3, 3–6, 6–3
Women's singles
Virginia Wade defeated Billie Jean King, 6–4, 6–2
Men's doubles
Bob Lutz / Stan Smith defeated Arthur Ashe / Andrés Gimeno, 11–9, 6–1, 7–5
Women's doubles
Maria Bueno / Margaret Court defeated Rosemary Casals / Billie Jean King, 4–6, 9–7, 8–6

1969

1969 NATIONAL FOOTBALL LEAGUE SEASON
STANDINGS

EAST CAPITOL	W	L	T	WEST COASTAL	W	L	T
Dallas	11	2	1	Los Angeles	11	3	0
Washington	7	5	2	Baltimore	8	5	1
New Orleans	5	9	0	Atlanta	6	8	0
Philadelphia	4	9	1	San Francisco	4	8	2
EAST CENTURY	W	L	T	WEST CENT	W	L	T
Cleveland	10	3	1	Minnesota	12	2	0
NY Giants	6	8	0	Detroit	9	4	1
St. Louis	4	9	1	Green Bay	8	6	0
Pittsburgh	1	13	0	Chicago	1	13	0

1969 U.S. OPEN BADMINTON CHAMPIONSHIPS
WINNERS

Year	Men's singles	Women's singles	Men's doubles	Women's doubles	Mixed doubles
1969	Rudy Hartono	Minarni	Ng Boon Bee Punch Gunalan	Minarni Retno Kustijah	Erland Kops Pernille Molgaard Hansen

1969 NBA STANDINGS
DIVISION STANDINGS

Team	W	L	W/L%	GB	PS/G	PA/G	SRS
Eastern Division							
Baltimore Bullets*	57	25	.695	—	116.4	112.1	4.05
Philadelphia 76ers*	55	27	.671	2.0	118.9	113.8	4.79
New York Knicks*	54	28	.659	3.0	110.8	105.1	5.48
Boston Celtics*	48	34	.585	9.0	111.0	105.4	5.35
Cincinnati Royals	41	41	.500	16.0	114.5	115.6	-0.83
Detroit Pistons	32	50	.390	25.0	114.1	117.3	-2.79
Milwaukee Bucks	27	55	.329	30.0	110.2	115.4	-5.07
Western Division							
Los Angeles Lakers*	55	27	.671	—	112.2	108.1	3.84
Atlanta Hawks*	48	34	.585	7.0	111.3	109.0	2.06
San Francisco Warriors*	41	41	.500	14.0	109.1	110.7	-1.53
San Diego Rockets*	37	45	.451	18.0	115.3	115.5	-0.30
Chicago Bulls	33	49	.402	22.0	104.7	107.0	-2.11
Seattle SuperSonics	30	52	.366	25.0	112.1	116.9	-4.68
Phoenix Suns	16	66	.195	39.0	111.7	120.5	-8.26

AMERICAN HORSE OF THE YEAR
1969 ECLIPSE AWARD

Year	Horse	Trainer	Owner	Age	Gender
1969	Arts and Letters	J. Elliott Burch	Rokeby Stables	3	G

1969- NHL SEASON
FINAL STANDINGS

East Division	GP	W	L	T	Pts	GF	GA	PIM
Chicago Black Hawks	76	45	22	9	99	250	170	901
Boston Bruins	76	40	17	19	99	277	216	1196
Detroit Red Wings	76	40	21	15	95	246	199	907
New York Rangers	76	38	22	16	92	246	189	853
Montreal Canadiens	76	38	22	16	92	244	201	892
Toronto Maple Leafs	76	29	34	13	71	222	242	898
West Division	GP	W	L	T	Pts	GF	GA	PIM
St. Louis Blues	76	37	27	12	86	224	179	876
Pittsburgh Penguins	76	26	38	12	64	182	238	1038
Minnesota North Stars	76	19	35	22	60	224	257	1008
Oakland Seals	76	22	40	14	58	169	243	845
Philadelphia Flyers	76	17	35	24	58	197	225	1123
Los Angeles Kings	76	14	52	10	38	168	290	969

1969 MAJOR LEAGUE BASEBALL SEASON HISTORY

1969 American League Standings									
EAST	W	L	PCT	GB	HOME	ROAD	RS	RA	DIFF
*-Baltimore	109	53	.673	--	--	--	779	517	+262
Detroit	90	72	.556	19	--	--	701	601	+100
Boston	87	75	.537	22	--	--	743	736	+7
Washington	86	76	.531	23	--	--	694	644	+50
New York	80	81	.494	28.5	--	--	562	587	-25
Cleveland	62	99	.385	46.5	--	--	573	717	-144
WEST	W	L	PCT	GB	HOME	ROAD	RS	RA	DIFF
x-Minnesota	97	65	.599	--	--	--	790	618	+172
Oakland	88	74	.543	9	--	--	740	678	+62
California	71	91	.436	26	--	--	528	652	-124
Kansas City	69	93	.423	28	--	--	586	688	-102
Chicago	68	94	.420	29	--	--	625	723	-98
Seattle	64	98	.393	33	--	--	639	799	-160
1969 National League Standings									
EAST	W	L	PCT	GB	HOME	ROAD	RS	RA	DIFF
*-New York	100	62	.617	--	--	--	632	541	+91
Chicago	92	70	.564	8	--	--	720	611	+109
Pittsburgh	88	74	.543	12	--	--	725	652	+73
St. Louis	87	75	.537	13	--	--	595	540	+55
Philadelphia	63	99	.389	37	--	--	645	745	-100
Montreal	52	110	.321	48	--	--	582	791	-209
WEST	W	L	PCT	GB	HOME	ROAD	RS	RA	DIFF
x-Atlanta	93	69	.574	--	--	--	691	631	+60
San Francisco	90	72	.556	3	--	--	713	636	+77
Cincinnati	89	73	.546	4	--	--	798	768	+30
Los Angeles	85	77	.525	8	--	--	645	561	+84
Houston	81	81	.500	12	--	--	676	668	+8
San Diego	52	110	.321	41	--	--	468	746	-278

1969 U.S. NATIONAL TENNIS CHAMPIONSHIPS

Men's singles
Rod Laver defeated Tony Roche, 7–9, 6–1, 6–2, 6–2
Women's singles
Margaret Court defeated Nancy Richey, 6–2, 6–2
Men's doubles
Ken Rosewall / Fred Stolle defeated Charlie Pasarell / Dennis Ralston, 2–6, 7–5, 13–11, 6–3
Women's doubles
Françoise Dürr / Darlene Hard defeated Margaret Court / Virginia Wade, 0–6, 6–4, 6–4
Mixed doubles
Margaret Court / Marty Riessen defeated Françoise Dürr / Dennis Ralston, 7–5, 6–3

1970

1970 NATIONAL FOOTBALL LEAGUE SEASON
STANDINGS

AFC EAST	W	L	T	NFC EAST	W	L	T
Baltimore	11	2	1	Dallas	10	4	0
Miami	10	4	0	NY Giants	9	5	0
NY Jets	4	10	0	St. Louis	8	5	1
Buffalo	3	10	1	Washington	6	8	0
Boston	2	12	0	Philadelphia	3	10	1
AFC CENT	**W**	**L**	**T**	**NFC CENT**	**W**	**L**	**T**
Cincinnati	8	6	0	Minnesota	12	2	0
Cleveland	7	7	0	Detroit	10	4	0
Pittsburgh	5	9	0	Chicago	6	8	0
Houston	3	10	1	Green Bay	6	8	0
AFC WEST	**W**	**L**	**T**	**NFC WEST**	**W**	**L**	**T**
Oakland	8	4	2	San Francisco	10	3	1
Kansas City	7	5	2	Los Angeles	9	4	1
San Diego	5	6	3	Atlanta	4	8	2
Denver	5	8	1	New Orleans	2	11	1

1970 U.S. NATIONAL BADMINTON CHAMPIONSHIPS
WINNERS

Year	Men's singles	Women's singles	Men's doubles	Women's doubles	Mixed doubles
1970	Stan Hales	Tyna Barinaga	Don Paup Jim Poole	Tyna Barinaga Caroline Hein	Jim Poole Tyna Barinaga

1970 NBA STANDINGS
DIVISION STANDINGS

Team	W	L	W/L%	GB	PS/G	PA/G	SRS
Eastern Division							
New York Knicks*	60	22	.732	—	115.0	105.9	8.42
Milwaukee Bucks*	56	26	.683	4.0	118.8	114.2	4.25
Baltimore Bullets*	50	32	.610	10.0	120.7	118.6	1.94
Philadelphia 76ers*	42	40	.512	18.0	121.9	118.5	3.32
Cincinnati Royals	36	46	.439	24.0	117.3	120.2	-2.55
Boston Celtics	34	48	.415	26.0	114.9	116.8	-1.60
Detroit Pistons	31	51	.378	29.0	112.8	116.1	-2.94
Western Division							
Atlanta Hawks*	48	34	.585	—	117.6	117.2	0.31
Los Angeles Lakers*	46	36	.561	2.0	113.7	111.8	1.76
Chicago Bulls*	39	43	.476	9.0	114.9	116.7	-1.71
Phoenix Suns*	39	43	.476	9.0	119.3	121.1	-1.66
Seattle SuperSonics	36	46	.439	12.0	116.9	119.5	-2.43
San Francisco Warriors	30	52	.366	18.0	111.1	115.6	-4.15
San Diego Rockets	27	55	.329	21.0	118.7	121.8	-2.95

AMERICAN HORSE OF THE YEAR
1970 ECLIPSE AWARD

Year	Horse	Trainer	Owner	Age	Gender
1970	Fort Marcy	J. Elliott Burch	Rokeby Stables	6	G
1970	Personality	John W. Jacobs	Ethel D. Jacobs	3	C

1970- NHL SEASON
FINAL STANDINGS

East Division	GP	W	L	T	Pts	GF	GA	PIM
Boston Bruins	78	57	14	7	121	399	207	1154
New York Rangers	78	49	18	11	109	259	177	952
Montreal Canadiens	78	42	23	13	97	291	216	1271
Toronto Maple Leafs	78	37	33	8	82	248	211	1133
Buffalo Sabres	78	24	39	15	63	217	291	1188
Vancouver Canucks	78	24	46	8	56	229	296	1371
Detroit Red Wings	78	22	45	11	55	209	308	988
West Division	**GP**	**W**	**L**	**T**	**Pts**	**GF**	**GA**	**PIM**
Chicago Black Hawks	78	49	20	9	107	277	184	1280
St. Louis Blues	78	34	25	19	87	223	208	1092
Philadelphia Flyers	78	28	33	17	73	207	225	1060
Minnesota North Stars	78	28	34	16	72	191	223	898
Los Angeles Kings	78	25	40	13	63	239	303	775
Pittsburgh Penguins	78	21	37	20	62	221	240	1079
California Golden Seals	78	20	53	5	45	199	320	937

1970 MAJOR LEAGUE BASEBALL SEASON HISTORY

1970 American League Standings

EAST	W	L	PCT	GB	HOME	ROAD	RS	RA	DIFF
*-Baltimore	108	54	.667	--	--	--	792	574	+218
New York	93	69	.571	15	--	--	680	612	+68
Boston	87	75	.537	21	--	--	786	722	+64
Detroit	79	83	.488	29	--	--	666	731	-65
Cleveland	76	86	.469	32	--	--	649	675	-26
Washington	70	92	.432	38	--	--	626	689	-63
WEST	**W**	**L**	**PCT**	**GB**	**HOME**	**ROAD**	**RS**	**RA**	**DIFF**
x-Minnesota	98	64	.605	--	--	--	744	605	+139
Oakland	89	73	.549	9	--	--	678	593	+85
California	86	76	.531	12	--	--	631	630	+1
Milwaukee	65	97	.399	33	--	--	613	751	-138
Kansas City	65	97	.401	33	--	--	611	705	-94
Chicago	56	106	.346	42	--	--	633	822	-189

1970 National League Standings

EAST	W	L	PCT	GB	HOME	ROAD	RS	RA	DIFF
x-Pittsburgh	89	73	.549	--	--	--	729	664	+65
Chicago	84	78	.519	5	--	--	806	679	+127
New York	83	79	.512	6	--	--	695	630	+65
St. Louis	76	86	.469	13	--	--	744	747	-3
Philadelphia	73	88	.453	15.5	--	--	594	730	-136
Montreal	73	89	.451	16	--	--	687	807	-120

WEST	W	L	PCT	GB	HOME	ROAD	RS	RA	DIFF
*-Cincinnati	102	60	.630	--	--	--	775	681	+94
Los Angeles	87	74	.540	14.5	--	--	749	684	+65
San Francisco	86	76	.531	16	--	--	831	826	+5
Houston	79	83	.488	23	--	--	744	763	-19
Atlanta	76	86	.469	26	--	--	736	772	-36
San Diego	63	99	.389	39	--	--	681	788	-107

1970 U.S. NATIONAL TENNIS CHAMPIONSHIPS

Men's singles
Ken Rosewall def. Tony Roche, 2–6, 6–4, 7–6$^{(5-2)}$, 6–3
Women's singles
Main article: 1970 US Open – Women's Singles
Margaret Court defeated Rosemary Casals, 6–2, 2–6, 6–1
Men's doubles
Pierre Barthès / Nikola Pilić defeated Roy Emerson / Rod Laver, 6–3, 7–6, 4–6, 7–6
Women's doubles
Margaret Court / Judy Tegart Dalton defeated Rosemary Casals / Virginia Wade, 6–3, 6–4
Mixed doubles
Margaret Court / Marty Riessen defeated Judy Tegart Dalton / Frew McMillan, 6–4, 6–4

1971

1971 NATIONAL FOOTBALL LEAGUE SEASON
STANDINGS

AFC EAST	W	L	T	NFC EAST	W	L	T
Miami	10	3	1	Dallas	11	3	0
Baltimore	10	4	0	Washington	9	4	1
New England	6	8	0	Philadelphia	6	7	1
NY Jets	6	8	0	St. Louis	4	9	1
Buffalo	1	13	0	NY Giants	4	10	0
AFC CENT	**W**	**L**	**T**	**NFC CENT**	**W**	**L**	**T**
Cleveland	9	5	0	Minnesota	11	3	0
Pittsburgh	6	8	0	Detroit	7	6	1
Houston	4	9	1	Chicago	6	8	0
Cincinnati	4	10	0	Green Bay	4	8	2
AFC WEST	**W**	**L**	**T**	**NFC WEST**	**W**	**L**	**T**
Kansas City	10	3	1	San Francisco	9	5	0
Oakland	8	4	2	Los Angeles	8	5	1
San Diego	6	8	0	Atlanta	7	6	1
Denver	4	9	1	New Orleans	4	8	2

1971 U.S. NATIONAL BADMINTON CHAMPIONSHIPS
WINNERS

Year	Men's singles	Women's singles	Men's doubles	Women's doubles	Mixed doubles
1971	Stan Hales	Diane Hales	Don Paup Jim Poole	Caroline Hein Carlene Starkey	Don Paup Helen Tibbetts

1971 NBA STANDINGS
DIVISION STANDINGS

Eastern Conference	W	L	W/L%	GB	PS/G	PA/G	SRS
Atlantic Division							
New York Knicks* (1)	52	30	.634	—	110.1	105.0	5.05
Philadelphia 76ers* (3)	47	35	.573	5.0	114.8	113.3	1.81
Boston Celtics (5)	44	38	.537	8.0	117.2	115.1	2.30
Buffalo Braves (7)	22	60	.268	30.0	105.5	112.1	-8.02
Central Division							
Baltimore Bullets* (2)	42	40	.512	—	112.9	112.3	0.91
Atlanta Hawks* (4)	36	46	.439	6.0	114.0	115.8	-1.30
Cincinnati Royals (6)	33	49	.402	9.0	116.0	119.2	-2.96
Cleveland Cavaliers (8)	15	67	.183	27.0	102.1	113.3	-12.04
Western Conference	**W**	**L**	**W/L%**	**GB**	**PS/G**	**PA/G**	**SRS**
Midwest Division							
Milwaukee Bucks* (1)	66	16	.805	—	118.4	106.2	11.92
Chicago Bulls* (3)	51	31	.622	15.0	110.6	105.4	5.47
Phoenix Suns (5)	48	34	.585	18.0	113.8	111.9	2.33
Detroit Pistons (6)	45	37	.549	21.0	110.1	110.9	-0.33

Pacific Division							
Los Angeles Lakers* (2)	48	34	.585	—	114.8	111.7	3.27
San Francisco Warriors* (4)	41	41	.500	7.0	107.1	108.5	-0.83
San Diego Rockets (7)	40	42	.488	8.0	113.2	113.4	0.21
Seattle SuperSonics (8)	38	44	.463	10.0	115.0	117.0	-1.53
Portland Trail Blazers (9)	29	53	.354	19.0	115.5	120.0	-6.20

AMERICAN HORSE OF THE YEAR
1971 ECLIPSE AWARD

Year	Horse	Trainer	Owner	Age	Gender
1971	Ack Ack	Charlie Whittingham	Buddy Fogelson	5	C

1971- NHL SEASON
FINAL STANDINGS

East Division	GP	W	L	T	Pts	GF	GA	PIM
Boston Bruins	78	54	13	11	119	330	204	1112
New York Rangers	78	48	17	13	109	317	192	1010
Montreal Canadiens	78	46	16	16	108	307	205	783
Toronto Maple Leafs	78	33	31	14	80	209	208	887
Detroit Red Wings	78	33	35	10	76	261	262	850
Buffalo Sabres	78	16	43	19	51	203	289	831
Vancouver Canucks	78	20	50	8	48	203	297	1092
West Division	GP	W	L	T	Pts	GF	GA	PIM
Chicago Black Hawks	78	46	17	15	107	256	166	844
Minnesota North Stars	78	37	29	12	86	212	191	853
St. Louis Blues	78	28	39	11	67	208	247	1150
Pittsburgh Penguins	78	26	38	14	66	220	258	978
Philadelphia Flyers	78	26	38	14	66	200	236	1233
California Golden Seals	78	21	39	18	60	216	288	1007
Los Angeles Kings	78	20	49	9	49	206	305	719

1971 MAJOR LEAGUE BASEBALL SEASON HISTORY

1971 American League Standings									
EAST	W	L	PCT	GB	HOME	ROAD	RS	RA	DIFF
x-Baltimore	101	57	.639	--	--	--	742	530	+212
Detroit	91	71	.562	12	--	--	701	645	+56
Boston	85	77	.525	18	--	--	691	667	+24
New York	82	80	.506	21	--	--	648	641	+7
Washington	63	96	.396	38.5	--	--	537	660	-123
Cleveland	60	102	.370	43	--	--	543	747	-204
WEST	W	L	PCT	GB	HOME	ROAD	RS	RA	DIFF
x-Oakland	101	60	.627	--	--	--	691	564	+127
Kansas City	85	76	.528	16	--	--	603	566	+37
Chicago	79	83	.488	22.5	--	--	617	597	+20
California	76	86	.469	25.5	--	--	511	576	-65
Minnesota	74	86	.463	26.5	--	--	654	670	-16
Milwaukee	69	92	.429	32	--	--	534	609	-75

1971 National League Standings

EAST	W	L	PCT	GB	HOME	ROAD	RS	RA	DIFF
*-Pittsburgh	97	65	.599	--	--	--	788	599	+189
St. Louis	90	72	.552	7	--	--	739	699	+40
New York	83	79	.512	14	--	--	588	550	+38
Chicago	83	79	.512	14	--	--	637	648	-11
Montreal	71	90	.438	25.5	--	--	622	729	-107
Philadelphia	67	95	.414	30	--	--	558	688	-130
WEST	**W**	**L**	**PCT**	**GB**	**HOME**	**ROAD**	**RS**	**RA**	**DIFF**
x-San Francisco	90	72	.556	--	--	--	706	644	+62
Los Angeles	89	73	.549	1	--	--	663	587	+76
Atlanta	82	80	.506	8	--	--	643	699	-56
Houston	79	83	.488	11	--	--	585	567	+18
Cincinnati	79	83	.488	11	--	--	586	581	+5
San Diego	61	100	.379	28.5	--	--	486	610	-124

1971 U.S. NATIONAL TENNIS CHAMPIONSHIPS

Men's singles
Stan Smith defeated Jan Kodeš, 3–6, 6–3, 6–2, 7–6
Women's singles
Billie Jean King defeated Rosemary Casals, 6–4, 7–6
Men's doubles
John Newcombe / Roger Taylor defeated Stan Smith / Erik van Dillen, 6–7, 6–3, 7–6, 4–6, 7–6
Women's doubles
Rosemary Casals / Judy Tegart Dalton defeated Gail Chanfreau / Françoise Dürr, 6–3, 6–3
Mixed doubles
Billie Jean King / Owen Davidson defeated Betty Stöve / Robert Maud, 6–3, 7–5

1972

1972 NATIONAL FOOTBALL LEAGUE SEASON
STANDINGS

AFC EAST	W	L	T	NFC EAST	W	L	T
Miami	14	0	0	Washington	11	3	0
NY Jets	7	7	0	Dallas	10	4	0
Baltimore	5	9	0	NY Giants	8	6	0
Buffalo	4	9	1	St. Louis	4	9	1
New England	3	11	0	Philadelphia	2	11	1
AFC CENT	W	L	T	NFC CENT	W	L	T
Pittsburgh	11	3	0	Green Bay	10	4	0
Cleveland	10	4	0	Detroit	8	5	1
Cincinnati	8	6	0	Minnesota	7	7	0
Houston	1	13	0	Chicago	4	9	1
AFC WEST	W	L	T	NFC WEST	W	L	T
Oakland	10	3	1	San Francisco	8	5	1
Kansas City	8	6	0	Atlanta	7	7	0
Denver	5	9	0	Los Angeles	6	7	1
San Diego	4	9	1	New Orleans	2	11	1

1972 U.S. NATIONAL BADMINTON CHAMPIONSHIPS
WINNERS

Year	Men's singles	Women's singles	Men's doubles	Women's doubles	Mixed doubles
1972	Chris Kinard	Pam Brady	Don Paup Jim Poole	P. Bretzke Pam Brady	Thomas Carmichael sen. Pam Brady

1972 NBA STANDINGS
DIVISION STANDINGS

Eastern Conference	W	L	W/L%	GB	PS/G	PA/G	SRS
Atlantic Division							
Boston Celtics* (1)	56	26	.683	—	115.6	110.8	4.38
New York Knicks* (3)	48	34	.585	8.0	107.1	104.7	2.28
Philadelphia 76ers (6)	30	52	.366	26.0	112.2	115.9	-3.44
Buffalo Braves (8)	22	60	.268	34.0	102.0	111.3	-9.44
Central Division							
Baltimore Bullets* (2)	38	44	.463	—	107.1	108.3	-1.26
Atlanta Hawks* (4)	36	46	.439	2.0	109.5	111.3	-1.94
Cincinnati Royals (5)	30	52	.366	8.0	107.8	111.8	-4.13
Cleveland Cavaliers (7)	23	59	.280	15.0	105.8	113.4	-7.90
Western Conference	W	L	W/L%	GB	PS/G	PA/G	SRS
Midwest Division							
Milwaukee Bucks* (2)	63	19	.768	—	114.6	103.5	10.70
Chicago Bulls* (3)	57	25	.695	6.0	111.2	102.9	7.91
Phoenix Suns (5)	49	33	.598	14.0	116.3	110.8	5.57
Detroit Pistons (8)	26	56	.317	37.0	109.1	115.9	-6.11

Pacific Division							
Los Angeles Lakers* (1)	69	13	.841	—	121.0	108.7	11.65
Golden State Warriors* (4)	51	31	.622	18.0	108.2	107.4	0.92
Seattle SuperSonics (6)	47	35	.573	22.0	109.2	108.8	0.86
Houston Rockets (7)	34	48	.415	35.0	109.7	111.2	-1.22
Portland Trail Blazers (9)	18	64	.220	51.0	106.8	116.5	-8.84

AMERICAN HORSE OF THE YEAR
1972 ECLIPSE AWARD

Year	Horse	Trainer	Owner	Age	Gender
1972	Ack Ack	Charlie Whittingham	Buddy Fogelson	5	C

1972- NHL SEASON
FINAL STANDINGS

East Division	GP	W	L	T	Pts	GF	GA	PIM
Montreal Canadiens	78	52	10	16	120	329	184	783
Boston Bruins	78	51	22	5	107	330	235	1097
New York Rangers	78	47	23	8	102	297	208	765
Buffalo Sabres	78	37	27	14	88	257	219	940
Detroit Red Wings	78	37	29	12	86	265	243	893
Toronto Maple Leafs	78	27	41	10	64	247	279	716
Vancouver Canucks	78	22	47	9	53	233	339	943
New York Islanders	78	12	60	6	30	170	347	881
West Division	GP	W	L	T	Pts	GF	GA	PIM
Chicago Black Hawks	78	42	27	9	93	284	225	864
Philadelphia Flyers	78	37	30	11	85	296	256	1756
Minnesota North Stars	78	37	30	11	85	254	230	881
St. Louis Blues	78	32	34	12	76	233	251	1195
Pittsburgh Penguins	78	32	37	9	73	257	265	866
Los Angeles Kings	78	31	36	11	73	232	245	888
Atlanta Flames	78	25	38	15	65	191	239	852
California Golden Seals	78	16	46	16	48	213	323	840

1972 MAJOR LEAGUE BASEBALL SEASON HISTORY

1972 American League Standings									
EAST	W	L	PCT	GB	HOME	ROAD	RS	RA	DIFF
x-Detroit	86	70	.551	--	--	--	558	514	+44
Boston	85	70	.548	.5	--	--	640	620	+20
Baltimore	80	74	.519	5	--	--	519	430	+89
New York	79	76	.510	6.5	--	--	557	527	+30
Cleveland	72	84	.462	14	--	--	472	519	-47
Milwaukee	65	91	.417	21	--	--	493	595	-102
WEST	W	L	PCT	GB	HOME	ROAD	RS	RA	DIFF
*-Oakland	93	62	.600	--	--	--	604	457	+147
Chicago	87	67	.565	5.5	--	--	566	538	+28
Minnesota	77	77	.500	15.5	--	--	537	535	+2
Kansas City	76	78	.494	16.5	--	--	580	545	+35
California	75	80	.484	18	--	--	454	533	-79
Texas	54	100	.351	38.5	--	--	461	628	-167

1972 National League Standings									
EAST	W	L	PCT	GB	HOME	ROAD	RS	RA	DIFF
*-Pittsburgh	96	59	.619	--	--	--	691	512	+179
Chicago	85	70	.545	11	--	--	685	567	+118
New York	83	73	.532	13.5	--	--	528	578	-50
St. Louis	75	81	.481	21.5	--	--	568	600	-32
Montreal	70	86	.449	26.5	--	--	513	609	-96
Philadelphia	59	97	.378	37.5	--	--	503	635	-132
WEST	**W**	**L**	**PCT**	**GB**	**HOME**	**ROAD**	**RS**	**RA**	**DIFF**
x-Cincinnati	95	59	.617	--	--	--	707	557	+150
Houston	84	69	.549	10.5	--	--	708	636	+72
Los Angeles	85	70	.548	10.5	--	--	584	527	+57
Atlanta	70	84	.452	25	--	--	628	730	-102
San Francisco	69	86	.445	26.5	--	--	662	649	+13
San Diego	58	95	.379	36.5	--	--	488	665	-177

1972 U.S. NATIONAL TENNIS CHAMPIONSHIPS

Men's singles
Ilie Năstase defeated Arthur Ashe, 3–6, 6–3, 6–7$^{(1-5)}$, 6–4, 6–3
Women's singles
Billie Jean King defeated Kerry Melville, 6–3, 7–5
Men's doubles
Cliff Drysdale / Roger Taylor defeated Owen Davidson / John Newcombe, 6–4, 7–6, 6–3
Women's doubles
Françoise Dürr / Betty Stöve defeated Margaret Court / Virginia Wade, 6–3, 1–6, 6–3
Mixed doubles
Margaret Court / Marty Riessen defeated Rosemary Casals / Ilie Năstase, 6–3, 7–5

1973

1973 NATIONAL FOOTBALL LEAGUE SEASON
STANDINGS

AFC EAST	W	L	T	NFC EAST	W	L	T
Miami	12	2	0	Dallas	10	4	0
Buffalo	9	5	0	Washington	10	4	0
New England	5	9	0	Philadelphia	5	8	1
Baltimore	4	10	0	St. Louis	4	9	1
NY Jets	4	10	0	NY Giants	2	11	1
AFC CENT	**W**	**L**	**T**	**NFC CENT**	**W**	**L**	**T**
Cincinnati	10	4	0	Minnesota	12	2	0
Pittsburgh	10	4	0	Detroit	6	7	1
Cleveland	7	5	2	Green Bay	5	7	2
Houston	1	13	0	Chicago	3	11	0
AFC WEST	**W**	**L**	**T**	**NFC WEST**	**W**	**L**	**T**
Oakland	9	4	1	Los Angeles	12	2	0
Denver	7	5	2	Atlanta	9	5	0
Kansas City	7	5	2	New Orleans	5	9	0
San Diego	2	11	1	San Francisco	5	9	0

1973 U.S. OPEN BADMINTON CHAMPIONSHIPS
WINNERS

Year	Men's singles	Women's singles	Men's doubles	Women's doubles	Mixed doubles
1973	Sture Johnsson	Eva Twedberg	Jim Poole Don Paup	Pam Brady Diane Hales	Sture Johnsson Eva Twedberg

1973 NBA STANDINGS
DIVISION STANDINGS

Eastern Conference	W	L	W/L%	GB	PS/G	PA/G	SRS
Atlantic Division							
Boston Celtics* (1)	68	14	.829	—	112.7	104.5	7.35
New York Knicks* (3)	57	25	.695	11.0	105.0	98.2	6.07
Buffalo Braves (7)	21	61	.256	47.0	103.3	112.5	-8.85
Philadelphia 76ers (8)	9	73	.110	59.0	104.1	116.2	-11.50
Central Division							
Baltimore Bullets* (2)	52	30	.634	—	105.0	101.6	2.85
Atlanta Hawks* (4)	46	36	.561	6.0	112.4	112.3	-0.15
Houston Rockets (5)	33	49	.402	19.0	112.8	114.5	-1.81
Cleveland Cavaliers (6)	32	50	.390	20.0	102.7	105.3	-2.64
Western Conference	**W**	**L**	**W/L%**	**GB**	**PS/G**	**PA/G**	**SRS**
Midwest Division							
Milwaukee Bucks* (1)	60	22	.732	—	107.2	99.0	7.84
Chicago Bulls* (3)	51	31	.622	9.0	104.1	100.6	3.43
Detroit Pistons (5)	40	42	.488	20.0	110.3	110.0	0.54
Kansas City-Omaha Kings (7)	36	46	.439	24.0	107.6	110.5	-2.36

Pacific Division							
Los Angeles Lakers* (2)	60	22	.732	—	111.7	103.2	8.16
Golden State Warriors* (4)	47	35	.573	13.0	108.8	105.7	3.12
Phoenix Suns (6)	38	44	.463	22.0	111.6	112.9	-0.96
Seattle SuperSonics (8)	26	56	.317	34.0	103.7	109.6	-5.33
Portland Trail Blazers (9)	21	61	.256	39.0	106.2	112.4	-5.67

AMERICAN HORSE OF THE YEAR
1973 ECLIPSE AWARD

Year	Horse	Trainer	Owner	Age	Gender
1973	Secretariat	Lucien Laurin	Meadow Stable	3	C

1973- NHL SEASON
FINAL STANDINGS

East Division	GP	W	L	T	Pts	GF	GA	PIM
Boston Bruins	78	52	17	9	113	349	221	968
Montreal Canadiens	78	45	24	9	99	293	240	761
New York Rangers	78	40	24	14	94	300	251	782
Toronto Maple Leafs	78	35	27	16	86	274	230	903
Buffalo Sabres	78	32	34	12	76	242	250	787
Detroit Red Wings	78	29	39	10	68	255	319	917
Vancouver Canucks	78	24	43	11	59	224	296	952
New York Islanders	78	19	41	18	56	182	247	1075
West Division	**GP**	**W**	**L**	**T**	**Pts**	**GF**	**GA**	**PIM**
Philadelphia Flyers	78	50	16	12	112	273	164	1750
Chicago Black Hawks	78	41	14	23	105	272	164	877
Los Angeles Kings	78	33	33	12	78	233	231	1055
Atlanta Flames	78	30	34	14	74	214	238	841
Pittsburgh Penguins	78	28	41	9	65	242	273	950
St. Louis Blues	78	26	40	12	64	206	248	1147
Minnesota North Stars	78	23	38	17	63	235	275	821
California Golden Seals	78	13	55	10	36	195	342	651

1973 MAJOR LEAGUE BASEBALL SEASON HISTORY

1973 American League Standings									
EAST	W	L	PCT	GB	HOME	ROAD	RS	RA	DIFF
*-Baltimore	97	65	.599	--	--	--	754	561	+193
Boston	89	73	.549	8	--	--	738	647	+91
Detroit	85	77	.525	12	--	--	642	674	-32
New York	80	82	.494	17	--	--	641	610	+31
Milwaukee	74	88	.457	23	--	--	708	731	-23
Cleveland	71	91	.438	26	--	--	680	826	-146
WEST	W	L	PCT	GB	HOME	ROAD	RS	RA	DIFF
x-Oakland	94	68	.580	--	--	--	758	615	+143
Kansas City	88	74	.543	6	--	--	755	752	+3
Minnesota	81	81	.500	13	--	--	738	692	+46
California	79	83	.488	15	--	--	629	657	-28
Chicago	77	85	.475	17	--	--	652	705	-53
Texas	57	105	.352	37	--	--	619	844	-225

1973 National League Standings									
EAST	W	L	PCT	GB	HOME	ROAD	RS	RA	DIFF
x-New York	82	79	.509	--	--	--	608	588	+20
St. Louis	81	81	.500	1.5	--	--	643	603	+40
Pittsburgh	80	82	.494	2.5	--	--	704	693	+11
Montreal	79	83	.488	3.5	--	--	668	702	-34
Chicago	77	84	.478	5	--	--	614	655	-41
Philadelphia	71	91	.438	11.5	--	--	642	717	-75
WEST	W	L	PCT	GB	HOME	ROAD	RS	RA	DIFF
*-Cincinnati	99	63	.611	--	--	--	741	621	+120
Los Angeles	95	66	.586	3.5	--	--	675	565	+110
San Francisco	88	74	.543	11	--	--	739	702	+37
Houston	82	80	.506	17	--	--	681	672	+9
Atlanta	76	85	.469	22.5	--	--	799	774	+25
San Diego	60	102	.370	39	--	--	548	770	-222

1973 U.S. NATIONAL TENNIS CHAMPIONSHIPS

Men's singles
John Newcombe defeated Jan Kodeš, 6–4, 1–6, 4–6, 6–2, 6–3
Women's singles
Margaret Court defeated Evonne Goolagong, 7–6, 5–7, 6–2
Men's doubles
Owen Davidson / John Newcombe defeated Rod Laver / Ken Rosewall, 7–5, 2–6, 7–5, 7–5
Women's doubles
Margaret Court / Virginia Wade defeated Rosemary Casals / Billie Jean King, 3–6, 6–3, 7–5
Mixed doubles
Billie Jean King / Owen Davidson defeated Margaret Court / Marty Riessen, 6–3, 3–6, 7–6

1974

1974 NATIONAL FOOTBALL LEAGUE SEASON
STANDINGS

AFC EAST	W	L	T	NFC EAST	W	L	T
Miami	11	3	0	St. Louis	10	4	0
Buffalo	9	5	0	Washington	10	4	0
New England	7	7	0	Dallas	8	6	0
NY Jets	7	7	0	Philadelphia	7	7	0
Baltimore	2	12	0	NY Giants	2	12	0
AFC CENT	**W**	**L**	**T**	**NFC CENT**	**W**	**L**	**T**
Pittsburgh	10	3	1	Minnesota	10	4	0
Cincinnati	7	7	0	Detroit	7	7	0
Houston	7	7	0	Green Bay	6	8	0
Cleveland	4	10	0	Chicago	4	10	0
AFC WEST	**W**	**L**	**T**	**NFC WEST**	**W**	**L**	**T**
Oakland	12	2	0	Los Angeles	10	4	0
Denver	7	6	1	San Francisco	6	8	0
Kansas City	5	9	0	New Orleans	5	9	0
San Diego	5	9	0	Atlanta	3	11	0

1974 U.S. NATIONAL BADMINTON CHAMPIONSHIPS
WINNERS

Year	Men's singles	Women's singles	Men's doubles	Women's doubles	Mixed doubles
1974	Chris Kinard	Cindy Baker	Don Paup Jim Poole	Pam Brady Diane Hales	Mike Walker Judianne Kelly

1974 NBA STANDINGS
DIVISION STANDINGS

Eastern Conference	W	L	W/L%	GB	PS/G	PA/G	SRS
Atlantic Division							
Boston Celtics* (1)	56	26	.683	—	109.0	105.1	3.42
New York Knicks* (3)	49	33	.598	7.0	101.3	98.5	2.42
Buffalo Braves* (4)	42	40	.512	14.0	111.6	111.8	-0.19
Philadelphia 76ers (8)	25	57	.305	31.0	101.2	107.5	-5.94
Central Division							
Capital Bullets* (2)	47	35	.573	—	101.9	100.4	1.19
Atlanta Hawks (5)	35	47	.427	12.0	108.6	110.0	-1.47
Houston Rockets (6)	32	50	.390	15.0	107.4	107.6	-0.34
Cleveland Cavaliers (7)	29	53	.354	18.0	100.3	104.6	-4.16

Western Conference	W	L	W/L%	GB	PS/G	PA/G	SRS
Midwest Division							
Milwaukee Bucks* (1)	59	23	.720	—	107.1	99.0	7.61
Chicago Bulls* (3)	54	28	.659	5.0	102.0	98.7	3.20
Detroit Pistons* (4)	52	30	.634	7.0	104.4	100.3	4.02
Kansas City-Omaha Kings (7)	33	49	.402	26.0	102.0	105.8	-3.24
Pacific Division							
Los Angeles Lakers* (2)	47	35	.573	—	109.2	108.3	0.85
Golden State Warriors (5)	44	38	.537	3.0	109.9	107.3	2.42
Seattle SuperSonics (6)	36	46	.439	11.0	107.0	109.5	-2.29
Phoenix Suns (8)	30	52	.366	17.0	107.9	111.5	-3.20
Portland Trail Blazers (9)	27	55	.329	20.0	106.8	111.6	-4.30

AMERICAN HORSE OF THE YEAR
1974 ECLIPSE AWARD

Year	Horse	Trainer	Owner	Age	Gender
1974	Forego	Sherrill W. Ward	Lazy F. Ranch	4	G

1974- NHL SEASON
FINAL STANDINGS

Prince of Wales Conference								
Adams Division	GP	W	L	T	Pts	GF	GA	PIM
Buffalo Sabres	80	49	16	15	113	354	240	1229
Boston Bruins	80	40	26	14	94	345	245	1153
Toronto Maple Leafs	80	31	33	16	78	280	309	1079
California Golden Seals	80	19	48	13	51	212	316	1101
Norris Division	GP	W	L	T	Pts	GF	GA	PIM
Montreal Canadiens	80	47	14	19	113	374	225	1155
Los Angeles Kings	80	42	17	21	105	269	185	1185
Pittsburgh Penguins	80	37	28	15	89	326	289	1119
Detroit Red Wings	80	23	45	12	58	259	335	1078
Washington Capitals	80	8	67	5	21	181	446	1085
Clarence Campbell Conference								
Patrick Division	GP	W	L	T	Pts	GF	GA	PIM
Philadelphia Flyers	80	51	18	11	113	293	181	1969
New York Rangers	80	37	29	14	88	319	276	1053
New York Islanders	80	33	25	22	88	264	221	1118
Atlanta Flames	80	34	31	15	83	243	233	915
Smythe Division	GP	W	L	T	Pts	GF	GA	PIM
Vancouver Canucks	80	38	32	10	86	271	254	965
St. Louis Blues	80	35	31	14	84	269	267	1275
Chicago Black Hawks	80	37	35	8	82	268	241	1112
Minnesota North Stars	80	23	50	7	53	221	341	1106

1974 MAJOR LEAGUE BASEBALL SEASON HISTORY

1974 American League Standings

EAST	W	L	PCT	GB	HOME	ROAD	RS	RA	DIFF
*-Baltimore	91	71	.562	--	--	--	659	612	+47
New York	89	73	.549	2	--	--	671	623	+48
Boston	84	78	.519	7	--	--	696	661	+35
Cleveland	77	85	.475	14	--	--	662	694	-32
Milwaukee	76	86	.469	15	--	--	647	660	-13
Detroit	72	90	.444	19	--	--	620	768	-148
WEST	**W**	**L**	**PCT**	**GB**	**HOME**	**ROAD**	**RS**	**RA**	**DIFF**
x-Oakland	90	72	.556	--	--	--	689	551	+138
Texas	84	76	.522	5	--	--	690	698	-8
Minnesota	82	80	.503	8	--	--	673	669	+4
Chicago	80	80	.491	9	--	--	684	721	-37
Kansas City	77	85	.475	13	--	--	667	662	+5
California	68	94	.417	22	--	--	618	657	-39

1974 National League Standings

EAST	W	L	PCT	GB	HOME	ROAD	RS	RA	DIFF
x-Pittsburgh	88	74	.543	--	--	--	751	657	+94
St. Louis	86	75	.534	1.5	--	--	677	643	+34
Philadelphia	80	82	.494	8	--	--	676	701	-25
Montreal	79	82	.491	8.5	--	--	662	657	+5
New York	71	91	.438	17	--	--	572	646	-74
Chicago	66	96	.407	22	--	--	669	826	-157
WEST	**W**	**L**	**PCT**	**GB**	**HOME**	**ROAD**	**RS**	**RA**	**DIFF**
*-Los Angeles	102	60	.630	--	--	--	798	561	+237
Cincinnati	98	64	.601	4	--	--	776	631	+145
Atlanta	88	74	.540	14	--	--	661	563	+98
Houston	81	81	.500	21	--	--	653	632	+21
San Francisco	72	90	.444	30	--	--	634	723	-89
San Diego	60	102	.370	42	--	--	541	830	-289

1974 U.S. NATIONAL TENNIS CHAMPIONSHIPS

Men's singles
Jimmy Connors defeated Ken Rosewall, 6–1, 6–0, 6–1
Women's singles
Billie Jean King defeated Evonne Goolagong, 3–6, 6–3, 7–5
Men's doubles
Bob Lutz / Stan Smith defeated Patricio Cornejo / Jaime Fillol, 6–3, 6–3
Women's doubles
Rosemary Casals / Billie Jean King defeated Françoise Dürr / Betty Stöve, 7–6, 6–7, 6–4
Mixed doubles
Pam Teeguarden / Geoff Masters defeated Chris Evert / Jimmy Connors, 6–1, 7–6

1975

1975 NATIONAL FOOTBALL LEAGUE SEASON
STANDINGS

AFC EAST	W	L	T	NFC EAST	W	L	T
Baltimore	10	4	0	St. Louis	11	3	0
Miami	10	4	0	Dallas	10	4	0
Buffalo	8	6	0	Washington	8	6	0
New England	3	11	0	NY Giants	5	9	0
NY Jets	3	11	0	Philadelphia	4	10	0
AFC CENT	**W**	**L**	**T**	**NFC CENT**	**W**	**L**	**T**
Pittsburgh	12	2	0	Minnesota	12	2	0
Cincinnati	11	3	0	Detroit	7	7	0
Houston	10	4	0	Chicago	4	10	0
Cleveland	3	11	0	Green Bay	4	10	0
AFC WEST	**W**	**L**	**T**	**NFC WEST**	**W**	**L**	**T**
Oakland	11	3	0	Los Angeles	12	2	0
Denver	6	8	0	San Francisco	5	9	0
Kansas City	5	9	0	Atlanta	4	10	0
San Diego	2	12	0	New Orleans	2	12	0

1975 U.S. NATIONAL BADMINTON CHAMPIONSHIPS
WINNERS

Year	Men's singles	Women's singles	Men's doubles	Women's doubles	Mixed doubles
1975	Mike Adams	Judianne Kelly	Don Paup / Jim Poole	Diane Hales / Carlene Starkey	Mike Walker / Judianne Kelly

1975 NBA STANDINGS
DIVISION STANDINGS

Eastern Conference	W	L	W/L%	GB	PS/G	PA/G	SRS
Atlantic Division							
Boston Celtics* (1)	60	22	.732	—	106.5	100.8	5.40
Buffalo Braves* (3)	49	33	.598	11.0	107.8	105.6	2.16
New York Knicks* (5)	40	42	.488	20.0	100.4	101.7	-0.92
Philadelphia 76ers (7)	34	48	.415	26.0	99.8	102.8	-2.60
Central Division							
Washington Bullets* (2)	60	22	.732	—	104.7	97.5	6.53
Houston Rockets* (4)	41	41	.500	19.0	103.9	102.9	0.84
Cleveland Cavaliers (6)	40	42	.488	20.0	99.0	99.4	-0.31
Atlanta Hawks (8)	31	51	.378	29.0	105.1	106.5	-1.32
New Orleans Jazz (9)	23	59	.280	37.0	101.5	109.3	-7.30

Western Conference	W	L	W/L%	GB	PS/G	PA/G	SRS
Midwest Division							
Chicago Bulls* (2)	47	35	.573	—	98.1	95.0	2.88
Kansas City-Omaha Kings* (3)	44	38	.537	3.0	101.4	101.6	-0.16
Detroit Pistons* (5)	40	42	.488	7.0	98.9	100.3	-1.19
Milwaukee Bucks (7)	38	44	.463	9.0	100.7	100.5	0.25
Pacific Division							
Golden State Warriors* (1)	48	34	.585	—	108.5	105.2	2.86
Seattle SuperSonics* (4)	43	39	.524	5.0	103.1	104.1	-1.19
Portland Trail Blazers (6)	38	44	.463	10.0	103.8	103.3	0.27
Phoenix Suns (8)	32	50	.390	16.0	101.2	103.6	-2.36
Los Angeles Lakers (9)	30	52	.366	18.0	103.2	107.2	-3.94

AMERICAN HORSE OF THE YEAR
1975 ECLIPSE AWARD

Year	Horse	Trainer	Owner	Age	Gender
1975	Forego	Sherrill W. Ward	Lazy F. Ranch	5	G

1975- NHL SEASON
FINAL STANDINGS

Prince of Wales Conference							
Adams Division	GP	W	L	T	Pts	GF	GA	PIM
Boston Bruins	80	48	15	17	113	313	237	1195
Buffalo Sabres	80	46	21	13	105	339	240	943
Toronto Maple Leafs	80	34	31	15	83	294	276	1368
California Golden Seals	80	27	42	11	65	250	278	1058
Norris Division	GP	W	L	T	Pts	GF	GA	PIM
Montreal Canadiens	80	58	11	11	127	337	174	977
Los Angeles Kings	80	38	33	9	85	263	265	1022
Pittsburgh Penguins	80	35	33	12	82	339	303	1004
Detroit Red Wings	80	26	44	10	62	226	300	1922
Washington Capitals	80	11	59	10	32	224	394	951
Clarence Campbell Conference							
Patrick Division	GP	W	L	T	Pts	GF	GA	PIM
Philadelphia Flyers	80	51	13	16	118	348	209	1980
New York Islanders	80	42	21	17	101	297	190	1277
Atlanta Flames	80	35	33	12	82	262	237	928
New York Rangers	80	29	42	9	67	262	333	911
Smythe Division	GP	W	L	T	Pts	GF	GA	PIM
Chicago Black Hawks	80	32	30	18	82	254	261	944
Vancouver Canucks	80	33	32	15	81	271	272	1122
St. Louis Blues	80	29	37	14	72	249	290	1274
Minnesota North Stars	80	20	53	7	47	195	303	1191
Kansas City Scouts	80	12	56	12	36	190	351	984

1975 MAJOR LEAGUE BASEBALL SEASON HISTORY

1975 American League Standings

EAST	W	L	PCT	GB	HOME	ROAD	RS	RA	DIFF
x-Boston	95	65	.594	--	--	--	796	709	+87
Baltimore	90	69	.566	4.5	--	--	682	553	+129
New York	83	77	.519	12	--	--	681	588	+93
Cleveland	79	80	.497	15.5	--	--	688	703	-15
Milwaukee	68	94	.420	28	--	--	675	792	-117
Detroit	57	102	.358	37.5	--	--	570	786	-216
WEST	**W**	**L**	**PCT**	**GB**	**HOME**	**ROAD**	**RS**	**RA**	**DIFF**
*-Oakland	98	64	.605	--	--	--	758	606	+152
Kansas City	91	71	.562	7	--	--	710	649	+61
Texas	79	83	.488	19	--	--	714	733	-19
Minnesota	76	83	.478	20.5	--	--	724	736	-12
Chicago	75	86	.466	22.5	--	--	655	703	-48
California	72	89	.447	25.5	--	--	628	723	-95

1975 National League Standings

EAST	W	L	PCT	GB	HOME	ROAD	RS	RA	DIFF
x-Pittsburgh	92	69	.571	--	--	--	712	565	+147
Philadelphia	86	76	.531	6.5	--	--	735	694	+41
New York	82	80	.506	10.5	--	--	646	625	+21
St. Louis	82	80	.503	10.5	--	--	662	689	-27
Montreal	75	87	.463	17.5	--	--	601	690	-89
Chicago	75	87	.463	17.5	--	--	712	827	-115
WEST	**W**	**L**	**PCT**	**GB**	**HOME**	**ROAD**	**RS**	**RA**	**DIFF**
*-Cincinnati	108	54	.667	--	--	--	840	586	+254
Los Angeles	88	74	.543	20	--	--	648	534	+114
San Francisco	80	81	.497	27.5	--	--	659	671	-12
San Diego	71	91	.438	37	--	--	552	683	-131
Atlanta	67	94	.416	40.5	--	--	583	739	-156
Houston	64	97	.395	43.5	--	--	664	711	-47

1975 U.S. NATIONAL TENNIS CHAMPIONSHIPS

Men's singles
Manuel Orantes defeated Jimmy Connors, 6–4, 6–3, 6–4
Women's singles
Chris Evert defeated Evonne Goolagong Cawley, 5–7, 6–4, 6–2
Men's doubles
Jimmy Connors / Ilie Năstase defeated Tom Okker / Marty Riessen, 6–4, 7–6
Women's doubles
Margaret Court / Virginia Wade defeated Rosemary Casals / Billie Jean King, 7–5, 2–6, 7–6
Mixed doubles
Rosemary Casals / Dick Stockton defeated Billie Jean King / Fred Stolle, 6–3, 7–6

1976

1976 NATIONAL FOOTBALL LEAGUE SEASON
STANDINGS

AFC EAST	W	L	T	NFC EAST	W	L	T
Baltimore	11	3	0	Dallas	11	3	0
New England	11	3	0	Washington	10	4	0
Miami	6	8	0	St. Louis	10	4	0
NY Jets	3	11	0	Philadelphia	4	10	0
Buffalo	2	12	0	NY Giants	3	11	0
AFC CENT	**W**	**L**	**T**	**NFC CENT**	**W**	**L**	**T**
Pittsburgh	10	4	0	Minnesota	11	2	1
Cincinnati	10	4	0	Chicago	7	7	0
Cleveland	9	5	0	Detroit	6	8	0
Houston	5	9	0	Green Bay	5	9	0
AFC WEST	**W**	**L**	**T**	**NFC WEST**	**W**	**L**	**T**
Oakland	13	1	0	Los Angeles	10	3	1
Denver	9	5	0	San Francisco	8	6	0
San Diego	6	8	0	Atlanta	4	10	0
Kansas City	5	9	0	New Orleans	4	10	0
Tampa Bay	0	14	0	Seattle	2	12	0

1976 U.S. NATIONAL BADMINTON CHAMPIONSHIPS
WINNERS

Year	Men's singles	Women's singles	Men's doubles	Women's doubles	Mixed doubles
1976	Chris Kinard	Pam Brady	Don Paup Bruce Pontow	Pam Brady Rosine Lemon	Mike Walker Judianne Kelly

1976 NBA STANDINGS
DIVISION STANDINGS

Eastern Conference	W	L	W/L%	GB	PS/G	PA/G	SRS
Atlantic Division							
Boston Celtics* (1)	54	28	.659	—	106.2	103.9	2.25
Philadelphia 76ers* (4)	46	36	.561	8.0	106.5	106.3	0.33
Buffalo Braves* (5)	46	36	.561	8.0	107.3	106.4	0.85
New York Knicks (7)	38	44	.463	16.0	102.7	103.9	-1.05
Central Division							
Cleveland Cavaliers* (2)	49	33	.598	—	101.7	99.2	2.34
Washington Bullets* (3)	48	34	.585	1.0	102.8	100.4	2.20
Houston Rockets (6)	40	42	.488	9.0	106.2	107.0	-0.71
New Orleans Jazz (8)	38	44	.463	11.0	104.1	105.0	-0.74
Atlanta Hawks (9)	29	53	.354	20.0	102.6	105.5	-2.66

Western Conference	W	L	W/L%	GB	PS/G	PA/G	SRS
Midwest Division							
Milwaukee Bucks* (2)	38	44	.463	—	101.8	103.3	-1.55
Detroit Pistons* (5)	36	46	.439	2.0	104.9	106.0	-1.18
Kansas City Kings (8)	31	51	.378	7.0	103.3	106.2	-2.83
Chicago Bulls (9)	24	58	.293	14.0	95.9	98.8	-2.89
Pacific Division							
Golden State Warriors* (1)	59	23	.720	—	109.8	103.1	6.23
Seattle SuperSonics* (3)	43	39	.524	16.0	106.4	106.7	-0.15
Phoenix Suns* (4)	42	40	.512	17.0	105.1	104.5	0.59
Los Angeles Lakers (6)	40	42	.488	19.0	106.9	106.8	0.18
Portland Trail Blazers (7)	37	45	.451	22.0	104.1	105.3	-1.11

AMERICAN HORSE OF THE YEAR
1976 ECLIPSE AWARD

Year	Horse	Trainer	Owner	Age	Gender
1976	Forego	Frank Y. Whiteley, Jr.	Lazy F. Ranch	6	G

1976- NHL SEASON
FINAL STANDINGS

Prince of Wales Conference								
Adams Division	GP	W	L	T	Pts	GF	GA	PIM
Boston Bruins	80	49	23	8	106	312	240	1065
Buffalo Sabres	80	48	24	8	104	301	220	848
Toronto Maple Leafs	80	33	32	15	81	301	285	1200
Cleveland Barons	80	25	42	13	63	240	292	1011
Norris Division	GP	W	L	T	Pts	GF	GA	PIM
Montreal Canadiens	**80**	**60**	**8**	**12**	**132**	**387**	**171**	**764**
Los Angeles Kings	80	34	31	15	83	271	241	1186
Pittsburgh Penguins	80	34	33	13	81	240	252	669
Washington Capitals	80	24	42	14	62	221	307	1231
Detroit Red Wings	80	16	55	9	41	183	309	1332
Clarence Campbell Conference								
Patrick Division	GP	W	L	T	Pts	GF	GA	PIM
Philadelphia Flyers	80	48	16	16	112	323	213	1547
New York Islanders	80	47	21	12	106	288	193	1012
Atlanta Flames	80	34	34	12	80	264	265	889
New York Rangers	80	29	37	14	72	272	310	1164
Smythe Division	GP	W	L	T	Pts	GF	GA	PIM
St. Louis Blues	80	32	39	9	73	239	276	877
Minnesota North Stars	80	23	39	18	64	240	310	774
Chicago Black Hawks	80	26	43	11	63	240	298	1104
Vancouver Canucks	80	25	42	13	63	235	294	1078
Colorado Rockies	80	20	46	14	54	226	307	978

1976 MAJOR LEAGUE BASEBALL SEASON HISTORY

1976 American League Standings

EAST	W	L	PCT	GB	HOME	ROAD	RS	RA	DIFF
*-New York	97	62	.610	--	--	--	730	575	+155
Baltimore	88	74	.543	10.5	--	--	619	598	+21
Boston	83	79	.512	15.5	--	--	716	660	+56
Cleveland	81	78	.509	16	--	--	615	615	0
Detroit	74	87	.460	24	--	--	609	709	-100
Milwaukee	66	95	.410	32	--	--	570	655	-85
WEST	**W**	**L**	**PCT**	**GB**	**HOME**	**ROAD**	**RS**	**RA**	**DIFF**
x-Kansas City	90	72	.556	--	--	--	713	611	+102
Oakland	87	74	.540	2.5	--	--	686	598	+88
Minnesota	85	77	.525	5	--	--	743	704	+39
Texas	76	86	.469	14	--	--	616	652	-36
California	76	86	.469	14	--	--	550	631	-81
Chicago	64	97	.398	25.5	--	--	586	745	-159

1976 National League Standings

EAST	W	L	PCT	GB	HOME	ROAD	RS	RA	DIFF
x-Philadelphia	101	61	.623	--	--	--	770	557	+213
Pittsburgh	92	70	.568	9	--	--	708	630	+78
New York	86	76	.531	15	--	--	615	538	+77
Chicago	75	87	.463	26	--	--	611	728	-117
St. Louis	72	90	.444	29	--	--	629	671	-42
Montreal	55	107	.340	46	--	--	531	734	-203
WEST	**W**	**L**	**PCT**	**GB**	**HOME**	**ROAD**	**RS**	**RA**	**DIFF**
*-Cincinnati	102	60	.630	--	--	--	857	633	+224
Los Angeles	92	70	.568	10	--	--	608	543	+65
Houston	80	82	.494	22	--	--	625	657	-32
San Francisco	74	88	.457	28	--	--	595	686	-91
San Diego	73	89	.451	29	--	--	570	662	-92
Atlanta	70	92	.432	32	--	--	620	700	-80

1976 U.S. NATIONAL TENNIS CHAMPIONSHIPS

Men's singles
Jimmy Connors defeated Björn Borg, 6–4, 3–6, 7–6, 6–4
Women's singles
Chris Evert defeated Evonne Goolagong Cawley 6–3, 6–0
Men's doubles
Tom Okker / Marty Riessen defeated Paul Kronk / Cliff Letcher 6–4, 6–0
Women's doubles
Delina Boshoff / Ilana Kloss defeated Olga Morozova / Virginia Wade 6–1, 6–4
Mixed doubles
Billie Jean King / Phil Dent defeated Betty Stöve / Frew McMillan 3–6, 6–2, 7–5

1977

1977 NATIONAL FOOTBALL LEAGUE SEASON
STANDINGS

AFC EAST	W	L	T	NFC EAST	W	L	T
Baltimore	10	4	0	Dallas	12	2	0
Miami	10	4	0	Washington	9	5	0
New England	9	5	0	St. Louis	7	7	0
NY Jets	3	11	0	Philadelphia	5	9	0
Buffalo	3	11	0	NY Giants	5	9	0
AFC CENT	**W**	**L**	**T**	**NFC CENT**	**W**	**L**	**T**
Pittsburgh	9	5	0	Minnesota	9	5	0
Cincinnati	8	6	0	Chicago	9	5	0
Houston	8	6	0	Detroit	6	8	0
Cleveland	6	8	0	Green Bay	4	10	0
AFC WEST	**W**	**L**	**T**	Tampa Bay	2	12	0
Denver	12	2	0	**NFC WEST**	**W**	**L**	**T**
Oakland	11	3	0	Los Angeles	10	4	0
San Diego	7	7	0	Atlanta	7	7	0
Seattle	5	9	0	San Francisco	5	9	0
Kansas City	2	12	0	New Orleans	3	11	0

1977 U.S. NATIONAL BADMINTON CHAMPIONSHIPS
WINNERS

Year	Men's singles	Women's singles	Men's doubles	Women's doubles	Mixed doubles
1977	Chris Kinard	Pam Brady	Jim Poole Mike Walker	Diana Osterhues Janet Wilts	Bruce Pontow Pam Brady

1977 NBA STANDINGS
DIVISION STANDINGS

Eastern Conference	W	L	W/L%	GB	PS/G	PA/G	SRS
Atlantic Division							
Philadelphia 76ers* (1)	50	32	.610	—	110.2	106.2	3.78
Boston Celtics* (4)	44	38	.537	6.0	104.5	106.5	-1.90
New York Knicks (7)	40	42	.488	10.0	108.6	108.6	0.01
Buffalo Braves (10)	30	52	.366	20.0	105.0	109.5	-4.28
New York Nets (11)	22	60	.268	28.0	95.9	102.7	-6.54
Central Division							
Houston Rockets* (2)	49	33	.598	—	106.4	104.8	1.44
Washington Bullets* (3)	48	34	.585	1.0	105.5	104.5	0.90
San Antonio Spurs* (5)	44	38	.537	5.0	115.0	114.4	0.53
Cleveland Cavaliers* (6)	43	39	.524	6.0	102.1	101.0	1.08
New Orleans Jazz (8)	35	47	.427	14.0	104.6	107.4	-2.68
Atlanta Hawks (9)	31	51	.378	18.0	102.4	106.4	-3.87

Western Conference	W	L	W/L%	GB	PS/G	PA/G	SRS
Midwest Division							
Denver Nuggets* (2)	50	32	.610	—	112.6	107.4	4.95
Detroit Pistons* (5)	44	38	.537	6.0	109.4	110.4	-1.00
Chicago Bulls* (6)	44	38	.537	6.0	98.9	98.0	0.92
Kansas City Kings (8)	40	42	.488	10.0	107.7	106.8	0.93
Indiana Pacers (9)	36	46	.439	14.0	106.8	108.6	-1.68
Milwaukee Bucks (11)	30	52	.366	20.0	108.4	111.5	-2.99
Pacific Division							
Los Angeles Lakers* (1)	53	29	.646	—	106.9	104.1	2.64
Portland Trail Blazers* (3)	49	33	.598	4.0	111.7	106.2	5.39
Golden State Warriors* (4)	46	36	.561	7.0	110.9	107.7	3.10
Seattle SuperSonics (7)	40	42	.488	13.0	104.0	105.5	-1.43
Phoenix Suns (10)	34	48	.415	19.0	104.9	104.2	0.64

AMERICAN HORSE OF THE YEAR
1977 ECLIPSE AWARD

Year	Horse	Trainer	Owner	Age	Gender
1977	Seattle Slew	William H. Turner, Jr.	Karen & Mickey Taylor	3	C

1977- NHL SEASON
FINAL STANDINGS

Prince of Wales Conference								
Adams Division	GP	W	L	T	Pts	GF	GA	PIM
Boston Bruins	80	51	18	11	113	333	218	1237
Buffalo Sabres	80	44	19	17	105	288	215	800
Toronto Maple Leafs	80	41	29	10	92	271	237	1258
Cleveland Barons	80	22	45	13	57	230	325	1010
Norris Division	GP	W	L	T	Pts	GF	GA	PIM
Montreal Canadiens	80	59	10	11	129	359	183	745
Detroit Red Wings	80	32	34	14	78	252	266	1534
Los Angeles Kings	80	31	34	15	77	243	245	903
Pittsburgh Penguins	80	25	37	18	68	254	321	1300
Washington Capitals	80	17	49	14	48	195	321	1332
Clarence Campbell Conference								
Patrick Division	GP	W	L	T	Pts	GF	GA	PIM
New York Islanders	80	48	17	15	111	334	210	938
Philadelphia Flyers	80	45	20	15	105	296	200	1668
Atlanta Flames	80	34	27	19	87	274	252	984
New York Rangers	80	30	37	13	73	279	280	1057
Smythe Division	GP	W	L	T	Pts	GF	GA	PIM
Chicago Black Hawks	80	32	29	19	83	230	220	1308
Colorado Rockies	80	19	40	21	59	257	305	818
Vancouver Canucks	80	20	43	17	57	239	320	962
St. Louis Blues	80	20	47	13	53	195	304	845
Minnesota North Stars	80	18	53	9	45	218	325	1096

1977 MAJOR LEAGUE BASEBALL SEASON HISTORY

1977 American League Standings

EAST	W	L	PCT	GB	HOME	ROAD	RS	RA	DIFF
x-New York	100	62	.617	--	--	--	831	651	+180
Baltimore	97	64	.602	2.5	--	--	719	653	+66
Boston	97	64	.602	2.5	--	--	859	712	+147
Detroit	74	88	.457	26	--	--	714	751	-37
Cleveland	71	90	.441	28.5	--	--	676	739	-63
Milwaukee	67	95	.414	33	--	--	639	765	-126
Toronto	54	107	.335	45.5	--	--	605	822	-217
WEST	**W**	**L**	**PCT**	**GB**	**HOME**	**ROAD**	**RS**	**RA**	**DIFF**
*-Kansas City	102	60	.630	--	--	--	822	651	+171
Texas	94	68	.580	8	--	--	767	657	+110
Chicago	90	72	.556	12	--	--	844	771	+73
Minnesota	84	77	.522	17.5	--	--	867	776	+91
California	74	88	.457	28	--	--	675	695	-20
Seattle	64	98	.395	38	--	--	624	855	-231
Oakland	63	98	.391	38.5	--	--	605	749	-144

1977 National League Standings

EAST	W	L	PCT	GB	HOME	ROAD	RS	RA	DIFF
*-Philadelphia	101	61	.623	--	--	--	847	668	+179
Pittsburgh	96	66	.593	5	--	--	734	665	+69
St. Louis	83	79	.512	18	--	--	737	688	+49
Chicago	81	81	.500	20	--	--	692	739	-47
Montreal	75	87	.463	26	--	--	665	736	-71
New York	64	98	.395	37	--	--	587	663	-76
WEST	**W**	**L**	**PCT**	**GB**	**HOME**	**ROAD**	**RS**	**RA**	**DIFF**
x-Los Angeles	**98**	**64**	**.605**	**--**	**--**	**--**	**769**	**582**	**+187**
Cincinnati	88	74	.543	10	--	--	802	725	+77
Houston	81	81	.500	17	--	--	680	650	+30
San Francisco	75	87	.463	23	--	--	673	711	-38
San Diego	69	93	.426	29	--	--	692	834	-142
Atlanta	61	101	.377	37	--	--	678	895	-217

1977 U.S. NATIONAL TENNIS CHAMPIONSHIPS

Men's singles
Guillermo Vilas defeated Jimmy Connors 2–6, 6–3, 7–6$^{(7-4)}$, 6–0
Women's singles
Chris Evert defeated Wendy Turnbull 7–6, 6–2
Men's doubles
Bob Hewitt / Frew McMillan defeated Brian Gottfried / Raúl Ramírez 6–4, 6–0
Women's doubles
Martina Navratilova / Betty Stöve defeated Renee Richards / Betty-Ann Stuart 6–1, 7–6
Mixed doubles
Betty Stöve / Frew McMillan defeated Billie Jean King / Vitas Gerulaitis 6–2, 3–6, 6–3

1978

1978 NATIONAL FOOTBALL LEAGUE SEASON
STANDINGS

AFC EAST	W	L	T	NFC EAST	W	L	T
New England	11	5	0	Dallas	12	4	0
Miami	11	5	0	Philadelphia	9	7	0
NY Jets	8	8	0	Washington	8	8	0
Buffalo	5	11	0	St. Louis	6	10	0
Baltimore	5	11	0	NY Giants	6	10	0
AFC CENT	W	L	T	NFC CENT	W	L	T
Pittsburgh	14	2	0	Minnesota	8	7	1
Houston	10	6	0	Green Bay	8	7	1
Cleveland	8	8	0	Detroit	7	9	0
Cincinnati	4	12	0	Chicago	7	9	0
AFC WEST	W	L	T	Tampa Bay	5	11	0
Denver	10	6	0	NFC WEST	W	L	T
San Diego	9	7	0	Los Angeles	12	4	0
Seattle	9	7	0	Atlanta	9	7	0
Oakland	9	7	0	New Orleans	7	9	0
Kansas City	4	12	0	San Francisco	2	14	0

1978 U.S. NATIONAL BADMINTON CHAMPIONSHIPS
WINNERS

Year	Men's singles	Women's singles	Men's doubles	Women's doubles	Mixed doubles
1978	Mike Walker	Cheryl Carton	John Britton Charles Coakley	Diana Osterhues Janet Wilts	Bruce Pontow Pam Brady

1978 NBA STANDINGS
DIVISION STANDINGS

Eastern Conference	W	L	W/L%	GB	PS/G	PA/G	SRS
\multicolumn{8}{c}{Atlantic Division}
Philadelphia 76ers* (1)	55	27	.671	—	114.7	109.6	4.87
New York Knicks* (5)	43	39	.524	12.0	113.4	114.0	-0.53
Boston Celtics (8)	32	50	.390	23.0	105.7	107.7	-1.86
Buffalo Braves (10)	27	55	.329	28.0	105.3	109.0	-3.55
New Jersey Nets (11)	24	58	.293	31.0	106.7	112.5	-5.61
\multicolumn{8}{c}{Central Division}
San Antonio Spurs* (2)	52	30	.634	—	114.5	111.1	3.20
Washington Bullets* (3)	44	38	.537	8.0	110.3	109.4	0.82
Cleveland Cavaliers* (4)	43	39	.524	9.0	104.4	103.9	0.44
Atlanta Hawks* (6)	41	41	.500	11.0	103.7	103.9	-0.13
New Orleans Jazz (7)	39	43	.476	13.0	107.6	109.5	-1.80
Houston Rockets (9)	28	54	.341	24.0	103.8	107.8	-3.83

Western Conference	W	L	W/L%	GB	PS/G	PA/G	SRS
Midwest Division							
Denver Nuggets* (2)	48	34	.585	—	111.8	110.9	0.80
Milwaukee Bucks* (6)	44	38	.537	4.0	112.4	113.0	-0.59
Chicago Bulls (8)	40	42	.488	8.0	103.9	104.8	-0.79
Detroit Pistons (9)	38	44	.463	10.0	109.0	110.2	-1.22
Kansas City Kings (10)	31	51	.378	17.0	109.5	111.4	-1.76
Indiana Pacers (11)	31	51	.378	17.0	108.6	111.1	-2.37
Pacific Division							
Portland Trail Blazers* (1)	58	24	.707	—	107.7	101.5	5.92
Phoenix Suns* (3)	49	33	.598	9.0	112.3	108.6	3.50
Seattle SuperSonics* (4)	47	35	.573	11.0	104.5	102.9	1.48
Los Angeles Lakers* (5)	45	37	.549	13.0	110.3	107.6	2.59
Golden State Warriors (7)	43	39	.524	15.0	106.1	105.7	0.41

AMERICAN HORSE OF THE YEAR
1978 ECLIPSE AWARD

Year	Horse	Trainer	Owner	Age	Gender
1978	Affirmed	Laz Barrera	Harbor View Farm	3	C

1978- NHL SEASON
FINAL STANDINGS

Prince of Wales Conference								
Adams Division	GP	W	L	T	Pts	GF	GA	PIM
Boston Bruins	80	43	23	14	100	316	270	1222
Buffalo Sabres	80	36	28	16	88	280	263	1026
Toronto Maple Leafs	80	34	33	13	81	267	252	1440
Minnesota North Stars	80	28	40	12	68	257	289	1102
Norris Division	GP	W	L	T	Pts	GF	GA	PIM
Montreal Canadiens	80	52	17	11	115	337	204	803
Pittsburgh Penguins	80	36	31	13	85	281	279	1039
Los Angeles Kings	80	34	34	12	80	292	286	1134
Washington Capitals	80	24	41	15	63	273	338	1312
Detroit Red Wings	80	23	41	16	62	252	295	1359
Clarence Campbell Conference								
Patrick Division	GP	W	L	T	Pts	GF	GA	PIM
New York Islanders	80	51	15	14	116	358	214	1077
Philadelphia Flyers	80	40	25	15	95	281	248	1548
New York Rangers	80	40	29	11	91	316	292	1214
Atlanta Flames	80	41	31	8	90	327	280	1158
Smythe Division	GP	W	L	T	Pts	GF	GA	PIM
Chicago Black Hawks	80	29	36	15	73	244	277	1254
Vancouver Canucks	80	25	42	13	63	217	291	1134
St. Louis Blues	80	18	50	12	48	249	348	1055
Colorado Rockies	80	15	53	12	42	210	331	838

1978 MAJOR LEAGUE BASEBALL SEASON HISTORY

1978 American League Standings

EAST	W	L	PCT	GB	HOME	ROAD	RS	RA	DIFF
*-New York	100	63	.613	--	--	--	735	582	+153
Boston	99	64	.607	1	--	--	796	657	+139
Milwaukee	93	69	.574	6.5	--	--	804	650	+154
Baltimore	90	71	.559	9	--	--	659	633	+26
Detroit	86	76	.531	13.5	--	--	714	653	+61
Cleveland	69	90	.434	29	--	--	639	694	-55
Toronto	59	102	.366	40	--	--	590	775	-185
WEST	**W**	**L**	**PCT**	**GB**	**HOME**	**ROAD**	**RS**	**RA**	**DIFF**
x-Kansas City	92	70	.568	--	--	--	743	634	+109
Texas	87	75	.537	5	--	--	692	632	+60
California	87	75	.537	5	--	--	691	666	+25
Minnesota	73	89	.451	19	--	--	666	678	-12
Chicago	71	90	.441	20.5	--	--	634	731	-97
Oakland	69	93	.426	23	--	--	532	690	-158
Seattle	56	104	.350	35	--	--	614	834	-220

1978 National League Standings

EAST	W	L	PCT	GB	HOME	ROAD	RS	RA	DIFF
x-Philadelphia	90	72	.556	--	--	--	708	586	+122
Pittsburgh	88	73	.547	1.5	--	--	684	637	+47
Chicago	79	83	.488	11	--	--	664	724	-60
Montreal	76	86	.469	14	--	--	633	611	+22
St. Louis	69	93	.426	21	--	--	600	657	-57
New York	66	96	.407	24	--	--	607	690	-83
WEST	**W**	**L**	**PCT**	**GB**	**HOME**	**ROAD**	**RS**	**RA**	**DIFF**
*-Los Angeles	95	67	.586	--	--	--	727	573	+154
Cincinnati	92	69	.571	2.5	--	--	710	688	+22
San Francisco	89	73	.549	6	--	--	613	594	+19
San Diego	84	78	.519	11	--	--	591	598	-7
Houston	74	88	.457	21	--	--	605	634	-29
Atlanta	69	93	.426	26	--	--	600	750	-150

1978 U.S. NATIONAL TENNIS CHAMPIONSHIPS

Men's singles
Jimmy Connors defeated Björn Borg, 6–4, 6–2, 6–2
Women's singles
Chris Evert defeated Pam Shriver, 7–5, 6–4
Men's doubles
Bob Lutz / Stan Smith defeated Marty Riessen / Sherwood Stewart, 1–6, 7–5, 6–3
Women's doubles
Billie Jean King / Martina Navratilova defeated Kerry Melville Reid / Wendy Turnbull, 7–6, 6–4
Mixed doubles
Betty Stöve / Frew McMillan defeated Billie Jean King / Ray Ruffels, 6–3, 7-6

1979

1979 NATIONAL FOOTBALL LEAGUE SEASON
STANDINGS

AFC EAST	W	L	T	NFC EAST	W	L	T
Miami	10	6	0	Dallas	11	5	0
New England	9	7	0	Philadelphia	11	5	0
NY Jets	8	8	0	Washington	10	6	0
Buffalo	7	9	0	NY Giants	6	10	0
Baltimore	5	11	0	St. Louis	5	11	0
AFC CENT	W	L	T	NFC CENT	W	L	T
Pittsburgh	12	4	0	Tampa Bay	10	6	0
Houston	11	5	0	Chicago	10	6	0
Cleveland	9	7	0	Minnesota	7	9	0
Cincinnati	4	12	0	Green Bay	5	11	0
AFC WEST	W	L	T	Detroit	2	14	0
San Diego	12	4	0	NFC WEST	W	L	T
Denver	10	6	0	Los Angeles	9	7	0
Seattle	9	7	0	New Orleans	8	8	0
Oakland	9	7	0	Atlanta	6	10	0
Kansas City	7	9	0	San Francisco	2	14	0

1979 U.S. NATIONAL BADMINTON CHAMPIONSHIPS
WINNERS

Year	Men's singles	Women's singles	Men's doubles	Women's doubles	Mixed doubles
1979	Chris Kinard	Pam Brady	Jim Poole Mike Walker	Pam Brady Judianne Kelly	Mike Walker Judianne Kelly

1979 NBA STANDINGS
DIVISION STANDINGS

Eastern Conference	W	L	W/L%	GB	PS/G	PA/G	SRS
Atlantic Division							
Washington Bullets* (1)	54	28	.659	—	114.9	109.9	4.75
Philadelphia 76ers* (3)	47	35	.573	7.0	109.5	107.7	1.74
New Jersey Nets* (6)	37	45	.451	17.0	107.7	111.9	-4.00
New York Knicks (7)	31	51	.378	23.0	107.7	111.1	-3.29
Boston Celtics (10)	29	53	.354	25.0	108.2	113.3	-4.78
Central Division							
San Antonio Spurs* (2)	48	34	.585	—	119.3	114.1	4.97
Houston Rockets* (4)	47	35	.573	1.0	113.4	112.4	0.92
Atlanta Hawks* (5)	46	36	.561	2.0	109.1	107.1	1.92
Detroit Pistons (8)	30	52	.366	18.0	110.0	112.7	-2.60
Cleveland Cavaliers (9)	30	52	.366	18.0	106.5	110.2	-3.57
New Orleans Jazz (11)	26	56	.317	22.0	108.3	114.6	-5.97

Western Conference	W	L	W/L%	GB	PS/G	PA/G	SRS
Midwest Division							
Kansas City Kings* (2)	48	34	.585	—	113.1	110.2	2.73
Denver Nuggets* (4)	47	35	.573	1.0	110.7	109.5	1.24
Milwaukee Bucks (8)	38	44	.463	10.0	114.1	111.8	2.12
Indiana Pacers (10)	38	44	.463	10.0	108.6	110.2	-1.41
Chicago Bulls (11)	31	51	.378	17.0	104.7	108.7	-3.78
Pacific Division							
Seattle SuperSonics* (1)	52	30	.634	—	106.6	103.9	2.69
Phoenix Suns* (3)	50	32	.610	2.0	115.4	111.7	3.55
Los Angeles Lakers* (5)	47	35	.573	5.0	112.9	109.9	2.95
Portland Trail Blazers* (6)	45	37	.549	7.0	108.4	107.1	1.12
San Diego Clippers (7)	43	39	.524	9.0	113.1	114.9	-1.76
Golden State Warriors (9)	38	44	.463	14.0	105.1	104.8	0.46

AMERICAN HORSE OF THE YEAR
1979 ECLIPSE AWARD

Year	Horse	Trainer	Owner	Age	Gender
1979	Affirmed	Laz Barrera	Harbor View Farm	4	C

1979- NHL SEASON
FINAL STANDINGS

Prince of Wales Conference								
Adams Division	GP	W	L	T	Pts	GF	GA	PIM
Buffalo Sabres	80	47	17	16	110	318	201	967
Boston Bruins	80	46	21	13	105	310	234	1460
Minnesota North Stars	80	36	28	16	88	311	253	1064
Toronto Maple Leafs	80	35	40	5	75	304	327	1158
Quebec Nordiques	80	25	44	11	61	248	313	1062
Norris Division	GP	W	L	T	Pts	GF	GA	PIM
Montreal Canadiens	80	47	20	13	107	328	240	874
Los Angeles Kings	80	30	36	14	74	290	313	1124
Pittsburgh Penguins	80	30	37	13	73	251	303	1038
Hartford Whalers	80	27	34	19	73	303	312	875
Detroit Red Wings	80	26	43	11	63	268	306	1114
Clarence Campbell Conference								
Patrick Division	GP	W	L	T	Pts	GF	GA	PIM
Philadelphia Flyers	80	48	12	20	116	327	254	1844
New York Islanders	80	39	28	13	91	281	247	1298
New York Rangers	80	38	32	10	86	308	284	1342
Atlanta Flames	80	35	32	13	83	282	269	1048
Washington Capitals	80	27	40	13	67	261	293	1198
Smythe Division	GP	W	L	T	Pts	GF	GA	PIM
Chicago Black Hawks	80	34	27	19	87	241	250	1325
St. Louis Blues	80	34	34	12	80	266	278	1037
Vancouver Canucks	80	27	37	16	70	256	281	1808
Edmonton Oilers	80	28	39	13	69	301	322	1528
Winnipeg Jets	80	20	49	11	51	214	314	1251
Colorado Rockies	80	19	48	13	51	234	308	1020

1979 MAJOR LEAGUE BASEBALL SEASON HISTORY

1979 American League Standings

EAST	W	L	PCT	GB	HOME	ROAD	RS	RA	DIFF
*-Baltimore	102	57	.642	--	--	--	757	582	+175
Milwaukee	95	66	.590	8	--	--	807	722	+85
Boston	91	69	.569	11.5	--	--	841	711	+130
New York	89	71	.556	13.5	--	--	734	672	+62
Detroit	85	76	.528	18	--	--	770	738	+32
Cleveland	81	80	.503	22	--	--	760	805	-45
Toronto	53	109	.327	50.5	--	--	613	862	-249
WEST	**W**	**L**	**PCT**	**GB**	**HOME**	**ROAD**	**RS**	**RA**	**DIFF**
x-California	88	74	.543	--	--	--	866	768	+98
Kansas City	85	77	.525	3	--	--	851	816	+35
Texas	83	79	.512	5	--	--	750	698	+52
Minnesota	82	80	.506	6	--	--	764	725	+39
Chicago	73	87	.456	14	--	--	730	748	-18
Seattle	67	95	.414	21	--	--	711	820	-109
Oakland	54	108	.333	34	--	--	573	860	-287

1979 National League Standings

EAST	W	L	PCT	GB	HOME	ROAD	RS	RA	DIFF
*-Pittsburgh	98	64	.601	--	--	--	775	643	+132
Montreal	95	65	.594	2	--	--	701	581	+120
St. Louis	86	76	.528	12	--	--	731	693	+38
Philadelphia	84	78	.515	14	--	--	683	718	-35
Chicago	80	82	.494	18	--	--	706	707	-1
New York	63	99	.387	35	--	--	593	706	-113
WEST	**W**	**L**	**PCT**	**GB**	**HOME**	**ROAD**	**RS**	**RA**	**DIFF**
x-Cincinnati	90	71	.559	--	--	--	731	644	+87
Houston	89	73	.549	1.5	--	--	583	582	+1
Los Angeles	79	83	.488	11.5	--	--	739	717	+22
San Francisco	71	91	.438	19.5	--	--	672	751	-79
San Diego	68	93	.422	22	--	--	603	681	-78
Atlanta	66	94	.413	23.5	--	--	669	763	-94

1979 U.S. NATIONAL TENNIS CHAMPIONSHIPS

Men's singles
John McEnroe defeated Vitas Gerulaitis 7–5, 6–3, 6–3
Women's singles
Tracy Austin defeated Chris Evert 6–4, 6–3
Men's doubles
John McEnroe / Peter Fleming defeated Bob Lutz / Stan Smith 6–2, 6–4
Women's doubles
Betty Stöve / Wendy Turnbull defeated Billie Jean King Martina Navratilova 7–5, 6–3
Mixed doubles
Greer Stevens / Bob Hewitt defeated Betty Stöve / Frew McMillan 6–3, 7–5

1980

1980 NATIONAL FOOTBALL LEAGUE SEASON
STANDINGS

AFC EAST	W	L	T	NFC EAST	W	L	T
Buffalo	11	5	0	Philadelphia	12	4	0
New England	10	6	0	Dallas	12	4	0
Miami	8	8	0	Washington	6	10	0
Baltimore	7	9	0	St. Louis	5	11	0
NY Jets	4	12	0	NY Giants	4	12	0
AFC CENT	**W**	**L**	**T**	**NFC CENT**	**W**	**L**	**T**
Cleveland	11	5	0	Minnesota	9	7	0
Houston	11	5	0	Detroit	9	7	0
Pittsburgh	9	7	0	Chicago	7	9	0
Cincinnati	6	10	0	Tampa Bay	5	10	1
AFC WEST	**W**	**L**	**T**	Green Bay	5	10	1
San Diego	11	5	0	**NFC WEST**	**W**	**L**	**T**
Oakland	11	5	0	Atlanta	12	4	0
Kansas City	8	8	0	Los Angeles	11	5	0
Denver	8	8	0	San Francisco	6	10	0
Seattle	4	12	0	New Orleans	1	15	0

1980 U.S. NATIONAL BADMINTON CHAMPIONSHIPS
WINNERS

Year	Men's singles	Women's singles	Men's doubles	Women's doubles	Mixed doubles
1980	Gary Higgins	Cheryl Carton	Matt Fogarty Mike Walker	Pam Brady Judianne Kelly	Mike Walker Judianne Kelly

1980 NBA STANDINGS
DIVISION STANDINGS

Eastern Conference	W	L	W/L%	GB	PS/G	PA/G	SRS
Atlantic Division							
Boston Celtics* (1)	61	21	.744	—	113.5	105.7	7.37
Philadelphia 76ers* (3)	59	23	.720	2.0	109.1	104.9	4.04
Washington Bullets* (6)	39	43	.476	22.0	107.0	109.5	-2.27
New York Knicks (7)	39	43	.476	22.0	114.0	115.1	-0.96
New Jersey Nets (10)	34	48	.415	27.0	108.3	109.5	-0.98
Central Division							
Atlanta Hawks* (2)	50	32	.610	—	104.5	101.6	2.83
Houston Rockets* (4)	41	41	.500	9.0	110.8	110.6	0.27
San Antonio Spurs* (5)	41	41	.500	9.0	119.4	119.7	-0.24
Indiana Pacers (8)	37	45	.451	13.0	111.2	111.9	-0.54
Cleveland Cavaliers (9)	37	45	.451	13.0	114.1	113.8	0.43
Detroit Pistons (11)	16	66	.195	34.0	108.9	117.2	-7.57

Western Conference	W	L	W/L%	GB	PS/G	PA/G	SRS
Midwest Division							
Milwaukee Bucks* (2)	49	33	.598	—	110.1	106.1	3.57
Kansas City Kings* (5)	47	35	.573	2.0	108.0	104.9	2.82
Denver Nuggets (8)	30	52	.366	19.0	108.3	112.7	-4.22
Chicago Bulls (9)	30	52	.366	19.0	107.5	110.2	-2.63
Utah Jazz (11)	24	58	.293	25.0	102.4	108.4	-5.71
Pacific Division							
Los Angeles Lakers* (1)	60	22	.732	—	115.1	109.2	5.40
Seattle SuperSonics* (3)	56	26	.683	4.0	108.5	103.8	4.24
Phoenix Suns* (4)	55	27	.671	5.0	111.1	107.5	3.25
Portland Trail Blazers* (6)	38	44	.463	22.0	102.5	103.3	-0.87
San Diego Clippers (7)	35	47	.427	25.0	107.6	111.7	-3.97
Golden State Warriors (10)	24	58	.293	36.0	103.6	108.0	-4.20

AMERICAN HORSE OF THE YEAR
1980 ECLIPSE AWARD

Year	Horse	Trainer	Owner	Age	Gender
1980	Spectacular Bid	Bud Delp	Hawksworth Farm	4	C

1980- NHL SEASON
FINAL STANDINGS

Prince of Wales Conference								
Adams Division	GP	W	L	T	Pts	GF	GA	PIM
Buffalo Sabres	80	39	20	21	99	327	250	1194
Boston Bruins	80	37	30	13	87	316	272	1836
Minnesota North Stars	80	35	28	17	87	291	263	1624
Quebec Nordiques	80	30	32	18	78	314	318	1524
Toronto Maple Leafs	80	28	37	15	71	322	367	1830
Norris Division	GP	W	L	T	Pts	GF	GA	PIM
Montreal Canadiens	80	45	22	13	103	332	232	1398
Los Angeles Kings	80	43	24	13	99	337	290	1627
Chicago Blackhawks	80	31	33	16	78	304	315	1660
Pittsburgh Penguins	80	30	37	13	73	302	345	1807
Hartford Whalers	80	21	41	18	60	292	372	1584
Detroit Red Wings	80	19	43	18	56	252	339	1687
Clarence Campbell Conference								
Patrick Division	GP	W	L	T	Pts	GF	GA	PIM
New York Islanders	80	48	18	14	110	355	260	1442
Philadelphia Flyers	80	41	24	15	97	313	249	2621
Calgary Flames	80	39	27	14	92	329	298	1450
New York Rangers	80	30	36	14	74	312	317	1981
Washington Capitals	80	26	36	18	70	286	317	1872
Smythe Division	GP	W	L	T	Pts	GF	GA	PIM
St. Louis Blues	80	45	18	17	107	352	281	1657
Vancouver Canucks	80	28	32	20	76	289	301	1892
Edmonton Oilers	80	29	35	16	74	328	327	1544
Colorado Rockies	80	22	45	13	57	258	344	1418
Winnipeg Jets	80	9	57	14	32	246	400	1191

1980 MAJOR LEAGUE BASEBALL SEASON HISTORY

1980 American League Standings

EAST	W	L	PCT	GB	HOME	ROAD	RS	RA	DIFF
*-New York	103	59	.636	--	--	--	820	662	+158
Baltimore	100	62	.617	3	--	--	805	640	+165
Milwaukee	86	76	.531	17	--	--	811	682	+129
Boston	83	77	.519	19	--	--	757	767	-10
Detroit	84	78	.515	19	--	--	830	757	+73
Cleveland	79	81	.494	23	--	--	738	807	-69
Toronto	67	95	.414	36	--	--	624	762	-138
WEST	**W**	**L**	**PCT**	**GB**	**HOME**	**ROAD**	**RS**	**RA**	**DIFF**
x-Kansas City	97	65	.599	--	--	--	809	694	+115
Oakland	83	79	.512	14	--	--	686	642	+44
Minnesota	77	84	.478	19.5	--	--	670	724	-54
Texas	76	85	.466	20.5	--	--	756	752	+4
Chicago	70	90	.432	26	--	--	587	722	-135
California	65	95	.406	31	--	--	698	797	-99
Seattle	59	103	.362	38	--	--	610	793	-183

1980 National League Standings

EAST	W	L	PCT	GB	HOME	ROAD	RS	RA	DIFF
x-Philadelphia	91	71	.562	--	--	--	728	639	+89
Montreal	90	72	.556	1	--	--	694	629	+65
Pittsburgh	83	79	.512	8	--	--	666	646	+20
St. Louis	74	88	.457	17	--	--	738	710	+28
New York	67	95	.414	24	--	--	611	702	-91
Chicago	64	98	.395	27	--	--	614	728	-114
WEST	**W**	**L**	**PCT**	**GB**	**HOME**	**ROAD**	**RS**	**RA**	**DIFF**
*-Houston	93	70	.571	--	--	--	637	589	+48
Los Angeles	92	71	.564	1	--	--	663	591	+72
Cincinnati	89	73	.546	3.5	--	--	707	670	+37
Atlanta	81	80	.503	11	--	--	630	660	-30
San Francisco	75	86	.466	17	--	--	573	634	-61
San Diego	73	89	.448	19.5	--	--	591	654	-63

1980 U.S. NATIONAL TENNIS CHAMPIONSHIPS

Men's Singles
John McEnroe defeated Björn Borg 7–6 (7–4), 6–1, 6–7(5–7), 5–7,
Women's singles
Chris Evert-Lloyd defeated Hana Mandlíková 5–7, 6–1, 6–1
Men's Doubles
Bob Lutz / Stan Smith defeated John McEnroe / Peter Fleming 7–5, 3–6, 6–1, 3–6, 6–3
Women's Doubles
Billie Jean King / Martina Navratilova defeated Pam Shriver / Betty Stöve 7–6 (7–2), 7–5
Mixed Doubles
Wendy Turnbull / Marty Riessen defeated Betty Stöve / Frew McMillan 7–5, 6–2

1981

1981 NATIONAL FOOTBALL LEAGUE SEASON
STANDINGS

AFC EAST	W	L	T	NFC EAST	W	L	T
Miami	11	4	1	Dallas	12	4	0
NY Jets	10	5	1	Philadelphia	10	6	0
Buffalo	10	6	0	NY Giants	9	7	0
Baltimore	2	14	0	Washington	8	8	0
New England	2	14	0	St. Louis	7	9	0
AFC CENT	W	L	T	**NFC CENT**	W	L	T
Cincinnati	12	4	0	Tampa Bay	9	7	0
Pittsburgh	8	8	0	Detroit	8	8	0
Houston	7	9	0	Green Bay	8	8	0
Cleveland	5	11	0	Minnesota	7	9	0
AFC WEST	W	L	T	Chicago	6	10	0
San Diego	10	6	0	**NFC WEST**	W	L	T
Denver	10	6	0	San Francisco	13	3	0
Kansas City	9	7	0	Atlanta	7	9	0
Oakland	7	9	0	Los Angeles	6	10	0
Seattle	6	10	0	New Orleans	4	12	0

1981 U.S. NATIONAL BADMINTON CHAMPIONSHIPS
WINNERS

Year	Men's singles	Women's singles	Men's doubles	Women's doubles	Mixed doubles
1981	Chris Kinard	Utami Kinard	John Britton Gary Higgins	Pam Brady Judianne Kelly	Danny Brady Pam Brady

1981 NBA STANDINGS
DIVISION STANDINGS

Eastern Conference	W	L	W/L%	GB	PS/G	PA/G	SRS
Atlantic Division							
Boston Celtics* (1)	62	20	.756	—	109.9	104.0	6.05
Philadelphia 76ers* (3)	62	20	.756	—	111.7	103.8	7.76
New York Knicks* (4)	50	32	.610	12.0	107.9	106.3	2.00
Washington Bullets (7)	39	43	.476	23.0	105.6	105.6	0.42
New Jersey Nets (10)	24	58	.293	38.0	106.9	113.0	-5.15
Central Division							
Milwaukee Bucks* (2)	60	22	.732	—	113.1	105.9	7.14
Chicago Bulls* (5)	45	37	.549	15.0	109.0	107.0	2.34
Indiana Pacers* (6)	44	38	.537	16.0	107.6	106.2	1.72
Atlanta Hawks (8)	31	51	.378	29.0	104.9	108.0	-2.37
Cleveland Cavaliers (9)	28	54	.341	32.0	105.7	110.6	-4.15
Detroit Pistons (11)	21	61	.256	39.0	99.7	106.0	-5.58

Western Conference	W	L	W/L%	GB	PS/G	PA/G	SRS
	Midwest Division
San Antonio Spurs* (2)	52	30	.634	—	112.3	109.4	2.18
Kansas City Kings* (5)	40	42	.488	12.0	106.9	106.9	-0.49
Houston Rockets* (6)	40	42	.488	12.0	108.3	107.9	-0.20
Denver Nuggets (8)	37	45	.451	15.0	121.8	122.3	-0.95
Utah Jazz (11)	28	54	.341	24.0	101.2	107.1	-5.99
Dallas Mavericks (12)	15	67	.183	37.0	101.5	109.9	-8.33
	Pacific Division
Phoenix Suns* (1)	57	25	.695	—	110.0	104.5	4.83
Los Angeles Lakers* (3)	54	28	.659	3.0	111.2	107.3	3.27
Portland Trail Blazers* (4)	45	37	.549	12.0	110.7	109.8	0.52
Golden State Warriors (7)	39	43	.476	18.0	109.8	111.0	-1.41
San Diego Clippers (9)	36	46	.439	21.0	106.5	108.1	-1.78
Seattle SuperSonics (10)	34	48	.415	23.0	104.0	105.7	-1.84

AMERICAN HORSE OF THE YEAR
1981 ECLIPSE AWARD

Year	Horse	Trainer	Owner	Age	Gender
1981	John Henry	Ron McAnally	Dotsam Stable	6	G

1981- NHL SEASON
FINAL STANDINGS

Prince of Wales Conference							
Adams Division	GP	W	L	T	Pts	GF	GA	PIM
Montreal Canadiens	80	46	17	17	109	360	223	1463
Boston Bruins	80	43	27	10	96	323	285	1266
Buffalo Sabres	80	39	26	15	93	307	273	1425
Quebec Nordiques	80	33	31	16	82	356	345	1757
Hartford Whalers	80	21	41	18	60	264	351	1493
Patrick Division	GP	W	L	T	Pts	GF	GA	PIM
New York Islanders	80	54	16	10	118	385	250	1328
New York Rangers	80	39	27	14	92	316	306	1402
Philadelphia Flyers	80	38	31	11	87	325	313	2493
Pittsburgh Penguins	80	31	36	13	75	310	337	2212
Washington Capitals	80	26	41	13	65	319	338	1932
Clarence Campbell Conference							
Norris Division	GP	W	L	T	Pts	GF	GA	PIM
Minnesota North Stars	80	37	23	20	94	346	288	1358
Winnipeg Jets	80	33	33	14	80	319	332	1314
St. Louis Blues	80	32	40	8	72	315	349	1579
Chicago Blackhawks	80	30	38	12	72	332	363	1775
Toronto Maple Leafs	80	20	44	16	56	298	380	1888
Detroit Red Wings	80	21	47	12	54	270	351	1250
Smythe Division	GP	W	L	T	Pts	GF	GA	PIM
Edmonton Oilers	80	48	17	15	111	417	295	1473
Vancouver Canucks	80	30	33	17	77	290	286	1840
Calgary Flames	80	29	34	17	75	334	345	1331
Los Angeles Kings	80	24	41	15	63	314	396	1730
Colorado Rockies	80	18	49	13	49	241	362	1138

1981 MAJOR LEAGUE BASEBALL SEASON HISTORY

1981 American League Standings

EAST	W	L	PCT	GB	HOME	ROAD	RS	RA	DIFF
x-Milwaukee	62	47	.569	--	--	--	493	459	+34
Baltimore	59	46	.562	1	--	--	429	437	-8
New York	59	48	.551	2	--	--	421	343	+78
Detroit	60	49	.550	2	--	--	427	404	+23
Boston	59	49	.546	2.5	--	--	519	481	+38
Cleveland	52	51	.505	7	--	--	431	442	-11
Toronto	37	69	.349	23.5	--	--	329	466	-137
WEST	**W**	**L**	**PCT**	**GB**	**HOME**	**ROAD**	**RS**	**RA**	**DIFF**
*-Oakland	64	45	.587	--	--	--	458	403	+55
Texas	57	48	.543	5	--	--	452	389	+63
Chicago	54	52	.509	8.5	--	--	476	423	+53
Kansas City	50	53	.485	11	--	--	397	405	-8
California	51	59	.464	13.5	--	--	476	453	+23
Seattle	44	65	.400	20	--	--	426	521	-95
Minnesota	41	68	.373	23	--	--	378	486	-108

1981 National League Standings

EAST	W	L	PCT	GB	HOME	ROAD	RS	RA	DIFF
x-St. Louis	59	43	.573	--	--	--	464	417	+47
Montreal	60	48	.556	2	--	--	443	394	+49
Philadelphia	59	48	.551	2.5	--	--	491	472	+19
Pittsburgh	46	56	.447	13	--	--	407	425	-18
New York	41	62	.390	18.5	--	--	348	432	-84
Chicago	38	65	.358	21.5	--	--	370	483	-113
WEST	**W**	**L**	**PCT**	**GB**	**HOME**	**ROAD**	**RS**	**RA**	**DIFF**
*-Cincinnati	66	42	.611	--	--	--	464	440	+24
Los Angeles	63	47	.573	4	--	--	450	356	+94
Houston	61	49	.555	6	--	--	394	331	+63
San Francisco	56	55	.505	11.5	--	--	427	414	+13
Atlanta	50	56	.467	15	--	--	395	416	-21
San Diego	41	69	.373	26	--	--	382	455	-73

1981 U.S. NATIONAL TENNIS CHAMPIONSHIPS

Men's Singles
John McEnroe defeated Björn Borg 4–6, 6–2, 6–4, 6–3
Women's Singles
Tracy Austin defeated Martina Navratilova 1–6, 7–6$^{(7-4)}$, 7–6$^{(7-1)}$
Men's Doubles
Peter Fleming / John McEnroe defeated Heinz Günthardt / Peter McNamara by Walkover
Women's Doubles
Kathy Jordan / Anne Smith defeated Rosemary Casals / Wendy Turnbull 6–3, 6–3
Mixed Doubles
Anne Smith / Kevin Curren defeated JoAnne Russell / Steve Denton 6–4, 7–6

1982

1982 NATIONAL FOOTBALL LEAGUE SEASON
STANDINGS

AFC	W	L	T	NFC	W	L	T
LA Raiders	8	1	0	Washington	8	1	0
Miami	7	2	0	Dallas	6	3	0
Cincinnati	7	2	0	Green Bay	5	3	1
Pittsburgh	6	3	0	Minnesota	5	4	0
San Diego	6	3	0	Atlanta	5	4	0
NY Jets	6	3	0	St. Louis	5	4	0
New England	5	4	0	Tampa Bay	5	4	0
Cleveland	4	5	0	Detroit	4	5	0
Buffalo	4	5	0	NY Giants	4	5	0
Seattle	4	5	0	New Orleans	4	5	0
Kansas City	3	6	0	San Francisco	3	6	0
Denver	2	7	0	Chicago	3	6	0
Houston	1	8	0	Philadelphia	3	6	0
Baltimore	0	8	1	LA Rams	2	7	0

1982 U.S. NATIONAL BADMINTON CHAMPIONSHIPS
WINNERS

Year	Men's singles	Women's singles	Men's doubles	Women's doubles	Mixed doubles
1982	Gary Higgins	Cheryl Carton	Don Paup Bruce Pontow	Pam Brady Judianne Kelly	Danny Brady Pam Brady

1982 NBA STANDINGS
DIVISION STANDINGS

Eastern Conference	W	L	W/L%	GB	PS/G	PA/G	SRS
Atlantic Division							
Boston Celtics* (1)	63	19	.768	—	112.0	105.6	6.35
Philadelphia 76ers* (3)	58	24	.707	5.0	111.2	105.5	5.74
New Jersey Nets* (4)	44	38	.537	19.0	106.7	106.0	0.87
Washington Bullets* (5)	43	39	.524	20.0	103.5	102.6	1.06
New York Knicks (10)	33	49	.402	30.0	106.2	108.9	-2.15
Central Division							
Milwaukee Bucks* (2)	55	27	.671	—	108.4	102.9	5.38
Atlanta Hawks* (6)	42	40	.512	13.0	101.0	100.5	0.81
Detroit Pistons (7)	39	43	.476	16.0	111.1	112.0	-0.63
Indiana Pacers (8)	35	47	.427	20.0	102.2	104.0	-1.49
Chicago Bulls (9)	34	48	.415	21.0	106.6	108.6	-1.57
Cleveland Cavaliers (11)	15	67	.183	40.0	103.2	111.7	-7.77

Western Conference	W	L	W/L%	GB	PS/G	PA/G	SRS
Midwest Division							
San Antonio Spurs* (2)	48	34	.585	—	113.1	110.8	1.79
Denver Nuggets* (4)	46	36	.561	2.0	126.5	126.0	0.13
Houston Rockets* (6)	46	36	.561	2.0	105.9	105.9	-0.39
Kansas City Kings (9)	30	52	.366	18.0	107.1	110.2	-3.25
Dallas Mavericks (10)	28	54	.341	20.0	104.6	109.0	-4.48
Utah Jazz (11)	25	57	.305	23.0	110.9	116.6	-5.63
Pacific Division							
Los Angeles Lakers* (1)	57	25	.695	—	114.6	109.8	4.37
Seattle SuperSonics* (3)	52	30	.634	5.0	107.3	103.1	3.69
Phoenix Suns* (5)	46	36	.561	11.0	106.2	102.7	3.05
Golden State Warriors (7)	45	37	.549	12.0	110.9	109.8	0.80
Portland Trail Blazers (8)	42	40	.512	15.0	109.8	109.2	0.39
San Diego Clippers (12)	17	65	.207	40.0	108.5	115.9	-7.05

AMERICAN HORSE OF THE YEAR
1982 ECLIPSE AWARD

Year	Horse	Trainer	Owner	Age	Gender
1982	Conquistador Cielo	Woody Stephens	Henryk de Kwiatkowski	3	C

1980- NHL SEASON
FINAL STANDINGS

Prince of Wales Conference								
Adams Division	GP	W	L	T	Pts	GF	GA	PIM
Boston Bruins	80	50	20	10	110	327	228	1202
Montreal Canadiens	80	42	24	14	98	350	286	1116
Buffalo Sabres	80	38	29	13	89	318	285	1031
Quebec Nordiques	80	34	34	12	80	343	336	1648
Hartford Whalers	80	19	54	7	45	261	403	1392
Patrick Division	GP	W	L	T	Pts	GF	GA	PIM
Philadelphia Flyers	80	49	23	8	106	326	240	1337
New York Islanders	80	42	26	12	96	302	226	1266
Washington Capitals	80	39	25	16	94	306	283	1329
New York Rangers	80	35	35	10	80	306	287	1100
New Jersey Devils	80	17	49	14	48	230	338	1270
Pittsburgh Penguins	80	18	53	9	45	257	394	1859
Clarence Campbell Conference								
Norris Division	GP	W	L	T	Pts	GF	GA	PIM
Chicago Blackhawks	80	47	23	10	104	338	268	1185
Minnesota North Stars	80	40	24	16	96	321	290	1520
Toronto Maple Leafs	80	28	40	12	68	293	330	1481
St. Louis Blues	80	25	40	15	65	285	316	1281
Detroit Red Wings	80	21	44	15	57	263	344	1064
Smythe Division	GP	W	L	T	Pts	GF	GA	PIM
Edmonton Oilers	80	47	21	12	106	424	315	1771
Calgary Flames	80	32	34	14	78	321	317	1146

Vancouver Canucks	80	30	35	15	75	303	309	1639
Winnipeg Jets	80	33	39	8	74	311	333	1089
Los Angeles Kings	80	27	41	12	66	308	365	1367

1982 MAJOR LEAGUE BASEBALL SEASON HISTORY

1982 American League Standings

EAST	W	L	PCT	GB	HOME	ROAD	RS	RA	DIFF
*-Milwaukee	95	67	.583	--	--	--	891	717	+174
Baltimore	94	68	.577	1	--	--	774	687	+87
Boston	89	73	.549	6	--	--	753	713	+40
Detroit	83	79	.512	12	--	--	729	685	+44
New York	79	83	.488	16	--	--	709	716	-7
Toronto	78	84	.481	17	--	--	651	701	-50
Cleveland	78	84	.481	17	--	--	683	748	-65
WEST	**W**	**L**	**PCT**	**GB**	**HOME**	**ROAD**	**RS**	**RA**	**DIFF**
x-California	93	69	.574	--	--	--	814	670	+144
Kansas City	90	72	.556	3	--	--	784	717	+67
Chicago	87	75	.537	6	--	--	786	710	+76
Seattle	76	86	.469	17	--	--	651	712	-61
Oakland	68	94	.420	25	--	--	691	819	-128
Texas	64	98	.395	29	--	--	590	749	-159
Minnesota	60	102	.370	33	--	--	657	819	-162

1982 National League Standings

EAST	W	L	PCT	GB	HOME	ROAD	RS	RA	DIFF
*-St. Louis	92	70	.568	--	--	--	685	609	+76
Philadelphia	89	73	.549	3	--	--	664	654	+10
Montreal	86	76	.531	6	--	--	697	616	+81
Pittsburgh	84	78	.519	8	--	--	724	696	+28
Chicago	73	89	.451	19	--	--	676	709	-33
New York	65	97	.401	27	--	--	609	723	-114
WEST	**W**	**L**	**PCT**	**GB**	**HOME**	**ROAD**	**RS**	**RA**	**DIFF**
x-Atlanta	89	73	.549	--	--	--	739	702	+37
Los Angeles	88	74	.543	1	--	--	691	612	+79
San Francisco	87	75	.537	2	--	--	673	687	-14
San Diego	81	81	.500	8	--	--	675	658	+17
Houston	77	85	.475	12	--	--	569	620	-51
Cincinnati	61	101	.377	28	--	--	545	661	-116

1982 U.S. NATIONAL TENNIS CHAMPIONSHIPS

Men's Singles
Jimmy Connors defeated Ivan Lendl 6–3, 6–2, 4–6, 6–4
Women's Singles
Chris Evert-Lloyd defeated Hana Mandlíková 6–3, 6–1
Men's Doubles
Kevin Curren / Steve Denton defeated Victor Amaya / Hank Pfister 6–2, 6–7$^{(4-7)}$, 5–7, 6–2, 6–4
Women's Doubles
Rosemary Casals / Wendy Turnbull defeated Barbara Potter / Sharon Walsh 6–4, 6–4
Mixed Doubles
Anne Smith / Kevin Curren defeated Barbara Potter / Ferdi Taygan 6–7, 7–6 , 7–6

1983

1983 NATIONAL FOOTBALL LEAGUE SEASON
STANDINGS

AFC EAST	W	L	T	NFC EAST	W	L	T
Miami	12	4	0	Washington	14	2	0
New England	8	8	0	Dallas	12	4	0
Buffalo	8	8	0	St. Louis	8	7	1
Baltimore	7	9	0	Philadelphia	5	11	0
NY Jets	7	9	0	NY Giants	3	12	1
AFC CENT	**W**	**L**	**T**	**NFC CENT**	**W**	**L**	**T**
Pittsburgh	10	6	0	Detroit	9	7	0
Cleveland	9	7	0	Green Bay	8	8	0
Cincinnati	7	9	0	Chicago	8	8	0
Houston	2	14	0	Minnesota	8	8	0
AFC WEST	**W**	**L**	**T**	Tampa Bay	2	14	0
LA Raiders	12	4	0	**NFC WEST**	**W**	**L**	**T**
Seattle	9	7	0	San Francisco	10	6	0
Denver	9	7	0	LA Rams	9	7	0
San Diego	6	10	0	New Orleans	8	8	0
Kansas City	6	10	0	Atlanta	7	9	0

1983 U.S. NATIONAL BADMINTON CHAMPIONSHIPS
WINNERS

Year	Men's singles	Women's singles	Men's doubles	Women's doubles	Mixed doubles
1983	Rodney Barton	Cheryl Carton	John Britton Gary Higgins	Pam Brady Judianne Kelly	Mike Walker Judianne Kelly

1983 NBA STANDINGS
DIVISION STANDINGS

Eastern Conference	W	L	W/L%	GB	PS/G	PA/G	SRS
Atlantic Division							
Philadelphia 76ers* (1)	65	17	.793	—	112.1	104.4	7.53
Boston Celtics* (3)	56	26	.683	9.0	112.1	106.7	5.34
New Jersey Nets* (4)	49	33	.598	16.0	105.8	103.0	2.77
New York Knicks* (5)	44	38	.537	21.0	100.0	97.5	2.58
Washington Bullets (7)	42	40	.512	23.0	99.2	99.3	0.20
Central Division							
Milwaukee Bucks* (2)	51	31	.622	—	106.6	102.2	4.32
Atlanta Hawks* (6)	43	39	.524	8.0	101.6	102.6	-0.72
Detroit Pistons (8)	37	45	.451	14.0	112.7	113.1	-0.17
Chicago Bulls (9)	28	54	.341	23.0	111.0	115.9	-4.41
Cleveland Cavaliers (10)	23	59	.280	28.0	97.1	104.6	-6.78
Indiana Pacers (11)	20	62	.244	31.0	108.7	114.5	-5.36

Western Conference	W	L	W/L%	GB	PS/G	PA/G	SRS
Midwest Division								
San Antonio Spurs* (2)	53	29	.646	—	114.3	110.7	3.10
Denver Nuggets* (6)	45	37	.549	8.0	123.2	122.6	0.27
Kansas City Kings (7)	45	37	.549	8.0	113.8	112.3	1.04
Dallas Mavericks (8)	38	44	.463	15.0	112.7	113.1	-0.70
Utah Jazz (10)	30	52	.366	23.0	109.0	113.2	-4.22
Houston Rockets (12)	14	68	.171	39.0	99.3	110.9	-11.1
Pacific Division								
Los Angeles Lakers* (1)	58	24	.707	—	115.0	109.5	5.06
Phoenix Suns* (3)	53	29	.646	5.0	107.0	102.0	4.61
Seattle SuperSonics* (4)	48	34	.585	10.0	110.0	106.8	2.88
Portland Trail Blazers* (5)	46	36	.561	12.0	107.4	105.3	1.88
Golden State Warriors (9)	30	52	.366	28.0	108.6	112.3	-3.48
San Diego Clippers (11)	25	57	.305	33.0	108.6	113.4	-4.61

AMERICAN HORSE OF THE YEAR
1983 ECLIPSE AWARD

Year	Horse	Trainer	Owner	Age	Gender
1983	All Along	Patrick Biancone	Daniel Wildenstein	4	F

1983- NHL SEASON
FINAL STANDINGS

Prince of Wales Conference								
Adams Division	GP	W	L	T	Pts	GF	GA	PIM
Boston Bruins	80	49	25	6	104	336	261	1606
Buffalo Sabres	80	48	25	7	103	315	257	1190
Quebec Nordiques	80	42	28	10	94	360	278	1600
Montreal Canadiens	80	35	40	5	75	286	295	1371
Hartford Whalers	80	28	42	10	66	288	320	1184
Patrick Division	GP	W	L	T	Pts	GF	GA	PIM
New York Islanders	80	50	26	4	104	357	269	1157
Washington Capitals	80	48	27	5	101	308	226	1252
Philadelphia Flyers	80	44	26	10	98	350	290	1488
New York Rangers	80	42	29	9	93	314	304	1471
New Jersey Devils	80	17	56	7	41	231	350	1352
Pittsburgh Penguins	80	16	58	6	38	254	390	1695
Clarence Campbell Conference								
Norris Division	GP	W	L	T	Pts	GF	GA	PIM
Minnesota North Stars	80	39	31	10	88	345	344	1696
St. Louis Blues	80	32	41	7	71	293	316	1614
Detroit Red Wings	80	31	42	7	69	298	323	1546
Chicago Blackhawks	80	30	42	8	68	277	311	1358
Toronto Maple Leafs	80	26	45	9	61	303	387	1682
Smythe Division	GP	W	L	T	Pts	GF	GA	PIM
Edmonton Oilers	80	57	18	5	119	446	314	1577
Calgary Flames	80	34	32	14	82	311	314	1390

Vancouver Canucks				80	32	39	9	73	306	328	1474
Winnipeg Jets				80	31	38	11	73	340	374	1579
Los Angeles Kings				80	23	44	13	59	309	376	1265

1983 MAJOR LEAGUE BASEBALL SEASON HISTORY

1983 American League Standings

EAST	W	L	PCT	GB	HOME	ROAD	RS	RA	DIFF
x-Baltimore	98	64	.605	--	--	--	799	652	+147
Detroit	92	70	.568	6	--	--	789	679	+110
New York	91	71	.562	7	--	--	770	703	+67
Toronto	89	73	.549	9	--	--	795	726	+69
Milwaukee	87	75	.537	11	--	--	764	708	+56
Boston	78	84	.481	20	--	--	724	775	-51
Cleveland	70	92	.432	28	--	--	704	785	-81
WEST	W	L	PCT	GB	HOME	ROAD	RS	RA	DIFF
*-Chicago	99	63	.611	--	--	--	800	650	+150
Kansas City	79	83	.485	20	--	--	696	767	-71
Texas	77	85	.472	22	--	--	639	609	+30
Oakland	74	88	.457	25	--	--	708	782	-74
California	70	92	.432	29	--	--	722	779	-57
Minnesota	70	92	.432	29	--	--	709	822	-113
Seattle	60	102	.370	39	--	--	558	740	-182

1983 National League Standings

EAST	W	L	PCT	GB	HOME	ROAD	RS	RA	DIFF
x-Philadelphia	90	72	.552	--	--	--	696	635	+61
Pittsburgh	84	78	.519	6	--	--	659	648	+11
Montreal	82	80	.503	8	--	--	677	646	+31
St. Louis	79	83	.488	11	--	--	679	710	-31
Chicago	71	91	.438	19	--	--	701	719	-18
New York	68	94	.420	22	--	--	575	680	-105
WEST	W	L	PCT	GB	HOME	ROAD	RS	RA	DIFF
*-Los Angeles	91	71	.558	--	--	--	654	609	+45
Atlanta	88	74	.543	3	--	--	746	640	+106
Houston	85	77	.525	6	--	--	643	646	-3
San Diego	81	81	.497	10	--	--	653	653	0
San Francisco	79	83	.488	12	--	--	687	697	-10
Cincinnati	74	88	.457	17	--	--	623	710	-87

1983 U.S. NATIONAL TENNIS CHAMPIONSHIPS

Men's Singles
Jimmy Connors defeated Ivan Lendl 6–3, 6–7, 7–5, 6–0
Women's Singles
Martina Navratilova defeated Chris Evert 6–1, 6–3
Men's Doubles
Peter Fleming / John McEnroe defeated Fritz Buehning / Van Winitsky 6–3, 6–4, 6–2
Women's Doubles
Martina Navratilova / Pam Shriver defeated Rosalyn Fairbank / Candy Reynolds 6–7, 6–1, 6–3
Mixed Doubles
Elizabeth Sayers / John Fitzgerald defeated Barbara Potter / Ferdi Taygan 3–6, 6–3, 6–4

1984

1984 NATIONAL FOOTBALL LEAGUE SEASON
STANDINGS

AFC EAST	W	L	T	NFC EAST	W	L	T
Miami	14	2	0	Washington	11	5	0
New England	9	7	0	NY Giants	9	7	0
NY Jets	7	9	0	St. Louis	9	7	0
Indianapolis	4	12	0	Dallas	9	7	0
Buffalo	2	14	0	Philadelphia	6	9	1
AFC CENT	W	L	T	NFC CENT	W	L	T
Pittsburgh	9	7	0	Chicago	10	6	0
Cincinnati	8	8	0	Green Bay	8	8	0
Cleveland	5	11	0	Tampa Bay	6	10	0
Houston	3	13	0	Detroit	4	11	1
AFC WEST	W	L	T	Minnesota	3	13	0
Denver	13	3	0	NFC WEST	W	L	T
Seattle	12	4	0	San Francisco	15	1	0
LA Raiders	11	5	0	LA Rams	10	6	0
Kansas City	8	8	0	New Orleans	7	9	0
San Diego	7	9	0	Atlanta	4	12	0

1984 U.S. NATIONAL BADMINTON CHAMPIONSHIPS
WINNERS

Year	Men's singles	Women's singles	Men's doubles	Women's doubles	Mixed doubles
1984	Rodney Barton	Cheryl Carton	Matt Fogarty Bruce Pontow	Pam Brady Monica Ortez	John Britton Cheryl Carton

1984 NBA STANDINGS
DIVISION STANDINGS

Eastern Conference	W	L	W/L%	GB	PS/G	PA/G	SRS
Atlantic Division							
Boston Celtics* (1)	62	20	.756	—	112.1	105.6	6.42
Philadelphia 76ers* (3)	52	30	.634	10.0	107.8	105.6	2.39
New York Knicks* (5)	47	35	.573	15.0	106.9	103.0	3.79
New Jersey Nets* (6)	45	37	.549	17.0	110.0	108.9	1.27
Washington Bullets* (8)	35	47	.427	27.0	102.7	105.6	-2.36
Central Division							
Milwaukee Bucks* (2)	50	32	.610	—	105.7	101.5	4.04
Detroit Pistons* (4)	49	33	.598	1.0	117.1	113.5	3.52
Atlanta Hawks* (7)	40	42	.488	10.0	101.5	102.8	-1.08
Cleveland Cavaliers (9)	28	54	.341	22.0	102.3	106.5	-3.71
Chicago Bulls (10)	27	55	.329	23.0	103.7	108.9	-4.69
Indiana Pacers (11)	26	56	.317	24.0	104.5	109.3	-4.25

Western Conference	W	L	W/L%	GB	PS/G	PA/G	SRS
Midwest Division							
Utah Jazz* (2)	45	37	.549	—	115.0	113.8	0.81
Dallas Mavericks* (4)	43	39	.524	2.0	110.4	110.0	0.15
Denver Nuggets* (7)	38	44	.463	7.0	123.7	124.8	-1.27
Kansas City Kings* (8)	38	44	.463	7.0	110.0	111.5	-1.62
San Antonio Spurs (10)	37	45	.451	8.0	120.3	120.5	-0.50
Houston Rockets (12)	29	53	.354	16.0	110.6	113.7	-3.12
Pacific Division							
Los Angeles Lakers* (1)	54	28	.659	—	115.6	111.8	3.32
Portland Trail Blazers* (3)	48	34	.585	6.0	113.1	109.6	3.13
Seattle SuperSonics* (5)	42	40	.512	12.0	108.1	108.3	-0.34
Phoenix Suns* (6)	41	41	.500	13.0	111.0	110.1	0.65
Golden State Warriors (9)	37	45	.451	17.0	109.9	113.3	-3.35
San Diego Clippers (11)	30	52	.366	24.0	110.7	114.0	-3.21

AMERICAN HORSE OF THE YEAR
1984 ECLIPSE AWARD

Year	Horse	Trainer	Owner	Age	Gender
1984	John Henry	Ron McAnally	Dotsam Stable	9	G

1984- NHL SEASON
FINAL STANDINGS

Prince of Wales Conference								
Adams Division	GP	W	L	T	Pts	GF	GA	PIM
Montreal Canadiens	80	41	27	12	94	309	262	1464
Quebec Nordiques	80	41	30	9	91	323	275	1643
Buffalo Sabres	80	38	28	14	90	290	237	1221
Boston Bruins	80	36	34	10	82	303	287	1825
Hartford Whalers	80	30	41	9	69	268	318	1606
Patrick Division	GP	W	L	T	Pts	GF	GA	PIM
Philadelphia Flyers	80	53	20	7	113	348	241	1540
Washington Capitals	80	46	25	9	101	322	240	1161
New York Islanders	80	40	34	6	86	345	312	1516
New York Rangers	80	26	44	10	62	295	345	1301
New Jersey Devils	80	22	48	10	54	264	346	1282
Pittsburgh Penguins	80	24	51	5	53	276	385	1493
Clarence Campbell Conference								
Norris Division	GP	W	L	T	Pts	GF	GA	PIM
St. Louis Blues	80	37	31	12	86	299	288	1301
Chicago Blackhawks	80	38	35	7	83	309	299	1432
Detroit Red Wings	80	27	41	12	66	313	357	1741
Minnesota North Stars	80	25	43	12	62	268	321	1735
Toronto Maple Leafs	80	20	52	8	48	253	358	1627
Smythe Division	GP	W	L	T	Pts	GF	GA	PIM
Edmonton Oilers	80	49	20	11	109	401	298	1567
Winnipeg Jets	80	43	27	10	96	358	332	1540

Calgary Flames	80	41	27	12	94	363	302	1400
Los Angeles Kings	80	34	32	14	82	339	326	1413
Vancouver Canucks	80	25	46	9	59	284	401	1451

1984 MAJOR LEAGUE BASEBALL SEASON HISTORY

1984 American League Standings

EAST	W	L	PCT	GB	HOME	ROAD	RS	RA	DIFF
*-Detroit	104	58	.642	--	--	--	829	643	+186
Toronto	89	73	.546	15	--	--	750	696	+54
New York	87	75	.537	17	--	--	758	679	+79
Boston	86	76	.531	18	--	--	810	764	+46
Baltimore	85	77	.525	19	--	--	681	667	+14
Cleveland	75	87	.460	29	--	--	761	766	-5
Milwaukee	67	94	.416	36.5	--	--	641	734	-93
WEST	W	L	PCT	GB	HOME	ROAD	RS	RA	DIFF
x-Kansas City	84	78	.519	--	--	--	673	686	-13
California	81	81	.500	3	--	--	696	697	-1
Minnesota	81	81	.500	3	--	--	673	675	-2
Oakland	77	85	.475	7	--	--	738	796	-58
Seattle	74	88	.457	10	--	--	682	774	-92
Chicago	74	88	.457	10	--	--	679	736	-57
Texas	69	92	.429	14.5	--	--	656	714	-58

1984 National League Standings

EAST	W	L	PCT	GB	HOME	ROAD	RS	RA	DIFF
*-Chicago	96	65	.596	--	--	--	762	658	+104
New York	90	72	.556	6.5	--	--	652	676	-24
St. Louis	84	78	.519	12.5	--	--	652	645	+7
Philadelphia	81	81	.500	15.5	--	--	720	690	+30
Montreal	78	83	.484	18	--	--	593	585	+8
Pittsburgh	75	87	.463	21.5	--	--	615	567	+48
WEST	W	L	PCT	GB	HOME	ROAD	RS	RA	DIFF
x-San Diego	92	70	.568	--	--	--	686	634	+52
Houston	80	82	.494	12	--	--	693	630	+63
Atlanta	80	82	.494	12	--	--	632	655	-23
Los Angeles	79	83	.488	13	--	--	580	600	-20
Cincinnati	70	92	.432	22	--	--	627	747	-120
San Francisco	66	96	.407	26	--	--	682	807	-125

1984 U.S. NATIONAL TENNIS CHAMPIONSHIPS

Men's Singles
John McEnroe defeated Ivan Lendl 6–3, 6–4, 6–1
Women's Singles
Martina Navratilova defeated Chris Evert-Lloyd 4–6, 6–4, 6–4
Men's Doubles
John Fitzgerald / Tomáš Šmíd defeated Stefan Edberg / Anders Järryd 7–6[7–5], 6–3, 6–3
Women's Doubles
Martina Navratilova / Pam Shriver defeated Anne Hobbs / Wendy Turnbull 6–2, 6–4
Mixed Doubles
Manuela Maleeva / Tom Gullikson defeated Elizabeth Sayers / John Fitzgerald 2–6, 7–5, 6–4

1985

1985 NATIONAL FOOTBALL LEAGUE SEASON
STANDINGS

AFC EAST	W	L	T	NFC EAST	W	L	T
Miami	12	4	0	Dallas	10	6	0
NY Jets	11	5	0	NY Giants	10	6	0
New England	11	5	0	Washington	10	6	0
Indianapolis	5	11	0	Philadelphia	7	9	0
Buffalo	2	14	0	St. Louis	5	11	0
AFC CENT	W	L	T	NFC CENT	W	L	T
Cleveland	8	8	0	Chicago	15	1	0
Cincinnati	7	9	0	Green Bay	8	8	0
Pittsburgh	7	9	0	Minnesota	7	9	0
Houston	5	11	0	Detroit	7	9	0
AFC WEST	W	L	T	Tampa Bay	2	14	0
LA Raiders	12	4	0	NFC WEST	W	L	T
Denver	11	5	0	LA Rams	11	5	0
Seattle	8	8	0	San Francisco	10	6	0
San Diego	8	8	0	New Orleans	5	11	0
Kansas City	6	10	0	Atlanta	4	12	0

1985 U.S. NATIONAL BADMINTON CHAMPIONSHIPS
WINNERS

Year	Men's singles	Women's singles	Men's doubles	Women's doubles	Mixed doubles
1985	Chris Jogis	Judianne Kelly	John Britton Gary Higgins	Pam Brady Judianne Kelly	Mike Walker Judianne Kelly

1985 NBA STANDINGS
DIVISION STANDINGS

Eastern Conference	W	L	W/L%	GB	PS/G	PA/G	SRS
Atlantic Division							
Boston Celtics* (1)	63	19	.768	—	114.8	108.1	6.47
Philadelphia 76ers* (3)	58	24	.707	5.0	112.9	108.8	4.17
New Jersey Nets* (5)	42	40	.512	21.0	109.5	109.2	0.64
Washington Bullets* (6)	40	42	.488	23.0	105.5	105.8	0.15
New York Knicks (10)	24	58	.293	39.0	105.2	109.8	-4.09
Central Division							
Milwaukee Bucks* (2)	59	23	.720	—	110.9	104.0	6.69
Detroit Pistons* (4)	46	36	.561	13.0	116.0	113.5	2.73
Chicago Bulls* (7)	38	44	.463	21.0	108.7	109.6	-0.50
Cleveland Cavaliers* (8)	36	46	.439	23.0	108.6	111.3	-2.27
Atlanta Hawks (9)	34	48	.415	25.0	106.6	108.1	-1.14
Indiana Pacers (11)	22	60	.268	37.0	108.3	114.5	-5.46

Western Conference	W	L	W/L%	GB	PS/G	PA/G	SRS
Midwest Division							
Denver Nuggets* (2)	52	30	.634	—	120.0	117.6	2.05
Houston Rockets* (3)	48	34	.585	4.0	111.2	109.5	1.38
Dallas Mavericks* (4)	44	38	.537	8.0	111.2	109.0	1.80
Utah Jazz* (6)	41	41	.500	11.0	109.0	109.1	-0.33
San Antonio Spurs* (7)	41	41	.500	11.0	114.8	113.9	0.63
Kansas City Kings (9)	31	51	.378	21.0	114.8	117.5	-2.71
Pacific Division							
Los Angeles Lakers* (1)	62	20	.756	—	118.2	110.9	6.48
Portland Trail Blazers* (5)	42	40	.512	20.0	115.5	112.1	2.80
Phoenix Suns* (8)	36	46	.439	26.0	108.0	110.1	-2.34
Seattle SuperSonics (10)	31	51	.378	31.0	102.1	107.6	-5.44
Los Angeles Clippers (11)	31	51	.378	31.0	107.1	111.6	-4.55
Golden State Warriors (12)	22	60	.268	40.0	110.4	117.7	-7.21

AMERICAN HORSE OF THE YEAR
1985 ECLIPSE AWARD

Year	Horse	Trainer	Owner	Age	Gender
1985	Spend A Buck	Cam Gambolati	Hunter Farm	3	C

1985- NHL SEASON
FINAL STANDINGS

Prince of Wales Conference								
Adams Division	GP	W	L	T	Pts	GF	GA	PIM
Quebec Nordiques	80	43	31	6	92	330	289	1847
Montreal Canadiens	80	40	33	7	87	330	280	1372
Boston Bruins	80	37	31	12	86	311	288	1919
Hartford Whalers	80	40	36	4	84	332	302	1759
Buffalo Sabres	80	37	37	6	80	296	291	1608
Patrick Division	GP	W	L	T	Pts	GF	GA	PIM
Philadelphia Flyers	80	53	23	4	110	335	241	2025
Washington Capitals	80	50	23	7	107	315	272	1418
New York Islanders	80	39	29	12	90	327	284	1343
New York Rangers	80	36	38	6	78	280	276	1496
Pittsburgh Penguins	80	34	38	8	76	313	305	1538
New Jersey Devils	80	28	49	3	59	300	374	1424
Clarence Campbell Conference								
Norris Division	GP	W	L	T	Pts	GF	GA	PIM
Chicago Blackhawks	80	39	33	8	86	351	349	1537
Minnesota North Stars	80	38	33	9	85	327	305	1672
St. Louis Blues	80	37	34	9	83	302	291	1478
Toronto Maple Leafs	80	25	48	7	57	311	386	1716
Detroit Red Wings	80	17	57	6	40	266	415	2393
Smythe Division	GP	W	L	T	Pts	GF	GA	PIM
Edmonton Oilers	80	56	17	7	119	426	310	1928
Calgary Flames	80	40	31	9	89	354	315	2297
Winnipeg Jets	80	26	47	7	59	295	372	1774

Vancouver Canucks	80	23	44	13	59	282	333	1813
Los Angeles Kings	80	23	49	8	54	284	389	2004

1985 MAJOR LEAGUE BASEBALL SEASON HISTORY

1985 American League Standings									
EAST	W	L	PCT	GB	HOME	ROAD	RS	RA	DIFF
*-Toronto	99	62	.615	--	--	--	759	588	+171
New York	97	64	.602	2	--	--	839	660	+179
Detroit	84	77	.522	15	--	--	729	688	+41
Baltimore	83	78	.516	16	--	--	818	764	+54
Boston	81	81	.497	18.5	--	--	800	720	+80
Milwaukee	71	90	.441	28	--	--	690	802	-112
Cleveland	60	102	.370	39.5	--	--	729	861	-132
WEST	W	L	PCT	GB	HOME	ROAD	RS	RA	DIFF
x-Kansas City	91	71	.562	--	--	--	687	639	+48
California	90	72	.556	1	--	--	732	703	+29
Chicago	85	77	.521	6	--	--	736	720	+16
Minnesota	77	85	.475	14	--	--	705	782	-77
Oakland	77	85	.475	14	--	--	757	787	-30
Seattle	74	88	.457	17	--	--	719	818	-99
Texas	62	99	.385	28.5	--	--	617	785	-168
1985 National League Standings									
EAST	W	L	PCT	GB	HOME	ROAD	RS	RA	DIFF
*-St. Louis	101	61	.623	--	--	--	747	572	+175
New York	98	64	.605	3	--	--	695	568	+127
Montreal	84	77	.522	16.5	--	--	633	636	-3
Chicago	77	84	.475	23.5	--	--	686	729	-43
Philadelphia	75	87	.463	26	--	--	667	673	-6
Pittsburgh	57	104	.354	43.5	--	--	568	708	-140
WEST	W	L	PCT	GB	HOME	ROAD	RS	RA	DIFF
x-Los Angeles	95	67	.586	--	--	--	682	579	+103
Cincinnati	89	72	.549	5.5	--	--	677	666	+11
San Diego	83	79	.512	12	--	--	650	622	+28
Houston	83	79	.512	12	--	--	706	691	+15
Atlanta	66	96	.407	29	--	--	632	781	-149
San Francisco	62	100	.383	33	--	--	556	674	-118

1985 U.S. NATIONAL TENNIS CHAMPIONSHIPS

Men's Singles
Ivan Lendl defeated John McEnroe 7–6$^{(7-1)}$, 6–3, 6–4
Women's Singles
Hana Mandlíková defeated Martina Navratilova 7–6$^{(7-3)}$, 1–6, 7–6$^{(7-2)}$
Men's Doubles
Ken Flach / Robert Seguso defeated Henri Leconte / Yannick Noah 6–7$^{(5-7)}$, 7–6$^{(7-1)}$, 7–6$^{(8-6)}$, 6–0
Women's Doubles
Claudia Kohde-Kilsch / Helena Suková defeated Martina Navratilova / Pam Shriver 6–7$^{(5-7)}$, 6–2, 6–3
Mixed Doubles
Martina Navratilova / Heinz Günthardt defeated Elizabeth Smylie / John Fitzgerald 6–3, 6–4

1986

1986 NATIONAL FOOTBALL LEAGUE SEASON
STANDINGS

AFC EAST	W	L	T	NFC EAST	W	L	T
New England	11	5	0	NY Giants	14	2	0
NY Jets	10	6	0	Washington	12	4	0
Miami	8	8	0	Dallas	7	9	0
Buffalo	4	12	0	Philadelphia	5	10	1
Indianapolis	3	13	0	St. Louis	4	11	1
AFC CENT	**W**	**L**	**T**	**NFC CENT**	**W**	**L**	**T**
Cleveland	12	4	0	Chicago	14	2	0
Cincinnati	10	6	0	Minnesota	9	7	0
Pittsburgh	6	10	0	Detroit	5	11	0
Houston	5	11	0	Green Bay	4	12	0
AFC WEST	**W**	**L**	**T**	Tampa Bay	2	14	0
Denver	11	5	0	**NFC WEST**	**W**	**L**	**T**
Kansas City	10	6	0	San Francisco	10	5	1
Seattle	10	6	0	LA Rams	10	6	0
LA Raiders	8	8	0	Atlanta	7	8	1
San Diego	4	12	0	New Orleans	7	9	0

1980 U.S. NATIONAL BADMINTON CHAMPIONSHIPS
WINNERS

Year	Men's singles	Women's singles	Men's doubles	Women's doubles	Mixed doubles
1986	Chris Jogis	Nina Lolk	Matt Fogarty Bruce Pontow	Linda French Nina Lolk	Mike Walker Judianne Kelly

1986 NBA STANDINGS
DIVISION STANDINGS

Eastern Conference	W	L	W/L%	GB	PS/G	PA/G	SRS
Boston Celtics* (1)	67	15	.817	—	114.1	104.7	9.06
Milwaukee Bucks* (2)	57	25	.695	—	114.5	105.5	8.69
Philadelphia 76ers* (3)	54	28	.659	13.0	110.4	108.0	2.46
Atlanta Hawks* (4)	50	32	.610	7.0	108.6	106.2	2.59
Detroit Pistons* (5)	46	36	.561	11.0	114.2	113.0	1.44
Washington Bullets* (6)	39	43	.476	28.0	103.0	104.8	-1.28
New Jersey Nets* (7)	39	43	.476	28.0	109.1	111.1	-1.39
Chicago Bulls* (8)	30	52	.366	27.0	109.3	113.1	-3.12
Cleveland Cavaliers (9)	29	53	.354	28.0	107.8	110.6	-2.19
Indiana Pacers (10)	26	56	.317	31.0	103.9	107.2	-2.66
New York Knicks (11)	23	59	.280	44.0	98.7	104.3	-4.82

Western Conference	W	L	W/L%	GB	PS/G	PA/G	SRS
Midwest Division							
Houston Rockets* (2)	51	31	.622	—	114.4	111.8	2.10
Denver Nuggets* (3)	47	35	.573	4.0	114.8	113.5	0.89
Dallas Mavericks* (4)	44	38	.537	7.0	115.3	114.2	0.70
Utah Jazz* (5)	42	40	.512	9.0	108.2	108.5	-0.67
Sacramento Kings* (7)	37	45	.451	14.0	108.8	111.9	-3.19
San Antonio Spurs* (8)	35	47	.427	16.0	111.2	113.1	-2.06
Pacific Division							
Los Angeles Lakers* (1)	62	20	.756	—	117.3	109.5	6.84
Portland Trail Blazers* (6)	40	42	.488	22.0	115.1	114.0	0.61
Phoenix Suns (9)	32	50	.390	30.0	110.0	113.0	-3.16
Los Angeles Clippers (10)	32	50	.390	30.0	108.6	115.5	-6.83
Seattle SuperSonics (11)	31	51	.378	31.0	104.4	104.5	-0.47
Golden State Warriors (12)	30	52	.366	32.0	113.4	116.9	-3.59

AMERICAN HORSE OF THE YEAR
1986 ECLIPSE AWARD

Year	Horse	Trainer	Owner	Age	Gender
1986	Lady's Secret	D. Wayne Lukas	Eugene V. Klein	4	F

1986- NHL SEASON
FINAL STANDINGS

Prince of Wales Conference								
Adams Division	GP	W	L	T	Pts	GF	GA	PIM
Hartford Whalers	80	43	30	7	93	287	270	1496
Montreal Canadiens	80	41	29	10	92	277	241	1802
Boston Bruins	80	39	34	7	85	301	276	1870
Quebec Nordiques	80	31	39	10	72	267	276	1741
Buffalo Sabres	80	28	44	8	64	280	308	1810
Patrick Division	GP	W	L	T	Pts	GF	GA	PIM
Philadelphia Flyers	80	46	26	8	100	310	245	2082
Washington Capitals	80	38	32	10	86	285	278	1720
New York Islanders	80	35	33	12	82	279	281	1857
New York Rangers	80	34	38	8	76	307	323	1718
Pittsburgh Penguins	80	30	38	12	72	297	290	1693
New Jersey Devils	80	29	45	6	64	293	368	1735
Clarence Campbell Conference								
Norris Division	GP	W	L	T	Pts	GF	GA	PIM
St. Louis Blues	80	32	33	15	79	281	293	1572
Detroit Red Wings	80	34	36	10	78	260	274	2209
Chicago Blackhawks	80	29	37	14	72	290	310	1692
Toronto Maple Leafs	80	32	42	6	70	286	319	1827
Minnesota North Stars	80	30	40	10	70	296	314	1936
Smythe Division	GP	W	L	T	Pts	GF	GA	PIM
Edmonton Oilers	80	50	24	6	106	372	284	1721
Calgary Flames	80	46	31	3	95	318	289	2036
Winnipeg Jets	80	40	32	8	88	279	271	1537

Los Angeles Kings	80	31	41	8	70	318	341	2038
Vancouver Canucks	80	29	43	8	66	282	314	1917

1986 MAJOR LEAGUE BASEBALL SEASON HISTORY

1986 American League Standings

EAST	W	L	PCT	GB	HOME	ROAD	RS	RA	DIFF
*-Boston	95	66	.590	--	--	--	794	696	+98
New York	90	72	.556	5.5	--	--	797	738	+59
Detroit	87	75	.537	8.5	--	--	798	714	+84
Toronto	86	76	.528	9.5	--	--	809	733	+76
Cleveland	84	78	.515	11.5	--	--	831	841	-10
Milwaukee	77	84	.478	18	--	--	667	734	-67
Baltimore	73	89	.451	22.5	--	--	708	760	-52
WEST	**W**	**L**	**PCT**	**GB**	**HOME**	**ROAD**	**RS**	**RA**	**DIFF**
x-California	92	70	.568	--	--	--	786	684	+102
Texas	87	75	.537	5	--	--	771	743	+28
Kansas City	76	86	.469	16	--	--	654	673	-19
Oakland	76	86	.469	16	--	--	731	760	-29
Chicago	72	90	.444	20	--	--	644	699	-55
Minnesota	71	91	.438	21	--	--	741	839	-98
Seattle	67	95	.414	25	--	--	718	835	-117

1986 National League Standings

EAST	W	L	PCT	GB	HOME	ROAD	RS	RA	DIFF
*-New York	108	54	.667	--	--	--	783	578	+205
Philadelphia	86	75	.534	21.5	--	--	739	713	+26
St. Louis	79	82	.491	28.5	--	--	601	611	-10
Montreal	78	83	.484	29.5	--	--	637	688	-51
Chicago	70	90	.438	37	--	--	680	781	-101
Pittsburgh	64	98	.395	44	--	--	663	700	-37
WEST	**W**	**L**	**PCT**	**GB**	**HOME**	**ROAD**	**RS**	**RA**	**DIFF**
x-Houston	96	66	.593	--	--	--	654	569	+85
Cincinnati	86	76	.531	10	--	--	732	717	+15
San Francisco	83	79	.512	13	--	--	698	618	+80
San Diego	74	88	.457	22	--	--	656	723	-67
Los Angeles	73	89	.451	23	--	--	638	679	-41
Atlanta	72	89	.447	23.5	--	--	615	719	-104

1986 U.S. NATIONAL TENNIS CHAMPIONSHIPS

Men's Singles
Ivan Lendl defeated Miloslav Mečíř 6–4, 6–2, 6–0
Women's Singles
Martina Navratilova defeated Helena Suková 6–3, 6–2
Men's Doubles
Andrés Gómez / Slobodan Živojinović defeated Joakim Nyström / Mats Wilander 4–6, 6–3, 6–3, 4–6, 6–3
Women's Doubles
Martina Navratilova / Pam Shriver defeated Hana Mandlíková / Wendy Turnbull 6–4, 3–6, 6–3
Mixed Doubles
Raffaella Reggi / Sergio Casal defeated Martina Navratilova / Peter Fleming 6–4, 6–4

1987

1987 NATIONAL FOOTBALL LEAGUE SEASON
STANDINGS

AFC EAST	W	L	T	NFC EAST	W	L	T
Indianapolis	9	6	0	Washington	11	4	0
New England	8	7	0	Dallas	7	8	0
Miami	8	7	0	St. Louis	7	8	0
Buffalo	7	8	0	Philadelphia	7	8	0
NY Jets	6	9	0	NY Giants	6	9	0
AFC CENT	**W**	**L**	**T**	**NFC CENT**	**W**	**L**	**T**
Cleveland	10	5	0	Chicago	11	4	0
Houston	9	6	0	Minnesota	8	7	0
Pittsburgh	8	7	0	Green Bay	5	9	1
Cincinnati	4	11	0	Tampa Bay	4	11	0
AFC WEST	**W**	**L**	**T**	Detroit	4	11	0
Denver	10	4	1	**NFC WEST**	**W**	**L**	**T**
Seattle	9	6	0	San Francisco	13	2	0
San Diego	8	7	0	New Orleans	12	3	0
LA Raiders	5	10	0	LA Rams	6	9	0
Kansas City	4	11	0	Atlanta	3	12	0

1987 U.S. NATIONAL BADMINTON CHAMPIONSHIPS
WINNERS

Year	Men's singles	Women's singles	Men's doubles	Women's doubles	Mixed doubles
1987	Tariq Wadood	Joy Kitzmiller	Chris Jogis Benny Lee	Linda French Nina Lolk	Chris Jogis Linda French

1987 NBA STANDINGS
DIVISION STANDINGS

Eastern Conference	W	L	W/L%	GB	PS/G	PA/G	SRS
Atlantic Division							
Boston Celtics* (1)	59	23	.720	—	112.6	106.0	6.57
Philadelphia 76ers* (5)	45	37	.549	14.0	106.5	106.6	0.11
Washington Bullets* (6)	42	40	.512	17.0	106.0	107.3	-1.02
New Jersey Nets (10)	24	58	.293	35.0	108.5	113.5	-4.42
New York Knicks (11)	24	58	.293	35.0	103.8	110.0	-5.42
Central Division							
Atlanta Hawks* (2)	57	25	.695	—	110.0	102.8	7.18
Detroit Pistons* (3)	52	30	.634	5.0	111.2	107.8	3.51
Milwaukee Bucks* (4)	50	32	.610	7.0	110.4	106.5	4.04
Indiana Pacers* (7)	41	41	.500	16.0	106.1	106.7	-0.17
Chicago Bulls* (8)	40	42	.488	17.0	104.8	103.9	1.26
Cleveland Cavaliers (9)	31	51	.378	26.0	104.4	108.2	-3.19

101

Western Conference	W	L	W/L%	GB	PS/G	PA/G	SRS
Midwest Division							
Dallas Mavericks* (2)	55	27	.671	—	116.7	110.4	5.54
Utah Jazz* (4)	44	38	.537	11.0	107.9	107.5	0.04
Houston Rockets* (6)	42	40	.512	13.0	106.9	105.9	0.60
Denver Nuggets* (8)	37	45	.451	18.0	116.7	117.6	-1.14
Sacramento Kings (10)	29	53	.354	26.0	110.9	114.1	-3.34
San Antonio Spurs (11)	28	54	.341	27.0	108.3	113.4	-5.09
Pacific Division							
Los Angeles Lakers* (1)	65	17	.793	—	117.8	108.5	8.32
Portland Trail Blazers* (3)	49	33	.598	16.0	117.9	114.8	2.57
Golden State Warriors* (5)	42	40	.512	23.0	112.0	114.4	-2.54
Seattle SuperSonics* (7)	39	43	.476	26.0	113.7	113.3	0.08
Phoenix Suns (9)	36	46	.439	29.0	111.1	113.5	-2.63
Los Angeles Clippers (12)	12	70	.146	53.0	104.5	115.9	-11.00

AMERICAN HORSE OF THE YEAR
1987 ECLIPSE AWARD

Year	Horse	Trainer	Owner	Age	Gender
1987	Ferdinand	Charlie Whittingham	Elizabeth A. Keck	4	C

1987- NHL SEASON
FINAL STANDINGS

Prince of Wales Conference								
Adams Division	GP	W	L	T	Pts	GF	GA	PIM
Montreal Canadiens	80	45	22	13	103	298	238	1830
Boston Bruins	80	44	30	6	94	300	251	2443
Buffalo Sabres	80	37	32	11	85	283	305	2277
Hartford Whalers	80	35	38	7	77	249	267	2046
Quebec Nordiques	80	32	43	5	69	271	306	2042
Patrick Division	GP	W	L	T	Pts	GF	GA	PIM
New York Islanders	80	39	31	10	88	308	267	1732
Philadelphia Flyers	80	38	33	9	85	292	292	2194
Washington Capitals	80	38	33	9	85	281	249	1680
New Jersey Devils	80	38	36	6	82	295	296	2315
New York Rangers	80	36	34	10	82	300	283	1775
Pittsburgh Penguins	80	36	35	9	81	319	316	2211
Clarence Campbell Conference								
Norris Division	GP	W	L	T	Pts	GF	GA	PIM
Detroit Red Wings	80	41	28	11	93	322	269	2391
St. Louis Blues	80	34	38	8	76	278	294	1919
Chicago Blackhawks	80	30	41	9	69	284	328	2228
Toronto Maple Leafs	80	21	49	10	52	273	345	1782
Minnesota North Stars	80	19	48	13	51	242	349	2313
Smythe Division	GP	W	L	T	Pts	GF	GA	PIM
Calgary Flames	80	48	23	9	105	397	305	2431
Edmonton Oilers	80	44	25	11	99	363	288	2173
Winnipeg Jets	80	33	36	11	77	292	310	2278

| Los Angeles Kings | | 80 | 30 | 42 | 8 | 68 | 318 | 359 | 2124 |
| Vancouver Canucks | | 80 | 25 | 46 | 9 | 59 | 272 | 320 | 2196 |

1987 MAJOR LEAGUE BASEBALL SEASON HISTORY

1987 American League Standings

EAST	W	L	PCT	GB	HOME	ROAD	RS	RA	DIFF
*-Detroit	98	64	.605	--	--	--	896	735	+161
Toronto	96	66	.593	2	--	--	845	655	+190
Milwaukee	91	71	.562	7	--	--	862	817	+45
New York	89	73	.549	9	--	--	788	758	+30
Boston	78	84	.481	20	--	--	842	825	+17
Baltimore	67	95	.414	31	--	--	729	880	-151
Cleveland	61	101	.377	37	--	--	742	957	-215
WEST	**W**	**L**	**PCT**	**GB**	**HOME**	**ROAD**	**RS**	**RA**	**DIFF**
x-Minnesota	85	77	.525	--	--	--	786	806	-20
Kansas City	83	79	.512	2	--	--	715	691	+24
Oakland	81	81	.500	4	--	--	806	789	+17
Seattle	78	84	.481	7	--	--	760	801	-41
Chicago	77	85	.475	8	--	--	748	746	+2
Texas	75	87	.463	10	--	--	823	849	-26
California	75	87	.463	10	--	--	770	803	-33

1987 National League Standings

EAST	W	L	PCT	GB	HOME	ROAD	RS	RA	DIFF
*-St. Louis	95	67	.586	--	--	--	798	693	+105
New York	92	70	.568	3	--	--	823	698	+125
Montreal	91	71	.562	4	--	--	741	720	+21
Pittsburgh	80	82	.494	15	--	--	723	744	-21
Philadelphia	80	82	.494	15	--	--	702	749	-47
Chicago	76	85	.472	18.5	--	--	720	801	-81
b	W	L	PCT	GB	HOME	ROAD	RS	RA	DIFF
x-San Francisco	90	72	.556	--	--	--	783	669	+114
Cincinnati	84	78	.519	6	--	--	783	752	+31
Houston	76	86	.469	14	--	--	648	678	-30
Los Angeles	73	89	.451	17	--	--	635	675	-40
Atlanta	69	92	.429	20.5	--	--	747	829	-82
San Diego	65	97	.401	25	--	--	668	763	-95

1987 U.S. NATIONAL TENNIS CHAMPIONSHIPS

Men's Singles
Ivan Lendl defeated Mats Wilander 6–7$^{(7-9)}$, 6–0, 7–6$^{(7-4)}$, 6–4
Women's Singles
Martina Navratilova defeated Steffi Graf 7–6$^{(7-4)}$, 6–1
Men's Doubles
Stefan Edberg / Anders Järryd defeated Ken Flach / Robert Seguso 7–6, 6–2, 4–6, 5–7, 7–6
Women's Doubles
Martina Navratilova / Pam Shriver defeated Kathy Jordan / Elizabeth Smylie 5–7, 6–4, 6–2
Mixed Doubles
Martina Navratilova / Emilio Sánchez defeated Betsy Nagelsen / Paul Annacone 6–4, 6–7, 7–6

1988

1988 NATIONAL FOOTBALL LEAGUE SEASON
STANDINGS

AFC EAST	W	L	T	NFC EAST	W	L	T
Buffalo	12	4	0	Philadelphia	10	6	0
Indianapolis	9	7	0	NY Giants	10	6	0
New England	9	7	0	Washington	7	9	0
NY Jets	8	7	1	Phoenix	7	9	0
Miami	6	10	0	Dallas	3	13	0
AFC CENT	**W**	**L**	**T**	**NFC CENT**	**W**	**L**	**T**
Cincinnati	12	4	0	Chicago	12	4	0
Cleveland	10	6	0	Minnesota	11	5	0
Houston	10	6	0	Tampa Bay	5	11	0
Pittsburgh	5	11	0	Detroit	4	12	0
AFC WEST	**W**	**L**	**T**	Green Bay	4	12	0
Seattle	9	7	0	**NFC WEST**	**W**	**L**	**T**
Denver	8	8	0	San Francisco	10	6	0
LA Raiders	7	9	0	LA Rams	10	6	0
San Diego	6	10	0	New Orleans	10	6	0
Kansas City	4	11	1	Atlanta	5	11	0

1988 U.S. NATIONAL BADMINTON CHAMPIONSHIPS
WINNERS

Year	Men's singles	Women's singles	Men's doubles	Women's doubles	Mixed doubles
1988	Chris Jogis	Joy Kitzmiller	Chris Jogis Benny Lee	Linda French Linda Safarik-Tong	Chris Jogis Linda French

1988 NBA STANDINGS
DIVISION STANDINGS

Eastern Conference	W	L	W/L%	GB	PS/G	PA/G	SRS
Atlantic Division							
Boston Celtics* (1)	57	25	.695	—	113.6	107.7	6.15
Washington Bullets* (7)	38	44	.463	19.0	105.5	106.3	-0.16
New York Knicks* (8)	38	44	.463	19.0	105.5	106.0	0.14
Philadelphia 76ers (10)	36	46	.439	21.0	105.7	107.1	-0.79
New Jersey Nets (11)	19	63	.232	38.0	100.4	108.5	-6.98
Central Division							
Detroit Pistons* (2)	54	28	.659	—	109.2	104.1	5.46
Chicago Bulls* (3)	50	32	.610	4.0	105.0	101.6	3.76
Atlanta Hawks* (4)	50	32	.610	4.0	107.9	104.3	4.02
Milwaukee Bucks* (5)	42	40	.512	12.0	106.1	105.5	1.21
Cleveland Cavaliers* (6)	42	40	.512	12.0	104.5	103.7	1.28
Indiana Pacers (9)	38	44	.463	16.0	104.6	105.4	-0.18

Western Conference	W	L	W/L%	GB	PS/G	PA/G	SRS
Midwest Division							
Denver Nuggets* (2)	54	28	.659	—	116.7	112.7	3.32
Dallas Mavericks* (3)	53	29	.646	1.0	109.3	104.9	3.59
Utah Jazz* (5)	47	35	.573	7.0	108.5	104.8	2.96
Houston Rockets* (6)	46	36	.561	8.0	109.0	107.6	0.82
San Antonio Spurs* (8)	31	51	.378	23.0	113.6	118.5	-5.02
Sacramento Kings (10)	24	58	.293	30.0	108.0	113.7	-5.84
Pacific Division							
Los Angeles Lakers* (1)	62	20	.756	—	112.8	107.0	4.81
Portland Trail Blazers* (4)	53	29	.646	9.0	116.1	111.5	3.59
Seattle SuperSonics* (7)	44	38	.537	18.0	111.4	109.3	1.29
Phoenix Suns (9)	28	54	.341	34.0	108.5	113.0	-4.80
Golden State Warriors (11)	20	62	.244	42.0	107.0	115.3	-8.38
Los Angeles Clippers (12)	17	65	.207	45.0	98.8	109.1	-10.24

AMERICAN HORSE OF THE YEAR
1988 ECLIPSE AWARD

Year	Horse	Trainer	Owner	Age	Gender
1988	Alysheba	Jack Van Berg	Dorothy & Pamela Scharbauer	4	C

1988- NHL SEASON
FINAL STANDINGS

Prince of Wales Conference								
Adams Division	GP	W	L	T	Pts	GF	GA	PIM
Montreal Canadiens	80	53	18	9	115	315	218	1537
Boston Bruins	80	37	29	14	88	289	256	1929
Buffalo Sabres	80	38	35	7	83	291	299	2034
Hartford Whalers	80	37	38	5	79	299	290	1672
Quebec Nordiques	80	27	46	7	61	269	342	2004
Patrick Division	GP	W	L	T	Pts	GF	GA	PIM
Washington Capitals	80	41	29	10	92	305	259	1836
Pittsburgh Penguins	80	40	33	7	87	347	349	2670
New York Rangers	80	37	35	8	82	310	307	1891
Philadelphia Flyers	80	36	36	8	80	307	285	2317
New Jersey Devils	80	27	41	12	66	281	325	2499
New York Islanders	80	28	47	5	61	265	325	1822
Clarence Campbell Conference								
Norris Division	GP	W	L	T	Pts	GF	GA	PIM
Detroit Red Wings	80	34	34	12	80	313	316	2245
St. Louis Blues	80	33	35	12	78	275	285	1675
Minnesota North Stars	80	27	37	16	70	258	278	1972
Chicago Blackhawks	80	27	41	12	66	297	335	2496
Toronto Maple Leafs	80	28	46	6	62	259	342	1740
Smythe Division	GP	W	L	T	Pts	GF	GA	PIM
Calgary Flames	80	54	17	9	117	354	226	2444
Los Angeles Kings	80	42	31	7	91	376	335	2215
Edmonton Oilers	80	38	34	8	84	325	306	1931

| Vancouver Canucks | 80 | 33 | 39 | 8 | 74 | 251 | 253 | 1569 |
| Winnipeg Jets | 80 | 26 | 42 | 12 | 64 | 300 | 355 | 1843 |

1988 MAJOR LEAGUE BASEBALL SEASON HISTORY

1988 American League Standings

EAST	W	L	PCT	GB	HOME	ROAD	RS	RA	DIFF
x-Boston	89	73	.549	--	--	--	813	689	+124
Detroit	88	74	.543	1	--	--	703	658	+45
Toronto	87	75	.537	2	--	--	763	680	+83
Milwaukee	87	75	.537	2	--	--	682	616	+66
New York	85	76	.528	3.5	--	--	772	748	+24
Cleveland	78	84	.481	11	--	--	666	731	-65
Baltimore	54	107	.335	34.5	--	--	550	789	-239
WEST	**W**	**L**	**PCT**	**GB**	**HOME**	**ROAD**	**RS**	**RA**	**DIFF**
*-Oakland	104	58	.642	--	--	--	800	620	+180
Minnesota	91	71	.562	13	--	--	759	672	+87
Kansas City	84	77	.522	19.5	--	--	704	648	+56
California	75	87	.463	29	--	--	714	771	-57
Chicago	71	90	.441	32.5	--	--	631	757	-126
Texas	70	91	.435	33.5	--	--	637	735	-98
Seattle	68	93	.422	35.5	--	--	664	744	-80

1988 National League Standings

EAST	W	L	PCT	GB	HOME	ROAD	RS	RA	DIFF
*-New York	100	60	.625	--	--	--	703	532	+171
Pittsburgh	85	75	.531	15	--	--	651	616	+35
Montreal	81	81	.497	20	--	--	628	592	+36
Chicago	77	85	.472	24	--	--	660	694	-34
St. Louis	76	86	.469	25	--	--	578	633	-55
Philadelphia	65	96	.401	35.5	--	--	597	734	-137
WEST	**W**	**L**	**PCT**	**GB**	**HOME**	**ROAD**	**RS**	**RA**	**DIFF**
x-Los Angeles	94	67	.580	--	--	--	628	544	+84
Cincinnati	87	74	.540	7	--	--	641	596	+45
San Diego	83	78	.516	11	--	--	594	583	+11
San Francisco	83	79	.512	11.5	--	--	670	626	+44
Houston	82	80	.506	12.5	--	--	617	631	-14
Atlanta	54	106	.338	39.5	--	--	555	741	-186

1988 U.S. NATIONAL TENNIS CHAMPIONSHIPS

Men's Singles
Mats Wilander defeated Ivan Lendl 6–4, 4–6, 6–3, 5–7, 6–4
Women's Singles
Steffi Graf defeated Gabriela Sabatini 6–3, 3–6, 6–1
Men's Doubles
Sergio Casal / Emilio Sánchez defeated Rick Leach / Jim Pugh by Walkover
Women's Doubles
Gigi Fernández / Robin White defeated Patty Fendick / Jill Hetherington 6–4, 6–1
Mixed Doubles
Jana Novotná / Jim Pugh defeated Elizabeth Smylie / Patrick McEnroe 7–5, 6–3

1989

1989 NATIONAL FOOTBALL LEAGUE SEASON
STANDINGS

AFC EAST	W	L	T	NFC EAST	W	L	T
Buffalo	9	7	0	NY Giants	12	4	0
Indianapolis	8	8	0	Philadelphia	11	5	0
Miami	8	8	0	Washington	10	6	0
New England	5	11	0	Phoenix	5	11	0
NY Jets	4	12	0	Dallas	1	15	0
AFC CENT	**W**	**L**	**T**	**NFC CENT**	**W**	**L**	**T**
Cleveland	9	6	1	Minnesota	10	6	0
Houston	9	7	0	Green Bay	10	6	0
Pittsburgh	9	7	0	Detroit	7	9	0
Cincinnati	8	8	0	Chicago	6	10	0
AFC WEST	**W**	**L**	**T**	Tampa Bay	5	11	0
Denver	11	5	0	**NFC WEST**	**W**	**L**	**T**
Kansas City	8	7	1	San Francisco	14	2	0
LA Raiders	8	8	0	LA Rams	11	5	0
Seattle	7	9	0	New Orleans	9	7	0
San Diego	6	10	0	Atlanta	3	13	0

1989 U.S. NATIONAL BADMINTON CHAMPIONSHIPS
WINNERS

Year	Men's singles	Women's singles	Men's doubles	Women's doubles	Mixed doubles
1989	Tariq Wadood	Linda Safarik-Tong	Chris Jogis Benny Lee	Linda French Linda Safarik-Tong	Tariq Wadood Linda French

1989 NBA STANDINGS
DIVISION STANDINGS

Eastern Conference	W	L	W/L%	GB	PS/G	PA/G	SRS
Atlantic Division							
New York Knicks* (2)	52	30	.634	—	116.7	112.9	3.62
Philadelphia 76ers* (7)	46	36	.561	6.0	111.9	110.4	1.68
Boston Celtics* (8)	42	40	.512	10.0	109.2	108.1	1.26
Washington Bullets (9)	40	42	.488	12.0	108.3	110.4	-1.77
New Jersey Nets (11)	26	56	.317	26.0	103.7	110.1	-5.69
Charlotte Hornets (12)	20	62	.244	32.0	104.5	113.0	-7.74
Central Division							
Detroit Pistons* (1)	63	19	.768	—	106.6	100.8	6.24
Cleveland Cavaliers* (3)	57	25	.695	6.0	108.8	101.2	7.95
Atlanta Hawks* (4)	52	30	.634	11.0	111.0	106.1	5.26
Milwaukee Bucks* (5)	49	33	.598	14.0	108.9	105.3	4.11
Chicago Bulls* (6)	47	35	.573	16.0	106.4	105.0	2.13
Indiana Pacers (10)	28	54	.341	35.0	106.9	111.1	-3.00

Western Conference	W	L	W/L%	GB	PS/G	PA/G	SRS
Midwest Division							
Utah Jazz* (2)	51	31	.622	—	104.7	99.7	4.01
Houston Rockets* (5)	45	37	.549	6.0	108.5	107.5	0.22
Denver Nuggets* (6)	44	38	.537	7.0	118.0	116.3	0.91
Dallas Mavericks (9)	38	44	.463	13.0	103.5	104.7	-1.79
San Antonio Spurs (12)	21	61	.256	30.0	105.5	112.8	-7.45
Miami Heat (13)	15	67	.183	36.0	97.8	109.0	-11.13
Pacific Division							
Los Angeles Lakers* (1)	57	25	.695	—	114.7	107.5	6.38
Phoenix Suns* (3)	55	27	.671	2.0	118.6	110.9	6.84
Seattle SuperSonics* (4)	47	35	.573	10.0	112.1	109.2	2.44
Golden State Warriors* (7)	43	39	.524	14.0	116.6	116.9	-0.59
Portland Trail Blazers* (8)	39	43	.476	18.0	114.6	113.1	0.92
Sacramento Kings (10)	27	55	.329	30.0	105.5	111.0	-5.35
Los Angeles Clippers (11)	21	61	.256	36.0	106.2	116.2	-9.50

AMERICAN HORSE OF THE YEAR
1989 ECLIPSE AWARD

Year	Horse	Trainer	Owner	Age	Gender
1989	Sunday Silence	Charlie Whittingham	H-G-W Partners	3	C

1989 – NHL SEASON
FINAL STANDINGS

Prince of Wales Conference								
Adams Division	GP	W	L	T	Pts	GF	GA	PIM
Boston Bruins	80	46	25	9	101	289	232	1458
Buffalo Sabres	80	45	27	8	98	286	248	1449
Montreal Canadiens	80	41	28	11	93	288	234	1590
Hartford Whalers	80	38	33	9	85	275	268	2102
Quebec Nordiques	80	12	61	7	31	240	407	2104
Patrick Division	GP	W	L	T	Pts	GF	GA	PIM
New York Rangers	80	36	31	13	85	279	267	2021
New Jersey Devils	80	37	34	9	83	295	288	1659
Washington Capitals	80	36	38	6	78	284	275	2204
New York Islanders	80	31	38	11	73	281	288	1777
Pittsburgh Penguins	80	32	40	8	72	318	359	2132
Philadelphia Flyers	80	30	39	11	71	290	297	2067
Clarence Campbell Conference								
Norris Division	GP	W	L	T	Pts	GF	GA	PIM
Chicago Blackhawks	80	41	33	6	88	316	294	2426
St. Louis Blues	80	37	34	9	83	295	279	1809
Toronto Maple Leafs	80	38	38	4	80	337	358	2419
Minnesota North Stars	80	36	40	4	76	284	291	2041
Detroit Red Wings	80	28	38	14	70	288	323	2140
Smythe Division	GP	W	L	T	Pts	GF	GA	PIM
Calgary Flames	80	42	23	15	99	348	265	1751
Edmonton Oilers	80	38	28	14	90	315	283	2046

Winnipeg Jets	80	37	32	11	85	298	290	1639
Los Angeles Kings	80	34	39	7	75	338	337	1844
Vancouver Canucks	80	25	41	14	64	245	306	1644

1989 MAJOR LEAGUE BASEBALL SEASON HISTORY

1989 American League Standings									
EAST	W	L	PCT	GB	HOME	ROAD	RS	RA	DIFF
x-Toronto	89	73	.549	--	--	--	731	651	+80
Baltimore	87	75	.537	2	--	--	708	686	+22
Boston	83	79	.512	6	--	--	774	735	+39
Milwaukee	81	81	.500	8	--	--	707	679	+28
New York	74	87	.460	14.5	--	--	698	792	-94
Cleveland	73	89	.451	16	--	--	604	654	-50
Detroit	59	103	.364	30	--	--	617	816	-199
WEST	W	L	PCT	GB	HOME	ROAD	RS	RA	DIFF
*-Oakland	99	63	.611	--	--	--	712	576	+136
Kansas City	92	70	.568	7	--	--	690	635	+55
California	91	71	.562	8	--	--	669	578	+91
Texas	83	79	.512	16	--	--	695	714	-19
Minnesota	80	82	.494	19	--	--	740	738	+2
Seattle	73	89	.451	26	--	--	694	728	-34
Chicago	69	92	.429	29.5	--	--	693	750	-57
1989 National League Standings									
EAST	W	L	PCT	GB	HOME	ROAD	RS	RA	DIFF
*-Chicago	93	69	.574	--	--	--	702	623	+79
New York	87	75	.537	6	--	--	683	595	+88
St. Louis	86	76	.524	7	--	--	632	608	+24
Montreal	81	81	.500	12	--	--	632	630	+2
Pittsburgh	74	88	.451	19	--	--	637	680	-43
Philadelphia	67	95	.411	26	--	--	629	735	-106
WEST	W	L	PCT	GB	HOME	ROAD	RS	RA	DIFF
x-San Francisco	92	70	.568	--	--	--	699	600	+99
San Diego	89	73	.549	3	--	--	642	626	+16
Houston	86	76	.531	6	--	--	647	669	-22
Los Angeles	77	83	.481	14	--	--	554	536	+18
Cincinnati	75	87	.463	17	--	--	632	691	-59
Atlanta	63	97	.391	28	--	--	584	680	-96

1989 U.S. NATIONAL TENNIS CHAMPIONSHIPS

Men's Singles
Boris Becker defeated Ivan Lendl 7–6$^{(7-2)}$, 1–6, 6–3, 7–6
Women's Singles
Steffi Graf defeated Martina Navratilova 3–6, 7–5, 6–1
Men's Doubles
John McEnroe / Mark Woodforde defeated Ken Flach / Robert Seguso 6–4, 4–6, 6–3, 6–3
Women's Doubles
Hana Mandlíková / Martina Navratilova defeated Mary Joe Fernández / Pam Shriver 5–7, 6–4, 6–4
Mixed Doubles
Robin White / Shelby Cannon defeated Meredith McGrath / Rick Leach 3–6, 6–2, 7–5

1990

1990 NATIONAL FOOTBALL LEAGUE SEASON
STANDINGS

AFC EAST	W	L	T	NFC EAST	W	L	T
Buffalo	13	3	0	NY Giants	13	3	0
Miami	12	4	0	Philadelphia	10	6	0
Indianapolis	7	9	0	Washington	10	6	0
NY Jets	6	10	0	Dallas	7	9	0
New England	1	15	0	Phoenix	5	11	0
AFC CENT	W	L	T	**NFC CENT**	W	L	T
Cincinnati	9	7	0	Chicago	11	5	0
Houston	9	7	0	Tampa Bay	6	10	0
Pittsburgh	9	7	0	Green Bay	6	10	0
Cleveland	3	13	0	Detroit	6	10	0
AFC WEST	W	L	T	Minnesota	6	10	0
LA Raiders	12	4	0	**NFC WEST**	W	L	T
Kansas City	11	5	0	San Francisco	14	2	0
Seattle	9	7	0	New Orleans	8	8	0
San Diego	6	10	0	LA Rams	5	11	0
Denver	5	11	0	Atlanta	5	11	0

1990 U.S. NATIONAL BADMINTON CHAMPIONSHIPS
WINNERS

Year	Men's singles	Women's singles	Men's doubles	Women's doubles	Mixed doubles
1990	Chris Jogis	Linda Safarik-Tong	Chris Jogis Benny Lee	Ann French Joy Kitzmiller	Tom Reidy Traci Britton

1990 NBA STANDINGS
DIVISION STANDINGS

Eastern Conference	W	L	W/L%	GB	PS/G	PA/G	SRS
Atlantic Division							
Philadelphia 76ers* (2)	53	29	.646	—	110.2	105.2	4.23
Boston Celtics* (4)	52	30	.634	1.0	110.0	106.0	3.23
New York Knicks* (5)	45	37	.549	8.0	108.3	106.9	0.78
Washington Bullets (10)	31	51	.378	22.0	107.7	109.9	-2.43
Miami Heat (11)	18	64	.220	35.0	100.6	110.3	-9.59
New Jersey Nets (13)	17	65	.207	36.0	100.1	108.0	-7.82
Central Division							
Detroit Pistons* (1)	59	23	.720	—	104.3	98.3	5.41
Chicago Bulls* (3)	55	27	.671	4.0	109.5	106.2	2.74
Milwaukee Bucks* (6)	44	38	.537	15.0	106.0	106.8	-1.06
Cleveland Cavaliers* (7)	42	40	.512	17.0	102.6	102.9	-0.62
Indiana Pacers* (8)	42	40	.512	17.0	109.3	109.1	-0.18
Atlanta Hawks (9)	41	41	.500	18.0	108.5	107.5	0.64
Orlando Magic (12)	18	64	.220	41.0	110.9	119.8	-8.73

Western Conference	W	L	W/L%	GB	PS/G	PA/G	SRS
Midwest Division							
San Antonio Spurs* (2)	56	26	.683	—	106.3	102.8	3.58
Utah Jazz* (4)	55	27	.671	1.0	106.8	102.0	4.82
Dallas Mavericks* (6)	47	35	.573	9.0	102.2	102.2	0.42
Denver Nuggets* (7)	43	39	.524	13.0	114.6	113.2	1.56
Houston Rockets* (8)	41	41	.500	15.0	106.7	105.3	1.71
Minnesota Timberwolves (13)	22	60	.268	34.0	95.2	99.4	-3.60
Charlotte Hornets (14)	19	63	.232	37.0	100.4	108.2	-7.00
Pacific Division							
Los Angeles Lakers* (1)	63	19	.768	—	110.7	103.9	6.74
Portland Trail Blazers* (3)	59	23	.720	4.0	114.2	107.9	6.48
Phoenix Suns* (5)	54	28	.659	9.0	114.9	107.8	7.09
Seattle SuperSonics (9)	41	41	.500	22.0	106.9	105.9	1.40
Golden State Warriors (10)	37	45	.451	26.0	116.3	119.4	-2.55
Los Angeles Clippers (11)	30	52	.366	33.0	103.8	107.2	-2.80
Sacramento Kings (12)	23	59	.280	40.0	101.7	106.8	-4.41

AMERICAN HORSE OF THE YEAR
1990 ECLIPSE AWARD

Year	Horse	Trainer	Owner	Age	Gender
1990	Criminal Type	D. Wayne Lukas	Calumet & Jurgen K. Arnemann	5	C

1990- NHL SEASON
FINAL STANDINGS

Wales Conference						
Adams Division						
Team	W	L	T	GF	GA	Pts
Boston Bruins	44	24	12	299	264	100
Montreal Canadiens	39	30	11	273	249	89
Buffalo Sabres	31	30	19	292	278	81
Hartford Whalers	31	38	11	238	276	73
Quebec Nordiques	16	50	14	236	354	46
Patrick Division						
Team	W	L	T	GF	GA	Pts
Pittsburgh Penguins	41	33	6	342	305	88
New York Rangers	36	31	13	297	265	85
Washington Capitals	37	36	7	258	258	81
New Jersey Devils	32	33	15	272	264	79
Philadelphia Flyers	33	37	10	252	267	76
New York Islanders	25	45	10	223	290	60

Campbell Conference						
Norris Division						
Team	W	L	T	GF	GA	Pts
Chicago Blackhawks	49	23	8	284	211	106
St. Louis Blues	47	22	11	310	250	105
Detroit Red Wings	34	38	8	273	298	76
Minnesota North Stars	27	39	14	256	266	68
Toronto Maple Leafs	23	46	11	241	318	57
Smythe Division						
Team	W	L	T	GF	GA	Pts
Los Angeles Kings	46	24	10	340	254	102
Calgary Flames	46	26	8	344	263	100
Edmonton Oilers	37	37	6	272	272	80
Vancouver Canucks	28	43	9	243	315	65
Winnipeg Jets	26	43	11	260	288	63

1990 MAJOR LEAGUE BASEBALL SEASON HISTORY

1990 American League Standings

EAST	W	L	PCT	GB	HOME	ROAD	RS	RA	DIFF
x-Boston	88	74	.543	--	--	--	699	664	+35
Toronto	86	76	.531	2	--	--	767	661	+106
Detroit	79	83	.488	9	--	--	750	754	-4
Cleveland	77	85	.475	11	--	--	732	737	-5
Baltimore	76	85	.472	11.5	--	--	669	698	-29
Milwaukee	74	88	.457	14	--	--	732	760	-28
New York	67	95	.414	21	--	--	603	749	-146
WEST	W	L	PCT	GB	HOME	ROAD	RS	RA	DIFF
*-Oakland	103	59	.636	--	--	--	733	570	+163
Chicago	94	68	.580	9	--	--	682	633	+49
Texas	83	79	.512	20	--	--	676	696	-20
California	80	82	.494	23	--	--	690	706	-16
Seattle	77	85	.475	26	--	--	640	680	-40
Kansas City	75	86	.466	27.5	--	--	707	709	-2
Minnesota	74	88	.457	29	--	--	666	729	-63

1990 National League Standings

EAST	W	L	PCT	GB	HOME	ROAD	RS	RA	DIFF
*-Pittsburgh	95	67	.586	--	--	--	733	619	+114
New York	91	71	.562	4	--	--	775	613	+162
Montreal	85	77	.525	10	--	--	662	598	+64
Philadelphia	77	85	.475	18	--	--	646	729	-83
Chicago	77	85	.475	18	--	--	690	774	-84
St. Louis	70	92	.432	25	--	--	599	698	-99
WEST	W	L	PCT	GB	HOME	ROAD	RS	RA	DIFF
x-Cincinnati	91	71	.562	--	--	--	693	597	+96
Los Angeles	86	76	.531	5	--	--	728	685	+43
San Francisco	85	77	.525	6	--	--	719	710	+9
San Diego	75	87	.463	16	--	--	673	673	0
Houston	75	87	.463	16	--	--	573	656	-83
Atlanta	65	97	.401	26	--	--	682	821	-139

1990 U.S. NATIONAL TENNIS CHAMPIONSHIPS

Men's Singles
Pete Sampras defeated Andre Agassi 6–4, 6–3, 6–2
Women's Singles
Gabriela Sabatini defeated Steffi Graf 6–2, 7–6$^{(7-4)}$
Men's Doubles
Pieter Aldrich / Danie Visser defeated Paul Annacone / David Wheaton 6–2, 7–6 (7–3), 6–2
Women's Doubles
Gigi Fernández / Martina Navratilova defeated Jana Novotná / Helena Suková 6–2, 6–4
Mixed Doubles
Elizabeth Smylie / Todd Woodbridge defeated Natasha Zvereva / Jim Pugh 6–4, 6–2

1991

1991 NATIONAL FOOTBALL LEAGUE SEASON
STANDINGS

AFC EAST	W	L	T	NFC EAST	W	L	T
Buffalo	13	3	0	Washington	14	2	0
NY Jets	8	8	0	Dallas	11	5	0
Miami	8	8	0	Philadelphia	10	6	0
New England	6	10	0	NY Giants	8	8	0
Indianapolis	1	15	0	Phoenix	4	12	0
AFC CENT	**W**	**L**	**T**	**NFC CENT**	**W**	**L**	**T**
Houston	11	5	0	Detroit	12	4	0
Pittsburgh	7	9	0	Chicago	11	5	0
Cleveland	6	10	0	Minnesota	8	8	0
Cincinnati	3	13	0	Green Bay	4	12	0
AFC WEST	**W**	**L**	**T**	Tampa Bay	3	13	0
Denver	12	4	0	**NFC WEST**	**W**	**L**	**T**
Kansas City	10	6	0	New Orleans	11	5	0
LA Raiders	9	7	0	Atlanta	10	6	0
Seattle	7	9	0	San Francisco	10	6	0
San Diego	4	12	0	LA Rams	3	13	0

1991 U.S. NATIONAL BADMINTON CHAMPIONSHIPS
WINNERS

Year	Men's singles	Women's singles	Men's doubles	Women's doubles	Mixed doubles
1991	Chris Jogis	Liz Aronsohn	John Britton Tom Reidy	Ann French Joy Kitzmiller	Tariq Wadood Traci Britton

1991 NBA STANDINGS
DIVISION STANDINGS

Eastern Conference	W	L	W/L%	GB	PS/G	PA/G	SRS
Atlantic Division							
Boston Celtics* (2)	56	26	.683	—	111.5	105.7	5.22
Philadelphia 76ers* (5)	44	38	.537	12.0	105.4	105.6	-0.39
New York Knicks* (8)	39	43	.476	17.0	103.1	103.3	-0.43
Washington Bullets (10)	30	52	.366	26.0	101.4	106.4	-4.84
New Jersey Nets (11)	26	56	.317	30.0	102.9	107.5	-4.53
Miami Heat (13)	24	58	.293	32.0	101.8	107.8	-5.91
Central Division							
Chicago Bulls* (1)	61	21	.744	—	110.0	101.0	8.57
Detroit Pistons* (3)	50	32	.610	11.0	100.1	96.8	3.08
Milwaukee Bucks* (4)	48	34	.585	13.0	106.4	104.0	2.33
Atlanta Hawks* (6)	43	39	.524	18.0	109.8	109.0	0.72
Indiana Pacers* (7)	41	41	.500	20.0	111.7	112.1	-0.37
Cleveland Cavaliers (9)	33	49	.402	28.0	101.7	104.2	-2.33
Charlotte Hornets (12)	26	56	.317	35.0	102.8	108.0	-4.95

Western Conference	W	L	W/L%	GB	PS/G	PA/G	SRS
Midwest Division							
San Antonio Spurs* (2)	55	27	.671	—	107.1	102.6	4.30
Utah Jazz* (5)	54	28	.659	1.0	104.0	100.7	3.18
Houston Rockets* (6)	52	30	.634	3.0	106.7	103.2	3.27
Orlando Magic (9)	31	51	.378	24.0	105.9	109.9	-3.79
Minnesota Timberwolves (11)	29	53	.354	26.0	99.6	103.5	-3.75
Dallas Mavericks (12)	28	54	.341	27.0	99.9	104.5	-4.27
Denver Nuggets (14)	20	62	.244	35.0	119.9	130.8	-10.31
Pacific Division							
Portland Trail Blazers* (1)	63	19	.768	—	114.7	106.0	8.47
Los Angeles Lakers* (3)	58	24	.707	5.0	106.3	99.6	6.73
Phoenix Suns* (4)	55	27	.671	8.0	114.0	107.5	6.49
Golden State Warriors* (7)	44	38	.537	19.0	116.6	115.0	1.72
Seattle SuperSonics* (8)	41	41	.500	22.0	106.6	105.4	1.31
Los Angeles Clippers (10)	31	51	.378	32.0	103.5	107.0	-3.16
Sacramento Kings (13)	25	57	.305	38.0	96.7	103.5	-6.27

AMERICAN HORSE OF THE YEAR
1991 ECLIPSE AWARD

Year	Horse	Trainer	Owner	Age	Gender
1991	Black Tie Affair	Ernie T. Poulos	Jeffrey Sullivan	5	C

1990- NHL SEASON
FINAL STANDINGS

Wales Conference						
Adams Division	GP	W	L	T	Pts	GF	GA
Montreal Canadiens	80	41	28	11	93	267	207
Boston Bruins	80	36	32	12	84	270	275
Buffalo Sabres	80	31	37	12	74	289	299
Hartford Whalers	80	26	41	13	65	247	283
Quebec Nordiques	80	20	48	12	52	255	318
Patrick Division	GP	W	L	T	Pts	GF	GA
New York Rangers	80	50	25	5	105	321	246
Washington Capitals	80	45	27	8	98	330	275
Pittsburgh Penguins	80	39	32	9	87	343	308
New Jersey Devils	80	38	31	11	87	289	259
New York Islanders	80	34	35	11	79	291	299
Philadelphia Flyers	80	32	37	11	75	252	273
Campbell Conference						
Norris Division	GP	W	L	T	Pts	GF	GA
Detroit Red Wings	80	43	25	12	98	320	256
Chicago Blackhawks	80	36	29	15	87	257	236
St. Louis Blues	80	36	33	11	83	279	266
Minnesota North Stars	80	32	42	6	70	246	278
Toronto Maple Leafs	80	30	43	7	67	234	294

Smythe Division	GP	W	L	T	Pts	GF	GA
Vancouver Canucks	80	42	26	12	96	285	250
Los Angeles Kings	80	35	31	14	84	287	296
Edmonton Oilers	80	36	34	10	82	295	297
Winnipeg Jets	80	33	32	15	81	251	244
Calgary Flames	80	31	37	12	74	296	305
San Jose Sharks	80	17	58	5	39	219	359

1991 MAJOR LEAGUE BASEBALL SEASON HISTORY

1991 American League Standings

EAST	W	L	PCT	GB	HOME	ROAD	RS	RA	DIFF
x-Toronto	91	71	.562	--	--	--	684	622	+62
Detroit	84	78	.519	7	--	--	817	794	+23
Boston	84	78	.519	7	--	--	731	712	+19
Milwaukee	83	79	.512	8	--	--	799	744	+55
New York	71	91	.438	20	--	--	674	777	-103
Baltimore	67	95	.414	24	--	--	686	796	-110
Cleveland	57	105	.352	34	--	--	576	759	-183
WEST	**W**	**L**	**PCT**	**GB**	**HOME**	**ROAD**	**RS**	**RA**	**DIFF**
*-Minnesota	95	67	.586	--	--	--	776	652	+124
Chicago	87	75	.537	8	--	--	758	681	+77
Texas	85	77	.525	10	--	--	829	814	+15
Oakland	84	78	.519	11	--	--	760	776	-16
Seattle	83	79	.512	12	--	--	702	674	+28
Kansas City	82	80	.506	13	--	--	727	722	+5
California	81	81	.500	14	--	--	653	649	+4

1991 National League Standings

EAST	W	L	PCT	GB	HOME	ROAD	RS	RA	DIFF
*-Pittsburgh	98	64	.605	--	--	--	768	632	+136
St. Louis	84	78	.519	14	--	--	651	648	+3
Philadelphia	78	84	.481	20	--	--	629	680	-51
Chicago	77	83	.481	20	--	--	695	734	-39
New York	77	84	.478	20.5	--	--	640	646	-6
WEST	**W**	**L**	**PCT**	**GB**	**HOME**	**ROAD**	**RS**	**RA**	**DIFF**
x-Atlanta	94	68	.580	--	--	--	749	644	+105
Los Angeles	93	69	.574	1	--	--	665	565	+100
San Diego	84	78	.519	10	--	--	636	646	-10
San Francisco	75	87	.463	19	--	--	649	697	-48
Cincinnati	74	88	.457	20	--	--	689	691	-2
Houston	65	97	.401	29	--	--	605	717	-112

1991 U.S. NATIONAL TENNIS CHAMPIONSHIPS

Men's Singles
Stefan Edberg defeated Jim Courier 6–2, 6–4, 6–0
Women's Singles
Monica Seles defeated Martina Navratilova 7–6$^{(7-1)}$, 6–1
Men's Doubles
John Fitzgerald / Anders Järryd defeated Scott Davis / David Pate 6–3, 3–6, 6–3, 6–3
Women's Doubles
Pam Shriver / Natasha Zvereva defeated Jana Novotná / Larisa Savchenko 6–4, 4–6, 7–6
Mixed Doubles
Manon Bollegraf / Tom Nijssen defeated Arantxa Sánchez Vicario / Emilio Sánchez 6–2, 7–6

1992

1992 NATIONAL FOOTBALL LEAGUE SEASON
STANDINGS

AFC EAST	W	L	T	NFC EAST	W	L	T
Miami	11	5	0	Dallas	13	3	0
Buffalo	11	5	0	Philadelphia	11	5	0
Indianapolis	9	7	0	Washington	9	7	0
NY Jets	4	12	0	NY Giants	6	10	0
New England	2	14	0	Phoenix	4	12	0
AFC CENT	**W**	**L**	**T**	**NFC CENT**	**W**	**L**	**T**
Pittsburgh	11	5	0	Minnesota	11	5	0
Houston	10	6	0	Green Bay	9	7	0
Cleveland	7	9	0	Tampa Bay	5	11	0
Cincinnati	5	11	0	Chicago	5	11	0
AFC WEST	**W**	**L**	**T**	Detroit	5	11	0
San Diego	11	5	0	**NFC WEST**	**W**	**L**	**T**
Kansas City	10	6	0	San Francisco	14	2	0
Denver	8	8	0	New Orleans	12	4	0
LA Raiders	7	9	0	Atlanta	6	10	0
Seattle	2	14	0	LA Rams	6	10	0

1992 U.S. NATIONAL BADMINTON CHAMPIONSHIPS
WINNERS

Year	Men's singles	Women's singles	Men's doubles	Women's doubles	Mixed doubles
1992	Chris Jogis	Joy Kitzmiller	Benny Lee Tom Reidy	Ann French Joy Kitzmiller	Andy Chong Linda French

1992 NBA STANDINGS
DIVISION STANDINGS

Eastern Conference	W	L	W/L%	GB	PS/G	PA/G	SRS
Atlantic Division							
Boston Celtics* (2)	51	31	.622	—	106.6	103.0	3.41
New York Knicks* (4)	51	31	.622	—	101.6	97.7	3.67
New Jersey Nets* (6)	40	42	.488	11.0	105.4	107.1	-1.54
Miami Heat* (8)	38	44	.463	13.0	105.0	109.2	-3.94
Philadelphia 76ers (10)	35	47	.427	16.0	101.9	103.2	-1.34
Washington Bullets (13)	25	57	.305	26.0	102.4	106.8	-4.35
Orlando Magic (14)	21	61	.256	30.0	101.6	108.5	-6.52
Central Division							
Chicago Bulls* (1)	67	15	.817	—	109.9	99.5	10.07
Cleveland Cavaliers* (3)	57	25	.695	10.0	108.9	103.4	5.34
Detroit Pistons* (5)	48	34	.585	19.0	98.9	96.9	2.06
Indiana Pacers* (7)	40	42	.488	27.0	112.2	110.3	1.85
Atlanta Hawks (9)	38	44	.463	29.0	106.2	107.7	-1.15
Milwaukee Bucks (11)	31	51	.378	36.0	105.0	106.7	-1.46
Charlotte Hornets (12)	31	51	.378	36.0	109.5	113.4	-3.57

Western Conference	W	L	W/L%	GB	PS/G	PA/G	SRS
Midwest Division							
Utah Jazz* (2)	55	27	.671	—	108.3	101.9	5.70
San Antonio Spurs* (5)	47	35	.573	8.0	104.0	100.6	2.81
Houston Rockets (9)	42	40	.512	13.0	102.0	103.7	-1.94
Denver Nuggets (11)	24	58	.293	31.0	99.7	107.6	-7.59
Dallas Mavericks (12)	22	60	.268	33.0	97.6	105.3	-7.47
Minnesota Timberwolves (13)	15	67	.183	40.0	100.5	107.5	-6.85
Pacific Division							
Portland Trail Blazers* (1)	57	25	.695	—	111.4	104.1	6.94
Golden State Warriors* (3)	55	27	.671	2.0	118.7	114.8	3.77
Phoenix Suns* (4)	53	29	.646	4.0	112.1	106.2	5.68
Seattle SuperSonics* (6)	47	35	.573	10.0	106.5	104.7	1.86
Los Angeles Clippers* (7)	45	37	.549	12.0	102.9	101.9	1.10
Los Angeles Lakers* (8)	43	39	.524	14.0	100.4	101.5	-0.95
Sacramento Kings (10)	29	53	.354	28.0	104.3	110.3	-5.63

AMERICAN HORSE OF THE YEAR
1992 ECLIPSE AWARD

Year	Horse	Trainer	Owner	Age	Gender
1992	A.P. Indy	Neil D. Drysdale	Tomonori Tsurumaki	3	C

1992- NHL SEASON
FINAL STANDINGS

Prince of Wales Conference							
Adams Division							
Team	GP	W	L	T	Pts	GF	GA
x - Boston Bruins	84	51	26	7	109	332	268
x - Quebec Nordiques	84	47	27	10	104	351	300
x - Montreal Canadiens	84	48	30	6	102	326	280
x - Buffalo Sabres	84	38	36	10	86	335	297
Hartford Whalers	84	26	52	6	58	284	369
Ottawa Senators	84	10	70	4	24	202	395
Patrick Division							
Team	GP	W	L	T	Pts	GF	GA
z - Pittsburgh Penguins	84	56	21	7	119	367	268
x - Washington Capitals	84	43	34	7	93	325	286
x - New York Islanders	84	40	37	7	87	335	297
x - New Jersey Devils	84	40	37	7	87	308	299
Philadelphia Flyers	84	36	37	11	83	319	319
New York Rangers	84	34	39	11	79	304	308
Clarence Campbell Conference							
Norris Division							
Team	GP	W	L	T	Pts	GF	GA
x - Chicago Blackhawks	84	47	25	12	106	279	230
x - Detroit Red Wings	84	47	28	9	103	369	280
x - Toronto Maple Leafs	84	44	29	11	99	288	241
x - St. Louis Blues	84	37	36	11	85	282	278
Minnesota North Stars	84	36	38	10	82	272	293
Tampa Bay Lightning	84	23	54	7	53	245	332

Smythe Division							
Team	GP	W	L	T	Pts	GF	GA
x - Vancouver Canucks	84	46	29	9	101	346	278
x - Calgary Flames	84	43	30	11	97	322	282
x - Los Angeles Kings	84	39	35	10	88	338	340
x - Winnipeg Jets	84	40	37	7	87	322	320
Edmonton Oilers	84	26	50	8	60	242	337
San Jose Sharks	84	11	71	2	24	218	414

1992 MAJOR LEAGUE BASEBALL SEASON HISTORY

1992 American League Standings									
EAST	W	L	PCT	GB	HOME	ROAD	RS	RA	DIFF
x-Toronto	96	66	.593	--	--	--	780	682	+98
Milwaukee	92	70	.568	4	--	--	740	604	+136
Baltimore	89	73	.549	7	--	--	705	656	+49
New York	76	86	.469	20	--	--	733	746	-13
Cleveland	76	86	.469	20	--	--	674	746	-72
Detroit	75	87	.463	21	--	--	791	794	-3
Boston	73	89	.451	23	--	--	599	669	-70
WEST	W	L	PCT	GB	HOME	ROAD	RS	RA	DIFF
x-Oakland	96	66	.593	--	--	--	745	672	+73
Minnesota	90	72	.556	6	--	--	747	653	+94
Chicago	86	76	.531	10	--	--	738	690	+48
Texas	77	85	.475	19	--	--	682	753	-71
Kansas City	72	90	.444	24	--	--	610	667	-57
California	72	90	.444	24	--	--	579	671	-92
Seattle	64	98	.395	32	--	--	679	799	-120

1992 National League Standings									
EAST	W	L	PCT	GB	HOME	ROAD	RS	RA	DIFF
x-Pittsburgh	96	66	.593	--	--	--	693	595	+98
Montreal	87	75	.537	9	--	--	648	581	+67
St. Louis	83	79	.512	13	--	--	631	604	+27
Chicago	78	84	.481	18	--	--	593	624	-31
New York	72	90	.444	24	--	--	599	653	-54
Philadelphia	70	92	.432	26	--	--	686	717	-31
WEST	W	L	PCT	GB	HOME	ROAD	RS	RA	DIFF
*-Atlanta	98	64	.605	--	--	--	682	569	+113
Cincinnati	90	72	.556	8	--	--	660	609	+51
San Diego	82	80	.506	16	--	--	617	636	-19
Houston	81	81	.500	17	--	--	608	668	-60
San Francisco	72	90	.444	26	--	--	574	647	-73
Los Angeles	63	99	.389	35	--	--	548	636	-88

1992 U.S. NATIONAL TENNIS CHAMPIONSHIPS

Men's Singles
Stefan Edberg defeated Pete Sampras 3–6, 6–4, 7–6, 6–2
Women's Singles
Monica Seles defeated Arantxa Sánchez Vicario 6–3, 6–3
Men's Doubles
Jim Grabb / Richey Reneberg defeated Kelly Jones / Rick Leach 3–6, 7–6, 6–3, 6–3
Women's Doubles
Gigi Fernández / Natasha Zvereva defeated Larisa Neiland / Jana Novotná 7–6$^{(7-4)}$, 6–1
Mixed Doubles
Nicole Provis / Mark Woodforde defeated Helena Suková / Tom Nijssen 4–6, 6–3, 6–3

1993

1993 NATIONAL FOOTBALL LEAGUE SEASON
STANDINGS

AFC EAST	W	L	T	NFC EAST	W	L	T
Buffalo	12	4	0	Dallas	12	4	0
Miami	9	7	0	NY Giants	11	5	0
NY Jets	8	8	0	Philadelphia	8	8	0
New England	5	11	0	Phoenix	7	9	0
Indianapolis	4	12	0	Washington	4	12	0
AFC CENT	W	L	T	NFC CENT	W	L	T
Houston	12	4	0	Detroit	10	6	0
Pittsburgh	9	7	0	Minnesota	9	7	0
Cleveland	7	9	0	Green Bay	9	7	0
Cincinnati	3	13	0	Chicago	7	9	0
AFC WEST	W	L	T	Tampa Bay	5	11	0
Kansas City	11	5	0	NFC WEST	W	L	T
LA Raiders	10	6	0	San Francisco	10	6	0
Denver	9	7	0	New Orleans	8	8	0
San Diego	8	8	0	Atlanta	6	10	0
Seattle	6	10	0	LA Rams	5	11	0

1993 U.S. NATIONAL BADMINTON CHAMPIONSHIPS
WINNERS

Year	Men's singles	Women's singles	Men's doubles	Women's doubles	Mixed doubles
1993	Andy Chong	Andrea Andersson	Benny Lee Tom Reidy	Andrea Andersson Traci Britton	Andy Chong Linda French

1993 NBA STANDINGS
DIVISION STANDINGS

Eastern Conference	W	L	W/L%	GB	PS/G	PA/G	SRS
Atlantic Division							
New York Knicks* (1)	60	22	.732	—	101.6	95.4	5.87
Boston Celtics* (4)	48	34	.585	12.0	103.7	102.8	0.93
New Jersey Nets* (6)	43	39	.524	17.0	102.8	101.6	1.20
Orlando Magic (9)	41	41	.500	19.0	105.5	104.2	1.35
Miami Heat (11)	36	46	.439	24.0	103.6	104.7	-0.93
Philadelphia 76ers (13)	26	56	.317	34.0	104.3	110.1	-5.25
Washington Bullets (14)	22	60	.268	38.0	101.9	108.9	-6.49
Central Division							
Chicago Bulls* (2)	57	25	.695	—	105.2	98.9	6.19
Cleveland Cavaliers* (3)	54	28	.659	3.0	107.7	101.3	6.30
Charlotte Hornets* (5)	44	38	.537	13.0	110.1	110.4	-0.02
Atlanta Hawks* (7)	43	39	.524	14.0	107.5	108.4	-0.67
Indiana Pacers* (8)	41	41	.500	16.0	107.8	106.1	1.77
Detroit Pistons (10)	40	42	.488	17.0	100.6	102.0	-1.10
Milwaukee Bucks (12)	28	54	.341	29.0	102.3	106.1	-3.26

Western Conference	W	L	W/L%	GB	PS/G	PA/G	SRS
Midwest Division							
Houston Rockets* (2)	55	27	.671	—	104.0	99.8	3.57
San Antonio Spurs* (5)	49	33	.598	6.0	105.5	102.8	2.21
Utah Jazz* (6)	47	35	.573	8.0	106.2	104.0	1.74
Denver Nuggets (9)	36	46	.439	19.0	105.2	106.9	-2.14
Minnesota Timberwolves (12)	19	63	.232	36.0	98.1	105.9	-7.62
Dallas Mavericks (13)	11	71	.134	44.0	99.3	114.5	-14.68
Pacific Division							
Phoenix Suns* (1)	62	20	.756	—	113.4	106.7	6.27
Seattle SuperSonics* (3)	55	27	.671	7.0	108.3	101.3	6.66
Portland Trail Blazers* (4)	51	31	.622	11.0	108.5	105.4	2.92
Los Angeles Clippers* (7)	41	41	.500	21.0	107.1	106.8	0.33
Los Angeles Lakers* (8)	39	43	.476	23.0	104.2	105.5	-1.20
Golden State Warriors (10)	34	48	.415	28.0	109.9	110.9	-0.94
Sacramento Kings (11)	25	57	.305	37.0	107.9	111.1	-3.00

AMERICAN HORSE OF THE YEAR
1993 ECLIPSE AWARD

Year	Horse	Trainer	Owner	Age	Gender
1993	Kotashaan	Richard Mandella	La Presle Farm	5	C

1993- NHL SEASON
FINAL STANDINGS

Eastern Conference							
Atlantic Division							
	GP	W	L	T	GF	GA	PTS
New York Rangers	84	52	24	8	299	231	112
New Jersey Devils	84	47	25	12	306	220	106
Washington Capitals	84	39	35	10	277	263	88
New York Islanders	84	36	36	12	282	264	84
Florida Panthers	84	33	34	17	233	233	83
Philadelphia Flyers	84	35	39	10	294	314	80
Tampa Bay Lightning	84	30	43	11	224	251	71
Northeast Division							
	GP	W	L	T	GF	GA	PTS
Pittsburgh Penguins	84	44	27	13	299	285	101
Boston Bruins	84	42	29	13	289	252	97
Montreal Canadiens	84	41	29	14	283	248	96
Buffalo Sabres	84	43	32	9	282	218	95
Quebec Nordiques	84	34	42	8	277	292	76
Hartford Whalers	84	27	48	9	227	288	63
Ottawa Senators	84	14	61	9	201	397	37
Western Conference							
Central Division							
	GP	W	L	T	GF	GA	Pts
Detroit Red Wings	84	46	30	8	356	275	100
Toronto Maple Leafs	84	43	29	12	280	243	98
Dallas Stars	84	42	29	13	286	265	97

St. Louis Blues	84	40	33	11	270	283	91
Chicago Blackhawks	84	39	36	9	254	240	87
Winnipeg Jets	84	24	51	9	245	344	57

Pacific Division							
	GP	W	L	T	GF	GA	Pts
Calgary Flames	84	42	29	13	302	256	97
Vancouver Canucks	84	41	40	3	279	276	85
San Jose Sharks	84	33	35	16	252	265	82
Mighty Ducks of Anaheim	84	33	46	5	229	251	71
Los Angeles Kings	84	27	45	12	294	322	66
Edmonton Oilers	84	25	45	14	261	305	6

1993 MAJOR LEAGUE BASEBALL SEASON HISTORY

1993 American League Standings									
EAST	W	L	PCT	GB	HOME	ROAD	RS	RA	DIFF
*-Toronto	95	67	.586	--	48-33	47-34	847	742	+105
New York	88	74	.543	7	50-31	38-43	821	761	+60
Baltimore	85	77	.525	10	48-33	37-44	786	745	+41
Detroit	85	77	.525	10	44-37	41-40	899	837	+62
Boston	80	82	.494	15	43-38	37-44	686	698	-12
Cleveland	76	86	.469	19	46-35	30-51	790	813	-23
Milwaukee	69	93	.426	26	38-43	31-50	733	792	-59
WEST	W	L	PCT	GB	HOME	ROAD	RS	RA	DIFF
x-Chicago	94	68	.580	--	45-36	49-32	776	664	+112
Texas	86	76	.531	8	50-31	36-45	835	751	+84
Kansas City	84	78	.519	10	43-38	41-40	675	694	-19
Seattle	82	80	.506	12	46-35	36-45	734	731	+3
California	71	91	.438	23	44-37	27-54	684	770	-86
Minnesota	71	91	.438	23	36-45	35-46	693	830	-137
Oakland	68	94	.420	26	38-43	30-51	715	846	-131
1993 National League Standings									
EAST	W	L	PCT	GB	HOME	ROAD	RS	RA	DIFF
x-Philadelphia	97	65	.599	--	52-29	45-36	877	740	+137
Montreal	94	68	.580	3	55-26	39-42	732	682	+50
St. Louis	87	75	.537	10	49-32	38-43	758	744	+14
Chicago	84	78	.519	13	43-38	41-40	738	739	-1
Pittsburgh	75	87	.463	22	40-41	35-46	707	806	-99
Florida	64	98	.395	33	35-46	29-52	581	724	-143
New York	59	103	.364	38	28-53	31-50	672	744	-72
WEST	W	L	PCT	GB	HOME	ROAD	RS	RA	DIFF
*-Atlanta	104	58	.642	--	51-30	53-28	767	559	+208
San Francisco	103	59	.636	1	50-31	53-28	808	636	+172
Houston	85	77	.525	19	44-37	41-40	716	630	+86
Los Angeles	81	81	.500	23	41-40	40-41	675	662	+13
Cincinnati	73	89	.451	31	41-40	32-49	722	785	-63
Colorado	67	95	.414	37	39-42	28-53	758	967	-209
San Diego	61	101	.377	43	34-47	27-54	679	772	-93

1993 U.S. NATIONAL TENNIS CHAMPIONSHIPS

Men's Singles
Pete Sampras defeated Cédric Pioline 6–4, 6–4, 6–3
Women's Singles
Steffi Graf defeated Helena Suková 6–3, 6–3
Men's Doubles
Ken Flach / Rick Leach defeated Karel Nováček / Martin Damm 6–7$^{(3–7)}$, 6–4, 6–2
Women's Doubles
Arantxa Sánchez Vicario / Helena Suková defeated Amanda Coetzer / Inés Gorrochategui 6–4, 6–2
Mixed Doubles
Helena Suková / Todd Woodbridge defeated Martina Navratilova / Mark Woodforde 6–3, 7–6

1994

1994 NATIONAL FOOTBALL LEAGUE SEASON
STANDINGS

AFC EAST	W	L	T	NFC EAST	W	L	T
Miami	10	6	0	Dallas	12	4	0
New England	10	6	0	NY Giants	9	7	0
Indianapolis	8	8	0	Arizona	8	8	0
Buffalo	7	9	0	Philadelphia	7	9	0
NY Jets	6	10	0	Washington	3	13	0
AFC CENT	W	L	T	NFC CENT	W	L	T
Pittsburgh	12	4	0	Minnesota	10	6	0
Cleveland	11	5	0	Green Bay	9	7	0
Cincinnati	3	13	0	Detroit	9	7	0
Houston	2	14	0	Chicago	9	7	0
AFC WEST	W	L	T	Tampa Bay	6	10	0
San Diego	11	5	0	NFC WEST	W	L	T
Kansas City	9	7	0	San Francisco	13	3	0
LA Raiders	9	7	0	New Orleans	7	9	0
Denver	7	9	0	Atlanta	7	9	0
Seattle	6	10	0	LA Rams	4	12	0

1994 U.S. NATIONAL BADMINTON CHAMPIONSHIPS
WINNERS

Year	Men's singles	Women's singles	Men's doubles	Women's doubles	Mixed doubles
1994	Kevin Han	Joy Kitzmiller	Benny Lee Tom Reidy	Andrea Andersson Liz Aronsohn	Andy Chong Linda French

1994 NBA STANDINGS
DIVISION STANDINGS

Eastern Conference	W	L	W/L%	GB	PS/G	PA/G	SRS
Atlantic Division								
New York Knicks* (2)	57	25	.695	—	98.5	91.5	6.48
Orlando Magic* (4)	50	32	.610	7.0	105.7	101.8	3.68
New Jersey Nets* (7)	45	37	.549	12.0	103.2	101.0	2.11
Miami Heat* (8)	42	40	.512	15.0	103.4	100.7	2.40
Boston Celtics (10)	32	50	.390	25.0	100.8	105.1	-4.28
Philadelphia 76ers (11)	25	57	.305	32.0	98.0	105.6	-7.37
Washington Bullets (12)	24	58	.293	33.0	100.4	107.7	-7.13
Central Division								
Atlanta Hawks* (1)	57	25	.695	—	101.4	96.2	4.94
Chicago Bulls* (3)	55	27	.671	2.0	98.0	94.9	2.87
Indiana Pacers* (5)	47	35	.573	10.0	101.0	97.5	3.26
Cleveland Cavaliers* (6)	47	35	.573	10.0	101.2	97.1	3.64
Charlotte Hornets (9)	41	41	.500	16.0	106.5	106.7	-0.23
Milwaukee Bucks (13)	20	62	.244	37.0	96.9	103.4	-6.24
Detroit Pistons (14)	20	62	.244	37.0	96.9	104.7	-7.46

Western Conference	W	L	W/L%	GB	PS/G	PA/G	SRS
Midwest Division							
Houston Rockets* (2)	58	24	.707	—	101.1	96.8	4.19
San Antonio Spurs* (4)	55	27	.671	3.0	100.0	94.8	5.05
Utah Jazz* (5)	53	29	.646	5.0	101.9	97.7	4.10
Denver Nuggets* (8)	42	40	.512	16.0	100.3	98.8	1.54
Minnesota Timberwolves (12)	20	62	.244	38.0	96.7	103.6	-6.55
Dallas Mavericks (13)	13	69	.159	45.0	95.1	103.8	-8.19
Pacific Division							
Seattle SuperSonics* (1)	63	19	.768	—	105.9	96.9	8.68
Phoenix Suns* (3)	56	26	.683	7.0	108.2	103.4	4.68
Golden State Warriors* (6)	50	32	.610	13.0	107.9	106.1	1.76
Portland Trail Blazers* (7)	47	35	.573	16.0	107.3	104.6	2.60
Los Angeles Lakers (9)	33	49	.402	30.0	100.4	104.7	-3.93
Sacramento Kings (10)	28	54	.341	35.0	101.1	106.9	-5.32
Los Angeles Clippers (11)	27	55	.329	36.0	103.0	108.7	-5.28

AMERICAN HORSE OF THE YEAR
1994 ECLIPSE AWARD

Year	Horse	Trainer	Owner	Age	Gender
1994	Holy Bull	Warren A. Croll, Jr.	Warren A. Croll, Jr.	3	C

1994- NHL SEASON
FINAL STANDINGS

Eastern Conference								
Northeast Division	GP	W	L	T	GF	GA	Pts
Quebec Nordiques	48	30	13	5	185	134	65
Pittsburgh Penguins	48	29	16	3	181	158	61
Boston Bruins	48	27	18	3	150	127	57
Buffalo Sabres	48	22	19	7	130	119	51
Hartford Whalers	48	19	24	5	127	141	43
Montreal Canadiens	48	18	23	7	125	148	43
Ottawa Senators	48	9	34	5	117	174	23
Atlantic Division	GP	W	L	T	GF	GA	Pts
Philadelphia Flyers	48	28	16	4	150	132	60
New Jersey Devils	48	22	18	8	136	121	52
Washington Capitals	48	22	18	8	136	120	52
New York Rangers	48	22	23	3	139	134	47
Florida Panthers	48	20	22	6	115	127	46
Tampa Bay Lightning	48	17	28	3	120	144	37
New York Islanders	48	15	28	5	126	158	35

Western Conference							
Central Division	GP	W	L	T	GF	GA	Pts
Detroit Red Wings	48	33	11	4	180	117	70
St. Louis Blues	48	28	15	5	178	135	61
Chicago Blackhawks	48	24	19	5	156	115	53
Toronto Maple Leafs	48	21	19	8	135	146	50
Dallas Stars	48	17	23	8	136	135	42
Winnipeg Jets	48	16	25	7	157	177	39
Pacific Division	GP	W	L	T	GF	GA	Pts
Calgary Flames	48	24	17	7	163	135	55
Vancouver Canucks	48	18	18	12	153	148	48
San Jose Sharks	48	19	25	4	129	161	42
Los Angeles Kings	48	16	23	9	142	174	41
Edmonton Oilers	48	17	27	4	136	183	38
Mighty Ducks of Anaheim	48	16	27	5	125	164	37

1994 MAJOR LEAGUE BASEBALL SEASON HISTORY

1994 American League Standings									
EAST	W	L	PCT	GB	HOME	ROAD	RS	RA	DIFF
New York	70	43	.619	--	33-24	37-19	670	534	+136
Baltimore	63	49	.563	6.5	28-27	35-22	589	497	+92
Toronto	55	60	.478	16	33-26	22-34	566	579	-13
Boston	54	61	.470	17	31-33	23-28	552	621	-69
Detroit	53	62	.461	18	34-24	19-38	652	671	-19
CENTRAL	W	L	PCT	GB	HOME	ROAD	RS	RA	DIFF
Chicago	67	46	.593	--	34-19	33-27	633	498	+135
Cleveland	66	47	.584	1	35-16	31-31	679	562	+117
Kansas City	64	51	.557	4	35-24	29-27	574	532	+42
Minnesota	53	60	.469	14	32-27	21-33	594	688	-94
Milwaukee	53	62	.461	15	24-32	29-30	547	586	-39
WEST	W	L	PCT	GB	HOME	ROAD	RS	RA	DIFF
Texas	52	62	.456	--	31-32	21-30	613	697	-84
Oakland	51	63	.447	1	24-32	27-31	549	589	-40
Seattle	49	63	.438	2	22-22	27-41	569	616	-47
California	47	68	.409	5.5	23-40	24-28	543	660	-117
1994 National League Standings									
EAST	W	L	PCT	GB	HOME	ROAD	RS	RA	DIFF
Montreal	74	40	.649	--	32-20	42-20	585	454	+131
Atlanta	68	46	.596	6	31-24	37-22	542	448	+94
New York	55	58	.487	18.5	23-30	32-28	506	526	-20
Philadelphia	54	61	.470	20.5	34-26	20-35	521	497	+24
Florida	51	64	.443	23.5	25-34	26-30	468	576	-108
CENTRAL	**W**	**L**	**PCT**	**GB**	**HOME**	**ROAD**	**RS**	**RA**	**DIFF**
Cincinnati	66	48	.579	--	37-22	29-26	609	490	+119
Houston	66	49	.574	.5	37-22	29-27	602	503	+99
St. Louis	53	61	.465	13	23-33	30-28	535	621	-86
Chicago	49	64	.434	16.5	20-39	29-25	500	549	-49
WEST	W	L	PCT	GB	HOME	ROAD	RS	RA	DIFF
Los Angeles	58	56	.509	--	33-22	25-34	532	509	+23
San Francisco	55	60	.478	3.5	29-31	26-29	504	500	+4
Colorado	53	64	.453	6.5	25-32	28-32	573	638	-65
San Diego	47	70	.402	12.5	26-31	21-39	479	531	-52

1994 U.S. NATIONAL TENNIS CHAMPIONSHIPS

Men's Singles
Andre Agassi defeated Michael Stich 6–1, 7–6$^{(7-5)}$, 7–5
Women's Singles
Arantxa Sánchez Vicario defeated Steffi Graf 1–6, 7–6$^{(7-3)}$, 6–4
Men's Doubles
Jacco Eltingh / Paul Haarhuis defeated Todd Woodbridge / Mark Woodforde 6–3, 7–6
Women's Doubles
Jana Novotná / Arantxa Sánchez Vicario defeated Katerina Maleeva / Robin White 6–3, 6–3
Mixed Doubles
Elna Reinach / Patrick Galbraith defeated Jana Novotná / Todd Woodbridge 6–2, 6–4

1995

1995 NATIONAL FOOTBALL LEAGUE SEASON
STANDINGS

AFC EAST	W	L	T	NFC EAST	W	L	T
Buffalo	10	6	0	Dallas	12	4	0
Indianapolis	9	7	0	Philadelphia	10	6	0
Miami	9	7	0	Washington	6	10	0
New England	6	10	0	NY Giants	5	11	0
NY Jets	3	13	0	Arizona	4	12	0
AFC CENT	**W**	**L**	**T**	**NFC CENT**	**W**	**L**	**T**
Pittsburgh	11	5	0	Green Bay	11	5	0
Cincinnati	7	9	0	Detroit	10	6	0
Houston	7	9	0	Chicago	9	7	0
Cleveland	5	11	0	Minnesota	8	8	0
Jacksonville	4	12	0	Tampa Bay	7	9	0
AFC WEST	**W**	**L**	**T**	**NFC WEST**	**W**	**L**	**T**
Kansas City	13	3	0	San Francisco	11	5	0
San Diego	9	7	0	Atlanta	9	7	0
Seattle	8	8	0	St. Louis	7	9	0
Denver	8	8	0	New Orleans	7	9	0
Oakland	8	8	0	Carolina	7	9	0

1995 U.S. NATIONAL BADMINTON CHAMPIONSHIPS
WINNERS

Year	Men's singles	Women's singles	Men's doubles	Women's doubles	Mixed doubles
1995	Kevin Han	Andrea Andersson	Benny Lee Tom Reidy	Andrea Andersson Liz Aronsohn	Andy Chong Linda French

1995 NBA STANDINGS
DIVISION STANDINGS

Eastern Conference	W	L	W/L%	GB	PS/G	PA/G	SRS
Atlantic Division							
Orlando Magic* (1)	57	25	.695	—	110.9	103.8	6.44
New York Knicks* (3)	55	27	.671	2.0	98.2	95.1	2.78
Boston Celtics* (8)	35	47	.427	22.0	102.8	104.7	-1.92
Miami Heat (10)	32	50	.390	25.0	101.1	102.8	-1.85
New Jersey Nets (11)	30	52	.366	27.0	98.1	101.2	-3.28
Philadelphia 76ers (13)	24	58	.293	33.0	95.4	100.4	-5.06
Washington Bullets (14)	21	61	.256	36.0	100.5	106.1	-5.56
Central Division							
Indiana Pacers* (2)	52	30	.634	—	99.2	95.5	3.35
Charlotte Hornets* (4)	50	32	.610	2.0	100.6	97.3	2.87
Chicago Bulls* (5)	47	35	.573	5.0	101.5	96.7	4.32
Cleveland Cavaliers* (6)	43	39	.524	9.0	90.5	89.8	0.55
Atlanta Hawks* (7)	42	40	.512	10.0	96.6	95.3	1.06
Milwaukee Bucks (9)	34	48	.415	18.0	99.3	103.7	-4.30
Detroit Pistons (12)	28	54	.341	24.0	98.2	105.5	-7.08

Western Conference	W	L	W/L%	GB	PS/G	PA/G	SRS
Midwest Division							
San Antonio Spurs* (1)	62	20	.756	—	106.6	100.6	5.90
Utah Jazz* (3)	60	22	.732	2.0	106.4	98.4	7.76
Houston Rockets* (6)	47	35	.573	15.0	103.5	101.4	2.32
Denver Nuggets* (8)	41	41	.500	21.0	101.3	100.5	0.96
Dallas Mavericks (10)	36	46	.439	26.0	103.2	106.1	-2.39
Minnesota Timberwolves (12)	21	61	.256	41.0	94.2	103.2	-8.22
Pacific Division							
Phoenix Suns* (2)	59	23	.720	—	110.6	106.8	3.86
Seattle SuperSonics* (4)	57	25	.695	2.0	110.4	102.2	7.91
Los Angeles Lakers* (5)	48	34	.585	11.0	105.1	105.3	-0.01
Portland Trail Blazers* (7)	44	38	.537	15.0	103.1	99.2	3.80
Sacramento Kings (9)	39	43	.476	20.0	98.2	99.2	-0.74
Golden State Warriors (11)	26	56	.317	33.0	105.7	111.1	-4.90
Los Angeles Clippers (13)	17	65	.207	42.0	96.7	105.8	-8.43

AMERICAN HORSE OF THE YEAR
1995 ECLIPSE AWARD

Year	Horse	Trainer	Owner	Age	Gender
1995	Cigar	William I. Mott	Allen E. Paulson	5	C

1995- NHL SEASON
FINAL STANDINGS

Eastern Conference						
Northeast Division						
Team	W	L	T	GF	GA	Pts
Pittsburgh Penguins	49	29	4	362	284	102
Boston Bruins	40	31	11	282	269	91
Montreal Canadiens	40	32	10	265	248	90
Hartford Whalers	34	39	9	237	259	77
Buffalo Sabres	33	42	7	247	262	73
Ottawa Senators	18	59	5	191	291	41
Atlantic Division						
Team	W	L	T	GF	GA	Pts
Philadelphia Flyers	45	24	13	282	208	103
New York Rangers	41	27	14	272	237	96
Florida Panthers	41	31	10	254	234	92
Washington Capitals	39	32	11	234	204	89
Tampa Bay Lightning	38	32	12	238	248	88
New Jersey Devils	37	33	12	215	202	86
New York Islanders	22	50	10	229	315	54

Western Conference						
Central Division						
Team	W	L	T	GF	GA	Pts
Detroit Red Wings	62	13	7	325	181	131
Chicago Blackhawks	40	28	14	273	220	94
Toronto Maple Leafs	34	36	12	247	252	80
St. Louis Blues	32	34	16	219	248	80
Winnipeg Jets	36	40	6	275	291	78
Dallas Stars	26	42	14	227	280	66
Pacific Division						
Team	W	L	T	GF	GA	Pts
Colorado Avalanche	47	25	10	326	240	104
Calgary Flames	34	37	11	241	240	79
Vancouver Canucks	32	35	15	278	278	79
Mighty Ducks of Anaheim	35	39	8	234	247	78
Edmonton Oilers	30	44	8	240	304	68
Los Angeles Kings	24	40	18	256	302	66
San Jose Sharks	20	55	7	252	357	47

1995 MAJOR LEAGUE BASEBALL SEASON HISTORY

1995 American League Standings								
EAST	W	L	PCT	GB	HOME	ROAD	RS	RA	DIFF
x-Boston	86	58	.597	--	42-30	44-28	791	698	+93
y-New York	79	65	.549	7	46-26	33-39	749	688	+61
Baltimore	71	73	.493	15	36-36	35-37	704	640	+64
Detroit	60	84	.417	26	35-37	25-47	654	844	-190
Toronto	56	88	.389	30	29-43	27-45	642	777	-135
CENTRAL	W	L	PCT	GB	HOME	ROAD	RS	RA	DIFF
*-Cleveland	100	44	.694	--	54-18	46-26	840	607	+233
Kansas City	70	74	.486	30	35-37	35-37	629	691	-62
Chicago	68	76	.472	32	38-34	30-42	755	758	-3
Milwaukee	65	79	.451	35	33-39	32-40	740	747	-7
Minnesota	56	88	.389	44	29-43	27-45	703	889	-186
WEST	W	L	PCT	GB	HOME	ROAD	RS	RA	DIFF
x-Seattle	79	66	.545	--	46-27	33-39	796	708	+88
California	78	67	.538	1	39-33	39-34	801	697	+104
Texas	74	70	.514	4.5	41-31	33-39	691	720	-29
Oakland	67	77	.465	11.5	38-34	29-43	730	761	-31
1995 National League Standings								
EAST	W	L	PCT	GB	HOME	ROAD	RS	RA	DIFF
*-Atlanta	90	54	.625	--	44-28	46-26	645	540	+105
New York	69	75	.479	21	40-32	29-43	657	618	+39
Philadelphia	69	75	.479	21	35-37	34-38	615	658	-43
Florida	67	76	.469	22.5	37-34	30-42	673	673	0
Montreal	66	78	.458	24	31-41	35-37	621	638	-17
CENTRAL	W	L	PCT	GB	HOME	ROAD	RS	RA	DIFF
x-Cincinnati	85	59	.590	--	44-28	41-31	747	623	+124
Houston	76	68	.528	9	36-36	40-32	747	674	+73
Chicago	73	71	.507	12	34-38	39-33	693	671	+22

St. Louis	62	81	.434	22.5	39-33	23-48	563	658	-95
Pittsburgh	58	86	.403	27	31-41	27-45	629	736	-107
WEST	**W**	**L**	**PCT**	**GB**	**HOME**	**ROAD**	**RS**	**RA**	**DIFF**
x-Los Angeles	78	66	.542	--	39-33	39-33	634	609	+25
y-Colorado	77	67	.535	1	44-28	33-39	785	783	+2
San Diego	70	74	.486	8	40-32	30-42	668	672	-4
San Francisco	67	77	.465	11	37-35	30-42	652	776	-124

1995 U.S. NATIONAL TENNIS CHAMPIONSHIPS

Men's Singles
Pete Sampras defeated Andre Agassi 6–4, 6–3, 4–6, 7–5
Women's Singles
Steffi Graf defeated Monica Seles 7–6$^{(8-6)}$, 0–6, 6–3
Men's Doubles
Todd Woodbridge / Mark Woodforde defeated Alex O'Brien / Sandon Stolle 6–3, 6–3
Women's Doubles
Gigi Fernández / Natasha Zvereva defeated Brenda Schultz-McCarthy / Rennae Stubbs 7–5, 6–3
Mixed Doubles
Meredith McGrath / Matt Lucena defeated Gigi Fernández / Cyril Suk 6–4, 6–4

1996

1996 NATIONAL FOOTBALL LEAGUE SEASON
STANDINGS

AFC EAST	W	L	T	NFC EAST	W	L	T
New England	11	5	0	Dallas	10	6	0
Buffalo	10	6	0	Philadelphia	10	6	0
Indianapolis	9	7	0	Washington	9	7	0
Miami	8	8	0	Arizona	7	9	0
NY Jets	1	15	0	NY Giants	6	10	0
AFC CENT	W	L	T	NFC CENT	W	L	T
Pittsburgh	10	6	0	Green Bay	13	3	0
Jacksonville	9	7	0	Minnesota	9	7	0
Cincinnati	8	8	0	Chicago	7	9	0
Houston	8	8	0	Tampa Bay	6	10	0
Baltimore	4	12	0	Detroit	5	11	0
AFC WEST	W	L	T	NFC WEST	W	L	T
Denver	13	3	0	Carolina	12	4	0
Kansas City	9	7	0	San Francisco	12	4	0
San Diego	8	8	0	St. Louis	6	10	0
Oakland	7	9	0	Atlanta	3	13	0
Seattle	7	9	0	New Orleans	3	13	0

1996 U.S. NATIONAL BADMINTON CHAMPIONSHIPS
WINNERS

Year	Men's singles	Women's singles	Men's doubles	Women's doubles	Mixed doubles
1996	Steve Butler	Zhao Ye Ping	Kevin Han Tom Reidy	Ann French Kathy Zimmerman	Andy Chong Zhao Ye Ping

1996 NBA STANDINGS
DIVISION STANDINGS

Eastern Conference	W	L	W/L%	GB	PS/G	PA/G	SRS
Atlantic Division							
Orlando Magic* (2)	60	22	.732	—	104.5	99.0	5.40
New York Knicks* (5)	47	35	.573	13.0	97.2	94.9	2.24
Miami Heat* (8)	42	40	.512	18.0	96.5	95.0	1.46
Washington Bullets (10)	39	43	.476	21.0	102.5	101.5	0.99
Boston Celtics (11)	33	49	.402	27.0	103.6	107.0	-3.37
New Jersey Nets (12)	30	52	.366	30.0	93.7	97.9	-4.14
Philadelphia 76ers (15)	18	64	.220	42.0	94.5	104.5	-9.45
Central Division							
Chicago Bulls* (1)	72	10	.878	—	105.2	92.9	11.80
Indiana Pacers* (3)	52	30	.634	20.0	99.3	96.1	3.11
Cleveland Cavaliers* (4)	47	35	.573	25.0	91.1	88.5	2.49
Atlanta Hawks* (6)	46	36	.561	26.0	98.3	97.1	1.29
Detroit Pistons* (7)	46	36	.561	26.0	95.4	92.9	2.45
Charlotte Hornets (9)	41	41	.500	31.0	102.8	103.4	-0.48
Milwaukee Bucks (13)	25	57	.305	47.0	95.6	100.9	-4.92
Toronto Raptors (14)	21	61	.256	51.0	97.5	105.0	-7.20

Western Conference	W	L	W/L%	GB	PS/G	PA/G	SRS
Midwest Division								
San Antonio Spurs* (2)	59	23	.720	—	103.4	97.1	5.98
Utah Jazz* (3)	55	27	.671	4.0	102.5	95.9	6.25
Houston Rockets* (5)	48	34	.585	11.0	102.5	100.7	1.63
Denver Nuggets (10)	35	47	.427	24.0	97.7	100.4	-2.62
Minnesota Timberwolves (12)	26	56	.317	33.0	97.9	103.2	-5.14
Dallas Mavericks (13)	26	56	.317	33.0	102.5	107.5	-4.71
Vancouver Grizzlies (14)	15	67	.183	44.0	89.8	99.8	-9.55
Pacific Division								
Seattle SuperSonics* (1)	64	18	.780	—	104.5	96.7	7.40
Los Angeles Lakers* (4)	53	29	.646	11.0	102.9	98.5	4.21
Portland Trail Blazers* (6)	44	38	.537	20.0	99.3	97.0	2.21
Phoenix Suns* (7)	41	41	.500	23.0	104.3	104.0	0.28
Sacramento Kings* (8)	39	43	.476	25.0	99.5	102.3	-2.62
Golden State Warriors (9)	36	46	.439	28.0	101.6	103.1	-1.42
Los Angeles Clippers (11)	29	53	.354	35.0	99.4	103.0	-3.46

AMERICAN HORSE OF THE YEAR
1996 ECLIPSE AWARD

Year	Horse	Trainer	Owner	Age	Gender
1996	Cigar	William I. Mott	Allen E. Paulson	6	C

1996 - NHL SEASON
FINAL STANDINGS

Eastern Conference							
Northeast Division							
Team	W	L	T	GF	GA	Pts	
Buffalo Sabres	40	30	12	237	208	92	
Pittsburgh Penguins	38	36	8	285	280	84	
Ottawa Senators	31	36	15	249	276	77	
Montreal Canadiens	31	36	15	249	276	77	
Hartford Whalers	32	39	11	226	256	75	
Boston Bruins	26	47	9	234	300	61	
Atlantic Division							
Team	W	L	T	GF	GA	Pts	
New Jersey Devils	45	23	14	231	182	104	
Philadelphia Flyers	45	24	13	274	217	103	
Florida Panthers	35	28	19	221	201	89	
New York Rangers	38	34	10	258	231	86	
Washington Capitals	33	40	9	214	231	75	
Tampa Bay Lightning	32	40	10	217	247	74	
New York Islanders	29	41	12	240	250	70	

Western Conference

Central Division

Team	W	L	T	GF	GA	Pts
Dallas Stars	48	26	8	252	198	104
Detroit Red Wings	38	26	18	253	197	94
Phoenix Coyotes	38	37	7	240	243	83
St. Louis Blues	36	35	11	236	239	83
Chicago Blackhawks	34	35	13	223	210	81
Toronto Maple Leafs	30	44	8	230	273	68

Pacific Division

Team	W	L	T	GF	GA	Pts
Colorado Avalanche	49	24	9	277	205	107
Mighty Ducks of Anaheim	36	33	13	243	231	85
Edmonton Oilers	36	37	9	252	247	81
Vancouver Canucks	35	40	7	257	273	77
Calgary Flames	32	41	9	214	239	73
Los Angeles Kings	28	43	11	214	268	67
San Jose Sharks	27	47	8	211	278	62

1996 MAJOR LEAGUE BASEBALL SEASON HISTORY

1996 American League Standings

EAST	W	L	PCT	GB	HOME	ROAD	RS	RA	DIFF
x-New York	92	70	.568	--	49-31	43-39	871	787	+84
y-Baltimore	88	74	.543	4	43-38	45-36	949	903	+46
Boston	85	77	.525	7	47-34	38-43	928	921	+7
Toronto	74	88	.457	18	35-46	39-42	766	809	-43
Detroit	53	109	.327	39	27-54	26-55	783	1103	-320
CENTRAL	W	L	PCT	GB	HOME	ROAD	RS	RA	DIFF
*-Cleveland	99	62	.615	--	51-29	48-33	952	769	+183
Chicago	85	77	.525	14.5	44-37	41-40	898	794	+104
Milwaukee	80	82	.494	19.5	38-43	42-39	894	899	-5
Minnesota	78	84	.481	21.5	39-43	39-41	877	900	-23
Kansas City	75	86	.466	24	37-43	38-43	746	786	-40
WEST	W	L	PCT	GB	HOME	ROAD	RS	RA	DIFF
x-Texas	90	72	.556	--	50-31	40-41	928	799	+129
Seattle	85	76	.528	4.5	43-38	42-38	993	895	+98
Oakland	78	84	.481	12	40-41	38-43	861	900	-39
California	70	91	.435	19.5	43-38	27-53	762	943	-181

1996 National League Standings

EAST	W	L	PCT	GB	HOME	ROAD	RS	RA	DIFF
*-Atlanta	96	66	.593	--	56-25	40-41	773	648	+125
Montreal	88	74	.543	8	50-31	38-43	741	668	+73
Florida	80	82	.494	16	52-29	28-53	688	703	-15
New York	71	91	.438	25	42-39	29-52	746	779	-33
Philadelphia	67	95	.414	29	35-46	32-49	650	790	-140
CENTRAL	W	L	PCT	GB	HOME	ROAD	RS	RA	DIFF
x-St. Louis	88	74	.543	--	48-33	40-41	759	706	+53
Houston	82	80	.506	6	48-33	34-47	753	792	-39
Cincinnati	81	81	.500	7	46-35	35-46	778	773	+5
Chicago	76	86	.469	12	43-38	33-48	772	771	+1
Pittsburgh	73	89	.451	15	36-44	37-45	776	833	-57

WEST	W	L	PCT	GB	HOME	ROAD	RS	RA	DIFF
x-San Diego	91	71	.562	--	45-36	46-35	771	682	+89
y-Los Angeles	90	72	.556	1	47-34	43-38	703	652	+51
Colorado	83	79	.512	8	55-26	28-53	961	964	-3
San Francisco	68	94	.420	23	38-44	30-50	752	862	-110

1996 U.S. NATIONAL TENNIS CHAMPIONSHIPS

Men's Singles	
Pete Sampras defeated Michael Chang 6–1, 6–4, 7–6$^{(7-3)}$	
Women's Singles	
Steffi Graf defeated Monica Seles 7–5, 6–4	
Men's Doubles	
Todd Woodbridge / Mark Woodforde defeated Jacco Eltingh / Paul Haarhuis 4–6, 7–6, 7–6	
Women's Doubles	
Gigi Fernández / Natasha Zvereva defeated Jana Novotná / Arantxa Sánchez Vicario 1–6, 6–1, 6–4	
Mixed Doubles	
Lisa Raymond / Patrick Galbraith defeated Manon Bollegraf / Rick Leach 7–6 (8–6), 7–6 (7–4)	

1997

1997 NATIONAL FOOTBALL LEAGUE SEASON
STANDINGS

AFC EAST	W	L	T	NFC EAST	W	L	T
New England	10	6	0	NY Giants	10	5	1
Miami	9	7	0	Washington	8	7	1
NY Jets	9	7	0	Philadelphia	6	9	1
Buffalo	6	10	0	Dallas	6	10	0
Indianapolis	3	13	0	Arizona	4	12	0
AFC CENT	**W**	**L**	**T**	**NFC CENT**	**W**	**L**	**T**
Pittsburgh	11	5	0	Green Bay	13	3	0
Jacksonville	11	5	0	Tampa Bay	10	6	0
Tennessee	8	8	0	Detroit	9	7	0
Cincinnati	7	9	0	Minnesota	9	7	0
Baltimore	6	9	1	Chicago	4	12	0
AFC WEST	**W**	**L**	**T**	**NFC WEST**	**W**	**L**	**T**
Kansas City	13	3	0	San Francisco	13	3	0
Denver	12	4	0	Carolina	7	9	0
Seattle	8	8	0	Atlanta	7	9	0
Oakland	4	12	0	New Orleans	6	10	0
San Diego	4	12	0	St. Louis	5	11	0

1997 U.S. NATIONAL BADMINTON CHAMPIONSHIPS
WINNERS

Year	Men's singles	Women's singles	Men's doubles	Women's doubles	Mixed doubles
1997	Kevin Han	Cindy Shi	Kevin Han Tom Reidy	Cindy Shi Zhao Ye Ping	Trisna Gunadi Eileen Tang

1997 NBA STANDINGS
DIVISION STANDINGS

Eastern Conference	W	L	W/L%	GB	PS/G	PA/G	SRS
Atlantic Division							
Miami Heat* (2)	61	21	.744	—	94.8	89.3	5.56
New York Knicks* (3)	57	25	.695	4.0	95.4	92.2	3.31
Orlando Magic* (7)	45	37	.549	16.0	94.1	94.5	-0.07
Washington Bullets* (8)	44	38	.537	17.0	99.4	97.7	1.77
New Jersey Nets (13)	26	56	.317	35.0	97.2	101.8	-3.89
Philadelphia 76ers (14)	22	60	.268	39.0	100.2	106.7	-5.89
Boston Celtics (15)	15	67	.183	46.0	100.6	107.9	-6.62
Central Division							
Chicago Bulls* (1)	69	13	.841	—	103.1	92.3	10.70
Atlanta Hawks* (4)	56	26	.683	13.0	94.8	89.4	5.52
Detroit Pistons* (5)	54	28	.659	15.0	94.2	88.9	5.45
Charlotte Hornets* (6)	54	28	.659	15.0	98.9	97.0	2.13
Cleveland Cavaliers (9)	42	40	.512	27.0	87.5	85.6	2.32
Indiana Pacers (10)	39	43	.476	30.0	95.4	94.4	1.49
Milwaukee Bucks (11)	33	49	.402	36.0	95.3	97.2	-1.38
Toronto Raptors (12)	30	52	.366	39.0	95.5	98.6	-2.56

Western Conference	W	L	W/L%	GB	PS/G	PA/G	SRS
Midwest Division							
Utah Jazz* (1)	64	18	.780	—	103.1	94.3	7.97
Houston Rockets* (3)	57	25	.695	7.0	100.6	96.1	3.85
Minnesota Timberwolves* (6)	40	42	.488	24.0	96.1	97.6	-1.82
Dallas Mavericks (11)	24	58	.293	40.0	90.6	97.0	-6.47
Denver Nuggets (12)	21	61	.256	43.0	97.8	104.1	-6.40
San Antonio Spurs (13)	20	62	.244	44.0	90.5	98.3	-7.93
Vancouver Grizzlies (14)	14	68	.171	50.0	89.2	99.4	-10.17
Pacific Division							
Seattle SuperSonics* (2)	57	25	.695	—	100.9	93.2	6.91
Los Angeles Lakers* (4)	56	26	.683	1.0	100.0	95.7	3.66
Portland Trail Blazers* (5)	49	33	.598	8.0	99.0	94.8	3.56
Phoenix Suns* (7)	40	42	.488	17.0	102.8	102.2	0.21
Los Angeles Clippers* (8)	36	46	.439	21.0	97.2	99.5	-2.66
Sacramento Kings (9)	34	48	.415	23.0	96.4	99.8	-3.64
Golden State Warriors (10)	30	52	.366	27.0	99.6	104.4	-4.90

AMERICAN HORSE OF THE YEAR
1997 ECLIPSE AWARD

Year	Horse	Trainer	Owner	Age	Gender
1997	Favorite Trick	Patrick B. Byrne	Joseph LaCombe	2	C

1997- NHL SEASON
FINAL STANDINGS

Eastern Conference							
Northeast Division							
Team	W	L	T	GF	GA	Pts
Pittsburgh Penguins	40	24	18	228	188	98
Boston Bruins	39	30	13	221	194	91
Buffalo Sabres	36	29	17	211	187	89
Montreal Canadiens	37	32	13	235	208	87
Ottawa Senators	34	33	15	193	200	83
Carolina Hurricanes	33	41	8	200	219	74
Atlantic Division							
Team	W	L	T	GF	GA	Pts
New Jersey Devils	48	23	11	225	166	107
Philadelphia Flyers	42	29	11	242	193	95
Washington Capitals	40	30	12	219	202	92
New York Islanders	30	41	11	212	225	71
New York Rangers	25	39	18	197	231	68
Florida Panthers	24	43	15	203	256	63
Tampa Bay Lightning	17	55	10	151	269	44

Western Conference							
Central Division							
Team	W	L	T	GF	GA	Pts
Dallas Stars	49	22	11	242	167	109
Detroit Red Wings	44	23	15	250	196	103
St. Louis Blues	45	29	8	256	204	98
Phoenix Coyotes	35	35	12	224	227	82
Chicago Blackhawks	30	39	13	192	199	73
Toronto Maple Leafs	30	43	9	194	237	69
Pacific Division							
Team	W	L	T	GF	GA	Pts
Colorado Avalanche	39	26	17	231	205	95
Los Angeles Kings	38	33	11	227	225	87
Edmonton Oilers	35	37	10	215	224	80
San Jose Sharks	34	38	10	210	216	78
Calgary Flames	26	41	15	217	252	67
Mighty Ducks of Anaheim	26	43	13	205	261	65
Vancouver Canucks	25	43	14	224	273	64

1997 MAJOR LEAGUE BASEBALL SEASON HISTORY

1997 American League Standings								
EAST	W	L	PCT	GB	HOME	ROAD	RS	RA	DIFF
*-Baltimore	98	64	.605	--	46-35	52-29	812	681	+131
y-New York	96	66	.593	2	47-33	49-33	891	688	+203
Detroit	79	83	.488	19	42-39	37-44	784	790	-6
Boston	78	84	.481	20	39-42	39-42	851	857	-6
Toronto	76	86	.469	22	42-39	34-47	654	694	-40
CENTRAL	W	L	PCT	GB	HOME	ROAD	RS	RA	DIFF
x-Cleveland	86	75	.534	--	44-37	42-38	868	815	+53
Chicago	80	81	.497	6	45-36	35-45	779	833	-54
Milwaukee	78	83	.484	8	47-33	31-50	681	742	-61
Minnesota	68	94	.420	18.5	35-46	33-48	772	861	-89
Kansas City	67	94	.416	19	33-47	34-47	747	820	-73
WEST	W	L	PCT	GB	HOME	ROAD	RS	RA	DIFF
x-Seattle	90	72	.556	--	45-36	45-36	925	833	+92
Anaheim	84	78	.519	6	46-36	38-42	829	794	+35
Texas	77	85	.475	13	39-42	38-43	807	823	-16
Oakland	65	97	.401	25	35-46	30-51	764	946	-182
1997 National League Standings								
EAST	W	L	PCT	GB	HOME	ROAD	RS	RA	DIFF
*-Atlanta	101	61	.623	--	50-31	51-30	791	581	+210
y-Florida	92	70	.568	9	52-29	40-41	740	669	+71
New York	88	74	.543	13	50-31	38-43	777	709	+68
Montreal	78	84	.481	23	45-36	33-48	691	740	-49
Philadelphia	68	94	.420	33	38-43	30-51	668	840	-172
CENTRAL	W	L	PCT	GB	HOME	ROAD	RS	RA	DIFF
x-Houston	84	78	.519	--	46-35	38-43	777	660	+117
Pittsburgh	79	83	.488	5	43-38	36-45	725	760	-35
Cincinnati	76	86	.469	8	40-41	36-45	651	764	-113
St. Louis	73	89	.451	11	41-40	32-49	689	708	-19
Chicago	68	94	.420	16	42-39	26-55	687	759	-72

WEST	W	L	PCT	GB	HOME	ROAD	RS	RA	DIFF
x-San Francisco	90	72	.556	--	48-33	42-39	784	793	-9
Los Angeles	88	74	.543	2	47-34	41-40	742	645	+97
Colorado	83	79	.512	7	47-34	36-45	923	908	+15
San Diego	76	86	.469	14	39-42	37-44	795	891	-96

1997 U.S. NATIONAL TENNIS CHAMPIONSHIPS

Men's Singles
Patrick Rafter defeated Greg Rusedski 6–3, 6–2, 4–6, 7–5
Women's Singles
Martina Hingis defeated Venus Williams 6–0, 6–4
Men's Doubles
Yevgeny Kafelnikov / Daniel Vacek defeated Jonas Björkman / Nicklas Kulti 7–6, 6–3
Women's Doubles
Lindsay Davenport / Jana Novotná defeated Gigi Fernández / Natasha Zvereva 6–3, 6–4
Mixed Doubles
Manon Bollegraf / Rick Leach defeated Mercedes Paz / Pablo Albano 3–6, 7–5, 7–6

1998

1998 NATIONAL FOOTBALL LEAGUE SEASON
STANDINGS

AFC EAST	W	L	T	NFC EAST	W	L	T
NY Jets	12	4	0	Dallas	10	6	0
Miami	10	6	0	Arizona	9	7	0
Buffalo	10	6	0	NY Giants	8	8	0
New England	9	7	0	Washington	6	10	0
Indianapolis	3	13	0	Philadelphia	3	13	0
AFC CENT	**W**	**L**	**T**	**NFC CENT**	**W**	**L**	**T**
Jacksonville	11	5	0	Minnesota	15	1	0
Tennessee	8	8	0	Green Bay	11	5	0
Pittsburgh	7	9	0	Tampa Bay	8	8	0
Baltimore	6	10	0	Detroit	5	11	0
Cincinnati	3	13	0	Chicago	4	12	0
AFC WEST	**W**	**L**	**T**	**NFC WEST**	**W**	**L**	**T**
Denver	14	2	0	Atlanta	14	2	0
Oakland	8	8	0	San Francisco	12	4	0
Seattle	8	8	0	New Orleans	6	10	0
Kansas City	7	9	0	Carolina	4	12	0
San Diego	5	11	0	St. Louis	4	12	0

1998 U.S. NATIONAL BADMINTON CHAMPIONSHIPS
WINNERS

Year	Men's singles	Women's singles	Men's doubles	Women's doubles	Mixed doubles
1998	Kevin Han	Yeping Tang	Andy Chong Benny Lee	Cindy Shi Yeping Tang	Andy Chong Yeping Tang

1998 NBA STANDINGS
DIVISION STANDINGS

Eastern Conference	W	L	W/L%	GB	PS/G	PA/G	SRS
Atlantic Division							
Miami Heat* (2)	55	27	.671	—	95.0	90.0	5.09
New York Knicks* (7)	43	39	.524	12.0	91.6	89.1	2.74
New Jersey Nets* (8)	43	39	.524	12.0	99.6	98.1	1.88
Washington Wizards (9)	42	40	.512	13.0	97.2	96.6	1.11
Orlando Magic (10)	41	41	.500	14.0	90.1	91.2	-0.53
Boston Celtics (12)	36	46	.439	19.0	95.9	98.5	-1.96
Philadelphia 76ers (14)	31	51	.378	24.0	93.3	95.7	-1.89
Central Division							
Chicago Bulls* (1)	62	20	.756	—	96.7	89.6	7.24
Indiana Pacers* (3)	58	24	.707	4.0	96.0	89.9	6.25
Charlotte Hornets* (4)	51	31	.622	11.0	96.6	94.6	2.45
Atlanta Hawks* (5)	50	32	.610	12.0	95.9	92.3	3.85
Cleveland Cavaliers* (6)	47	35	.573	15.0	92.5	89.8	3.06
Detroit Pistons (11)	37	45	.451	25.0	94.2	92.6	1.95
Milwaukee Bucks (13)	36	46	.439	26.0	94.5	96.4	-1.33
Toronto Raptors (15)	16	66	.195	46.0	94.9	104.2	-8.33

Western Conference	W	L	W/L%	GB	PS/G	PA/G	SRS
Midwest Division							
Utah Jazz* (1)	62	20	.756	—	101.0	94.4	5.73
San Antonio Spurs* (5)	56	26	.683	6.0	92.5	88.5	3.30
Minnesota Timberwolves* (7)	45	37	.549	17.0	101.1	100.4	0.17
Houston Rockets* (8)	41	41	.500	21.0	98.8	99.5	-1.23
Dallas Mavericks (10)	20	62	.244	42.0	91.4	97.5	-6.33
Vancouver Grizzlies (11)	19	63	.232	43.0	96.6	103.9	-7.47
Denver Nuggets (14)	11	71	.134	51.0	89.0	100.8	-11.74
Pacific Division							
Seattle SuperSonics* (2)	61	21	.744	—	100.6	93.4	6.33
Los Angeles Lakers* (3)	61	21	.744	—	105.5	97.8	6.88
Phoenix Suns* (4)	56	26	.683	5.0	99.6	94.4	4.44
Portland Trail Blazers* (6)	46	36	.561	15.0	94.3	92.9	0.83
Sacramento Kings (9)	27	55	.329	34.0	93.1	98.7	-5.83
Golden State Warriors (12)	19	63	.232	42.0	88.3	97.4	-9.20
Los Angeles Clippers (13)	17	65	.207	44.0	95.9	103.3	-7.53

AMERICAN HORSE OF THE YEAR
1998 ECLIPSE AWARD

Year	Horse	Trainer	Owner	Age	Gender
1998	Skip Away	Sonny Hine	Carolyn Hine	5	C

1998 - NHL SEASON
FINAL STANDINGS

Eastern Conference								
Atlantic Division	GP	W	L	T	Pts	GF	GA	PIM
New Jersey Devils	82	47	24	11	105	248	196	1355
Philadelphia Flyers	82	37	26	19	93	231	196	1075
Pittsburgh Penguins	82	38	30	14	90	242	225	977
New York Rangers	82	33	38	11	77	217	227	1087
New York Islanders	82	24	48	10	58	194	244	1111
Northeast Division	GP	W	L	T	Pts	GF	GA	PIM
Ottawa Senators	82	44	23	15	103	239	179	892
Toronto Maple Leafs	82	45	30	7	97	268	231	1095
Boston Bruins	82	39	30	13	91	214	181	1182
Buffalo Sabres	82	37	28	17	91	207	175	1561
Montreal Canadiens	82	32	39	11	75	184	209	1299
Southeast Division	GP	W	L	T	Pts	GF	GA	PIM
Carolina Hurricanes	82	34	30	18	86	210	202	1158
Florida Panthers	82	30	34	18	78	210	228	1522
Washington Capitals	82	31	45	6	68	200	218	1381
Western Conference								
Central Division	GP	W	L	T	Pts	GF	GA	PIM
Detroit Red Wings	82	43	32	7	93	245	202	1202
St. Louis Blues	82	37	32	13	87	237	209	1308
Chicago Blackhawks	82	29	41	12	70	202	248	1807
Nashville Predators	82	28	47	7	63	190	261	1420

Northwest Division	GP	W	L	T	Pts	GF	GA	PIM
Colorado Avalanche	82	44	28	10	98	239	205	1619
Edmonton Oilers	82	33	37	12	78	230	226	1373
Calgary Flames	82	30	40	12	72	211	234	1389
Vancouver Canucks	82	23	47	12	58	192	258	1764
Pacific Division	GP	W	L	T	Pts	GF	GA	PIM
Dallas Stars	82	51	19	12	114	236	168	1108
Phoenix Coyotes	82	39	31	12	90	205	197	1412
Anaheim Mighty Ducks	82	35	34	13	83	215	206	1323
San Jose Sharks	82	31	33	18	80	196	191	1423
Los Angeles Kings	82	32	45	5	69	189	222	1383

1998 MAJOR LEAGUE BASEBALL SEASON HISTORY

1998 American League Standings

EAST	W	L	PCT	GB	HOME	ROAD	RS	RA	DIFF
*-New York	114	48	.704	--	62-19	52-29	965	656	+309
y-Boston	92	70	.568	22	51-30	41-40	876	729	+147
Toronto	88	74	.543	26	51-30	37-44	816	768	+48
Baltimore	79	83	.488	35	42-39	37-44	817	785	+32
Tampa Bay	63	99	.389	51	33-48	30-51	620	751	-131
CENTRAL	W	L	PCT	GB	HOME	ROAD	RS	RA	DIFF
x-Cleveland	89	73	.549	--	46-35	43-38	850	779	+71
Chicago	80	82	.494	9	44-37	36-45	861	931	-70
Kansas City	72	89	.447	16.5	29-51	43-38	714	899	-185
Minnesota	70	92	.432	19	35-46	35-46	734	818	-84
Detroit	65	97	.401	24	32-49	33-48	722	863	-141
WEST	W	L	PCT	GB	HOME	ROAD	RS	RA	DIFF
x-Texas	88	74	.543	--	48-33	40-41	940	871	+69
Anaheim	85	77	.525	3	42-39	43-38	787	783	+4
Seattle	76	85	.472	11.5	42-39	34-46	859	855	+4
Oakland	74	88	.457	14	39-42	35-46	804	866	-62

1998 National League Standings

EAST	W	L	PCT	GB	HOME	ROAD	RS	RA	DIFF
*-Atlanta	106	56	.654	--	56-25	50-31	826	581	+245
New York	88	74	.543	18	47-34	41-40	706	645	+61
Philadelphia	75	87	.463	31	40-41	35-46	713	808	-95
Montreal	65	97	.401	41	39-42	26-55	644	783	-139
Florida	54	108	.333	52	31-50	23-58	667	923	-256
CENTRAL	W	L	PCT	GB	HOME	ROAD	RS	RA	DIFF
x-Houston	102	60	.630	--	55-26	47-34	874	620	+254
y-Chicago	90	73	.552	12.5	51-31	39-42	831	792	+39
St. Louis	83	79	.512	19	48-34	35-45	810	782	+28
Cincinnati	77	85	.475	25	39-42	38-43	750	760	-10
Milwaukee	74	88	.457	28	38-43	36-45	707	812	-105
Pittsburgh	69	93	.426	33	40-40	29-53	650	718	-68
WEST	W	L	PCT	GB	HOME	ROAD	RS	RA	DIFF
x-San Diego	98	64	.605	--	54-27	44-37	749	635	+114
San Francisco	89	74	.546	9.5	49-32	40-42	845	739	+106
Los Angeles	83	79	.512	15	48-33	35-46	669	678	-9
Colorado	77	85	.475	21	42-39	35-46	826	855	-29
Arizona	65	97	.401	33	34-47	31-50	665	812	-147

1998 U.S. NATIONAL TENNIS CHAMPIONSHIPS

Men's Singles
Patrick Rafter defeated Mark Philippoussis, 6–3, 3–6, 6–2, 6–0
Women's Singles
Lindsay Davenport defeated Martina Hingis, 6–3, 7–5
Men's Doubles
Sandon Stolle / Cyril Suk defeated Mark Knowles / Daniel Nestor, 4–6, 7–6, 6–2
Women's Doubles
Martina Hingis / Jana Novotná defeated Lindsay Davenport / Natasha Zvereva 6–3, 6–3
Mixed Doubles
Serena Williams / Max Mirnyi defeated Lisa Raymond / Patrick Galbraith 6–2, 6–2

1999

1999 NATIONAL FOOTBALL LEAGUE SEASON
STANDINGS

AFC EAST	W	L	T	NFC EAST	W	L	T
Indianapolis	13	3	0	Washington	10	6	0
Buffalo	11	5	0	Dallas	8	8	0
Miami	9	7	0	NY Giants	7	9	0
NY Jets	8	8	0	Arizona	6	10	0
New England	8	8	0	Philadelphia	5	11	0
AFC CENT	**W**	**L**	**T**	**NFC CENT**	**W**	**L**	**T**
Jacksonville	14	2	0	Tampa Bay	11	5	0
Tennessee	13	3	0	Minnesota	10	6	0
Baltimore	8	8	0	Detroit	8	8	0
Pittsburgh	6	10	0	Green Bay	8	8	0
Cincinnati	4	12	0	Chicago	6	10	0
Cleveland	2	14	0	**NFC WEST**	**W**	**L**	**T**
AFC WEST	**W**	**L**	**T**	St. Louis	13	3	0
Seattle	9	7	0	Carolina	8	8	0
Kansas City	9	7	0	Atlanta	5	11	0
San Diego	8	8	0	San Francisco	4	12	0
Oakland	8	8	0	New Orleans	3	13	0
Denver	6	10	0				

1999 U.S. NATIONAL BADMINTON CHAMPIONSHIPS
WINNERS

Year	Men's singles	Women's singles	Men's doubles	Women's doubles	Mixed doubles
1999	Kevin Han	Yeping Tang	Kevin Han Alex Liang	Cindy Shi Yeping Tang	Andy Chong Yeping Tang

1999 NBA STANDINGS
DIVISION STANDINGS

Eastern Conference	W	L	W/L%	GB	PS/G	PA/G	SRS
Atlantic Division							
Miami Heat* (1)	33	17	.660	—	89.0	84.0	5.11
Orlando Magic* (3)	33	17	.660	—	89.5	86.9	3.11
Philadelphia 76ers* (6)	28	22	.560	5.0	89.7	87.6	2.56
New York Knicks* (8)	27	23	.540	6.0	86.4	85.4	1.45
Boston Celtics (12)	19	31	.380	14.0	93.0	94.9	-1.75
Washington Wizards (13)	18	32	.360	15.0	91.2	93.4	-1.75
New Jersey Nets (14)	16	34	.320	17.0	91.4	95.2	-3.20
Central Division							
Indiana Pacers* (2)	33	17	.660	—	94.7	90.9	3.86
Atlanta Hawks* (4)	31	19	.620	2.0	86.3	83.4	2.82
Detroit Pistons* (5)	29	21	.580	4.0	90.4	86.9	3.97

Milwaukee Bucks* (7)	28	22	.560	5.0	91.7	90.0	1.66
Charlotte Hornets (9)	26	24	.520	7.0	92.9	93.0	0.63
Toronto Raptors (10)	23	27	.460	10.0	91.1	92.8	-1.32
Cleveland Cavaliers (11)	22	28	.440	11.0	86.4	88.2	-0.94
Chicago Bulls (15)	13	37	.260	20.0	81.9	91.4	-8.58
Western Conference	**W**	**L**	**W/L%**	**GB**	**PS/G**	**PA/G**	**SRS**
Midwest Division							
San Antonio Spurs* (1)	37	13	.740	—	92.8	84.7	7.12
Utah Jazz* (2)	37	13	.740	—	93.3	86.8	5.54
Houston Rockets* (5)	31	19	.620	6.0	94.2	91.9	1.39
Minnesota Timberwolves* (8)	25	25	.500	12.0	92.9	92.6	-0.17
Dallas Mavericks (11)	19	31	.380	18.0	91.6	94.0	-2.50
Denver Nuggets (12)	14	36	.280	23.0	93.5	100.1	-6.67
Vancouver Grizzlies (14)	8	42	.160	29.0	88.9	97.5	-8.94
Pacific Division							
Portland Trail Blazers* (3)	35	15	.700	—	94.8	88.5	5.67
Los Angeles Lakers* (4)	31	19	.620	4.0	99.0	96.0	2.68
Phoenix Suns* (6)	27	23	.540	8.0	95.6	93.3	2.15
Sacramento Kings* (7)	27	23	.540	8.0	100.2	100.6	-0.89
Seattle SuperSonics (9)	25	25	.500	10.0	94.9	95.9	-1.43
Golden State Warriors (10)	21	29	.420	14.0	88.3	90.8	-2.63
Los Angeles Clippers (13)	9	41	.180	26.0	90.4	99.2	-8.94

AMERICAN HORSE OF THE YEAR
1999 ECLIPSE AWARD

Year	Horse	Trainer	Owner	Age	Gender
1999	Charismatic	D. Wayne Lukas	Bob and Beverly Lewis	3	C

1999- NHL SEASON
FINAL STANDINGS

Eastern Conference								
Northeast Division	**GP**	**W**	**L**	**T**	**OTL**	**Pts**	**GF**	**GA**	**PIM**
Toronto Maple Leafs	82	45	27	7	3	100	246	222	1103
Ottawa Senators	82	41	28	11	2	95	244	210	850
Buffalo Sabres	82	35	32	11	4	85	213	204	1173
Montreal Canadiens	82	35	34	9	4	83	196	194	1067
Boston Bruins	82	24	33	19	6	73	210	248	865
Atlantic Division	**GP**	**W**	**L**	**T**	**OTL**	**Pts**	**GF**	**GA**	**PIM**
Philadelphia Flyers	82	45	22	12	3	105	237	179	1233
New Jersey Devils	82	45	24	8	5	103	251	203	1313
Pittsburgh Penguins	82	37	31	8	6	88	241	236	1221
New York Rangers	82	29	38	12	3	73	218	246	916
New York Islanders	82	24	48	9	1	58	194	275	1376
Southeast Division	**GP**	**W**	**L**	**T**	**OTL**	**Pts**	**GF**	**GA**	**PIM**
Washington Capitals	82	44	24	12	2	102	227	194	994
Florida Panthers	82	43	27	6	6	98	244	209	1329
Carolina Hurricanes	82	37	35	10	0	84	217	216	799
Tampa Bay Lightning	82	19	47	9	7	54	204	310	1733
Atlanta Thrashers	82	14	57	7	4	39	170	313	1422

Western Conference									
Central Division	GP	W	L	T	OTL	Pts	GF	GA	PIM
St. Louis Blues	82	51	19	11	1	114	248	165	1139
Detroit Red Wings	82	48	22	10	2	108	278	210	1014
Chicago Blackhawks	82	33	37	10	2	78	242	245	1444
Nashville Predators	82	28	40	7	7	70	199	240	946
Pacific Division	GP	W	L	T	OTL	Pts	GF	GA	PIM
Dallas Stars	82	43	23	10	6	102	211	184	1029
Los Angeles Kings	82	39	27	12	4	94	245	228	1313
Phoenix Coyotes	82	39	31	8	4	90	232	228	940
San Jose Sharks	82	35	30	10	7	87	225	214	1292
Mighty Ducks of Anaheim	82	34	33	12	3	83	217	227	926
Northwest Division	GP	W	L	T	OTL	Pts	GF	GA	PIM
Colorado Avalanche	82	42	28	11	1	96	233	201	1118
Edmonton Oilers	82	32	26	16	8	88	226	212	1344
Vancouver Canucks	82	30	29	15	8	83	227	237	1047
Calgary Flames	82	31	36	10	5	77	211	256	1267

1999 MAJOR LEAGUE BASEBALL SEASON HISTORY

1999 American League Standings									
EAST	W	L	PCT	GB	HOME	ROAD	RS	RA	DIFF
*-New York	98	64	.605	--	48-33	50-31	900	731	+169
y-Boston	94	68	.580	4	49-32	45-36	836	718	+118
Toronto	84	78	.519	14	40-41	44-37	883	862	+21
Baltimore	78	84	.481	20	41-40	37-44	851	815	+36
Tampa Bay	69	93	.426	29	33-48	36-45	772	913	-141
CENTRAL	W	L	PCT	GB	HOME	ROAD	RS	RA	DIFF
x-Cleveland	97	65	.599	--	47-34	50-31	1009	860	+149
Chicago	75	86	.466	21.5	38-42	37-44	777	870	-93
Detroit	69	92	.429	27.5	38-43	31-49	747	882	-135
Kansas City	64	97	.398	32.5	33-47	31-50	856	921	-65
Minnesota	63	97	.394	33	31-50	32-47	686	845	-159
WEST	W	L	PCT	GB	HOME	ROAD	RS	RA	DIFF
x-Texas	95	67	.586	--	51-30	44-37	945	859	+86
Oakland	87	75	.537	8	52-29	35-46	893	846	+47
Seattle	79	83	.488	16	43-38	36-45	859	905	-46
Anaheim	70	92	.432	25	37-44	33-48	711	826	-115
1999 National League Standings									
EAST	W	L	PCT	GB	HOME	ROAD	RS	RA	DIFF
*-Atlanta	103	59	.636	--	56-25	47-34	840	661	+179
y-New York	97	66	.595	6.5	49-32	48-34	853	711	+142
Philadelphia	77	85	.475	26	41-40	36-45	841	846	-5
Montreal	68	94	.420	35	35-46	33-48	718	853	-135
Florida	64	98	.395	39	35-45	29-53	691	852	-161
CENTRAL	W	L	PCT	GB	HOME	ROAD	RS	RA	DIFF
x-Houston	97	65	.599	--	50-32	47-33	823	675	+148
Cincinnati	96	67	.589	1.5	45-37	51-30	865	711	+154
Pittsburgh	78	83	.484	18.5	45-36	33-47	775	782	-7
St. Louis	75	86	.466	21.5	38-42	37-44	809	838	-29
Milwaukee	74	87	.460	22.5	32-48	42-39	815	886	-71
Chicago	67	95	.414	30	34-47	33-48	747	920	-173

WEST	W	L	PCT	GB	HOME	ROAD	RS	RA	DIFF
x-Arizona	100	62	.617	--	52-29	48-33	908	676	+232
San Francisco	86	76	.531	14	49-32	37-44	872	831	+41
Los Angeles	77	85	.475	23	37-44	40-41	793	787	+6
San Diego	74	88	.457	26	46-35	28-53	710	781	-71
Colorado	72	90	.444	28	39-42	33-48	906	1028	-122

1999 U.S. NATIONAL TENNIS CHAMPIONSHIPS

Men's Singles
Andre Agassi defeated Todd Martin, 6–4, 6–7$^{(5-7)}$, 6–7$^{(2-7)}$, 6–3, 6–2
Women's Singles
Serena Williams defeated Martina Hingis, 6–3, 7–6$^{(7-4)}$
Men's Doubles
Sébastien Lareau / Alex O'Brien defeated Mahesh Bhupathi / Leander Paes, 7–6$^{(9-7)}$, 6–4
Women's Doubles
Serena Williams / Venus Williams defeated Chanda Rubin / Sandrine Testud, 4–6, 6–1, 6–4
Mixed Doubles
Ai Sugiyama / Mahesh Bhupathi defeated Kimberly Po / Donald Johnson, 6–4, 6–4

2000

2000 NATIONAL FOOTBALL LEAGUE SEASON
STANDINGS

AFC EAST	W	L	T	NFC EAST	W	L	T
Miami	11	5	0	NY Giants	12	4	0
Indianapolis	10	6	0	Philadelphia	11	5	0
NY Jets	9	7	0	Washington	8	8	0
Buffalo	8	8	0	Dallas	5	11	0
New England	5	11	0	Arizona	3	13	0
AFC CENT	**W**	**L**	**T**	**NFC CENT**	**W**	**L**	**T**
Tennessee	13	3	0	Minnesota	11	5	0
Baltimore	12	4	0	Tampa Bay	10	6	0
Pittsburgh	9	7	0	Green Bay	9	7	0
Jacksonville	7	9	0	Detroit	9	7	0
Cincinnati	4	12	0	Chicago	5	11	0
Cleveland	3	13	0	**NFC WEST**	**W**	**L**	**T**
AFC WEST	**W**	**L**	**T**	New Orleans	10	6	0
Oakland	12	4	0	St. Louis	10	6	0
Denver	11	5	0	Carolina	7	9	0
Kansas City	7	9	0	San Francisco	6	10	0
Seattle	6	10	0	Atlanta	4	12	0
San Diego	1	15	0				

2000 U.S. NATIONAL BADMINTON CHAMPIONSHIPS
WINNERS

Year	Men's singles	Women's singles	Men's doubles	Women's doubles	Mixed doubles
2000	Alex Liang	Yeping Tang	Matt Fogarty Chibing Wu	Janis Tan Elie Wu	Chibing Wu Melinda Keszthelyi

2000 NBA STANDINGS
DIVISION STANDINGS

Eastern Conference	W	L	W/L%	GB	PS/G	PA/G	SRS
Atlantic Division							
Miami Heat* (2)	52	30	.634	—	94.4	91.3	2.75
New York Knicks* (3)	50	32	.610	2.0	92.1	90.7	1.30
Philadelphia 76ers* (5)	49	33	.598	3.0	94.8	93.4	1.02
Orlando Magic (9)	41	41	.500	11.0	100.1	99.4	0.43
Boston Celtics (10)	35	47	.427	17.0	99.3	100.1	-1.00
New Jersey Nets (12)	31	51	.378	21.0	98.0	99.0	-1.18
Washington Wizards (13)	29	53	.354	23.0	96.6	99.9	-3.47
Central Division							
Indiana Pacers* (1)	56	26	.683	—	101.3	96.7	4.15
Charlotte Hornets* (4)	49	33	.598	7.0	98.4	95.8	2.33
Toronto Raptors* (6)	45	37	.549	11.0	97.2	97.3	-0.46
Detroit Pistons* (7)	42	40	.512	14.0	103.5	102.0	1.13
Milwaukee Bucks* (8)	42	40	.512	14.0	101.2	101.0	-0.06
Cleveland Cavaliers (11)	32	50	.390	24.0	97.0	100.5	-3.64

Atlanta Hawks (14)	28	54	.341	28.0	94.3	99.7	-5.41
Chicago Bulls (15)	17	65	.207	39.0	84.8	94.2	-9.23
Western Conference	W	L	W/L%	GB	PS/G	PA/G	SRS
Midwest Division							
Utah Jazz* (2)	55	27	.671	—	96.5	92.0	4.52
San Antonio Spurs* (4)	53	29	.646	2.0	96.2	90.2	5.92
Minnesota Timberwolves* (6)	50	32	.610	5.0	98.5	96.0	2.67
Dallas Mavericks (9)	40	42	.488	15.0	101.4	102.0	-0.29
Denver Nuggets (10)	35	47	.427	20.0	99.0	101.1	-1.76
Houston Rockets (11)	34	48	.415	21.0	99.5	100.3	-0.57
Vancouver Grizzlies (12)	22	60	.268	33.0	93.9	99.5	-5.10
Pacific Division							
Los Angeles Lakers* (1)	67	15	.817	—	100.8	92.3	8.41
Portland Trail Blazers* (3)	59	23	.720	8.0	97.5	91.0	6.36
Phoenix Suns* (5)	53	29	.646	14.0	98.9	93.7	5.24
Seattle SuperSonics* (7)	45	37	.549	22.0	99.1	98.1	1.17
Sacramento Kings* (8)	44	38	.537	23.0	105.0	102.0	3.04
Golden State Warriors (13)	19	63	.232	48.0	95.5	103.8	-7.63
Los Angeles Clippers (14)	15	67	.183	52.0	92.0	103.5	-10.73

AMERICAN HORSE OF THE YEAR
2000 ECLIPSE AWARD

Year	Horse	Trainer	Owner	Age	Gender
2000	Tiznow	Jay M. Robbins	M. Cooper & Cecilia Straub-Rubens	3	C

2000- NHL SEASON
FINAL STANDINGS

Eastern Conference							
Northeast Division	GP	W	L	T	OTL	GF	GA	Pts
Ottawa Senators	82	48	21	9	4	274	205	109
Buffalo Sabres	82	46	30	5	1	218	184	98
Toronto Maple Leafs	82	37	29	11	5	232	207	90
Boston Bruins	82	36	30	8	8	227	249	88
Montreal Canadiens	82	28	40	8	6	206	232	70
Atlantic Division	GP	W	L	T	OTL	GF	GA	Pts
New Jersey Devils	82	48	19	12	3	295	195	111
Philadelphia Flyers	82	43	25	11	3	240	207	100
Pittsburgh Penguins	82	42	28	9	3	281	256	96
New York Rangers	82	33	43	5	1	250	290	72
New York Islanders	82	21	51	7	3	185	268	52
Southeast Division	GP	W	L	T	OTL	GF	GA	Pts
Washington Capitals	82	41	27	10	4	233	211	96
Carolina Hurricanes	82	38	32	9	3	212	225	88
Florida Panthers	82	22	38	13	9	200	246	66
Atlanta Thrashers	82	23	45	12	2	211	289	60
Tampa Bay Lightning	82	24	47	6	5	201	280	59

Western Conference

Central Division	GP	W	L	T	OTL	GF	GA	Pts
Detroit Red Wings	82	49	20	9	4	253	202	111
St. Louis Blues	82	43	22	12	5	249	195	103
Nashville Predators	82	34	36	9	3	186	200	80
Chicago Blackhawks	82	29	40	8	5	210	246	71
Columbus Blue Jackets	82	28	39	9	6	190	233	71
Pacific Division	GP	W	L	T	OTL	GF	GA	Pts
Dallas Stars	82	48	24	8	2	241	187	106
San Jose Sharks	82	40	27	12	3	217	192	95
Los Angeles Kings	82	38	28	13	3	252	228	92
Phoenix Coyotes	82	35	27	17	3	214	212	90
Mighty Ducks of Anaheim	82	25	41	11	5	188	245	66
Northwest Division	GP	W	L	T	OTL	GF	GA	Pts
Colorado Avalanche	82	52	16	10	4	270	192	118
Edmonton Oilers	82	39	28	12	3	243	222	93
Vancouver Canucks	82	36	28	11	7	239	238	90
Calgary Flames	82	27	36	15	4	197	236	73
Minnesota Wild	82	25	39	13	5	168	210	68

2000 MAJOR LEAGUE BASEBALL SEASON HISTORY

2000 American League Standings									
EAST	W	L	PCT	GB	HOME	ROAD	RS	RA	DIFF
x-New York	87	74	.540	--	44-36	43-38	871	814	+57
Boston	85	77	.525	2.5	42-39	43-38	792	745	+47
Toronto	83	79	.512	4.5	45-36	38-43	861	908	-47
Baltimore	74	88	.457	13.5	44-37	30-51	794	913	-119
Tampa Bay	69	92	.429	18	36-44	33-48	733	842	-109
CENTRAL	W	L	PCT	GB	HOME	ROAD	RS	RA	DIFF
*-Chicago	95	67	.586	--	46-35	49-32	978	839	+139
Cleveland	90	72	.556	5	48-33	42-39	950	816	+134
Detroit	79	83	.488	16	43-38	36-45	823	827	-4
Kansas City	77	85	.475	18	42-39	35-46	879	930	-51
Minnesota	69	93	.426	26	36-45	33-48	748	880	-132
WEST	W	L	PCT	GB	HOME	ROAD	RS	RA	DIFF
x-Oakland	91	70	.565	--	47-34	44-36	947	813	+134
y-Seattle	91	71	.562	.5	47-34	44-37	907	780	+127
Anaheim	82	80	.506	9.5	46-35	36-45	864	869	-5
Texas	71	91	.438	20.5	42-39	29-52	848	974	-126
2000 National League Standings									
EAST	W	L	PCT	GB	HOME	ROAD	RS	RA	DIFF
x-Atlanta	95	67	.586	--	51-30	44-37	810	714	+96
y-New York	94	68	.580	1	55-26	39-42	807	738	+69
Florida	79	82	.491	15.5	43-38	36-44	731	797	-66
Montreal	67	95	.414	28	37-44	30-51	738	902	-164
Philadelphia	65	97	.401	30	34-47	31-50	708	830	-122
CENTRAL	W	L	PCT	GB	HOME	ROAD	RS	RA	DIFF
x-St. Louis	95	67	.586	--	50-31	45-36	887	771	+116
Cincinnati	85	77	.525	10	43-38	42-39	825	765	+60
Milwaukee	73	89	.451	22	42-39	31-50	740	826	-86
Houston	72	90	.444	23	39-42	33-48	938	944	-6

	W	L	PCT	GB	HOME	ROAD	RS	RA	DIFF
Pittsburgh	69	93	.426	26	37-44	32-49	793	888	-95
Chicago	65	97	.401	30	38-43	27-54	764	904	-140
WEST	**W**	**L**	**PCT**	**GB**	**HOME**	**ROAD**	**RS**	**RA**	**DIFF**
*-San Francisco	97	65	.599	--	55-26	42-39	925	747	+178
Los Angeles	86	76	.531	11	44-37	42-39	798	729	+69
Arizona	85	77	.525	12	47-34	38-43	792	754	+38
Colorado	82	80	.506	15	48-33	34-47	968	897	+71
San Diego	76	86	.469	21	41-40	35-46	752	815	-63

2000 U.S. NATIONAL TENNIS CHAMPIONSHIPS

Men's singles
Marat Safin defeated Pete Sampras, 6–4, 6–3, 6–3
Women's singles
Venus Williams defeated Lindsay Davenport, 6–4, 7–5
Men's doubles
Lleyton Hewitt / Max Mirnyi defeated Ellis Ferreira / Rick Leach, 6–4, 5–7, 7–6
Women's doubles
Julie Halard-Decugis / Ai Sugiyama defeated Cara Black / Elena Likhovtseva, 6–0, 1–6, 6–1
Mixed doubles
Arantxa Sánchez Vicario / Jared Palmer defeated Anna Kournikova / Max Mirnyi, 6–4, 6–3

★★★ GRAYS ★★★
SPORTS ALMANAC

COMPLETES SPORTS STATISTICS
1950–2000

Made in the USA
Columbia, SC
18 April 2018